DIPLOMATIC TERRORISM

DIPLOMATIC TERRORISM

Anatomy of Iran's State Terror

Secretariat of the National Council of Resistance of Iran (NCRI)

Diplomatic Terrorism

Anatomy of Iran's State Terror

Copyright © 2022 National Council of Resistance of Iran

All rights reserved. No part of this book may be reproduced or used in any manner without proper attribution to the author. To request permissions, contact the publisher at

https://www.ncr-iran.org/en/contact-us/

First published in September 2022

National Council of Resistance of Iran (NCRI)

ISBN-10: 1-7396173-3-9 (Hardcover)

ISBN-13: 978-1-7396173-3-2 (Hardcover)

ISBN-10: 1-7396173-2-0 (Paperback)

ISBN-13: 978-1-7396173-2-5 (Paperback)

ISBN-10: 1-7396173-4-7 (eBook)

ISBN-13: 978-1-7396173-4-9 (eBook)

Printed by National Council of Resistance of Iran (NCRI)

www.ncr-iran.org

This book is dedicated to the victims of Iranian state terrorism.

ACKNOWLEDGMENTS

The compilation, writing, editing, and graphic design of this book was an arduous undertaking that could not have been done without the tireless efforts of the NCRI Judiciary, Foreign Affairs, and Security and Anti-Terrorism Committees. I would like to sincerely thank three persons in particular: Mohammad Mohaddessin, Chairman of the Foreign Affairs Committee, Sanabargh Zahedi, the Chairman of the Judiciary Committee, and Farzin Hashemi, NCRI Representative in International Court Affairs, for their keen insights, ongoing support, and valuable editorial help, and direction of the publishing team to bring this work to fruition.

Finally, to all those selfless colleagues in our struggle for democracy and freedom, the list of which is too long to mention here, who contributed to the completion of this seminal work.

Mahnaz Salimian

Senior Secretary

National Council of Resistance of Iran

Paris, August 2022

CONTENTS

FOREWORD 1

PREFACE 5

INTRODUCTION 9

CHAPTER 1 – The Plot 13

CHAPTER 2 – The Target 51

CHAPTER 3 – The Terrorists 63

CHAPTER 4 – State Terrorism 85

CHAPTER 5 – The Modus Operandi 105

CHAPTER 6 – The Response 121

CHAPTER 7 – The Judgment 149

CHAPTER 8 – The Silence 169

CHAPTER 9 – The Treaty 181

APPENDICES 193

ENDNOTES 259

LIST OF FIGURES

Figure 1 – Left to Right: Assadi, Arefani, Naami, Saadouni. 15
Figure 2 - Assadi's hand-written instruction about the bomb to the couple. 31
Figure 3 - Assadi walking through Luxembourg market area to meet with his accomplices. 35
Figure 4 - Assadi after leaving Luxembourg and during a police officer stop. 36
Figure 5 - Police: "Suspect T3 [Assadi] in Alima Bourse [Luxembourg], near Saadouni-Naami. T3 seems to have hidden something under his T-shirt." 37
Figure 6 - Schematic of Paris Nord Villepinte. 51
Figure 7 – Huge attendance of Iranians at the Free Iran World Summit on June 30, 2018, at the Villepinte exhibition center, near Paris. ...52
Figure 8 - Dignitaries at Free Iran 2018 gathering that sat within range of explosion, had the bomb exploded. 53
Figure 9 - Mrs. Rajavi passing by the VIP section, where the bomb was due to be detonated. 54
Figure 10 - Naami's toiletry bag containing bomb remote control. 60
Figure 11 - X-ray of explosive device found in Naami's toiletry bag that was neutralized by a robot on June 30 in Woluwe-Saint-Pierre. ...60
Figure 12 – A huge attendance of Iranians at the Free Iran World Summit in Villepinte, June 30, 2018. 62
Figure 13 - Assadollah Assadi, diplomat-terrorist, ringleader of the terrorist plot. 63
Figure 14 - Passport details of Assadi as confirmed by Belgian VSSE ...64
Figure 15 - Document from Embassy of Iraq in Tehran attesting to Assadi's role in Iranian Embassy in Baghdad. Translated below. ..66
Figure 16 - A page of police report listing evidence in Assadi's car. 68
Figure 17 - Sheets of paper containing monetary requests from the Naami-Saadouni couple. 71
Figure 18 - Amir Saadouni in prison. 73
Figure 19 – Nasimeh Naami in prison. 75

Figure 20: Naami's Iranian passport showing the number of her trips to Iran. 77
Figure 21: Naami in Brussels, Belgium. 78
Figure 22 - Mehrdad Arefani 79
Figure 23 - A 1080p HD glasses with camera, and a USB flash drive with audio recording capability (evidence no. 158) 81
Figure 24- Mohammad Reza Zaeri visiting Khamenei. 87
Figure 25 - Zaeri with regime's diplomacy cheif Mohammad Javad Zarif 88
Figure 26- Receipt of a €2,400 salary of €2,400 paid to an agent with pseudonym Kazemi. It also mentions €900 been deducted for a previous loan. 106
Figure 27 – Money transfer document. 111
Figure 28- Arefani's post 119
Figure 29 - Iranian passports issued in Brussels to Naami and Saadouni. 120
Figure 30 - Javad Zarif's tweet on the Villepinte bombing attempt 169
Figure 31 - NCRI activists outside EU Foreign Ministers meeting in Brussels, Friday, Jan. 10, 2020. (AP). 174
Figure 32 - Robabeh Assadi. 256
Figure 33 - Ali Assadi. 256
Figure 34 – Assadi's eldest son, Hossein. 257
Figure 35- Assadollah Assadi's passport showing his position in Vienna as the "third counsellor" 257
Figure 36 - Saadouni Naami couple's car under police inspection following their arrest. 258
Figure 37 - Decision making chart. 258

GLOSSARY

DOVO	Explosive Device Disposal and Destruction Service
FTO	Foreign Terrorist Organization
IED	Improvised Explosive Device
MEK	Persian acronym for PMOI (Mujahedin-e Khalq)
MFA	Ministry of Foreign Affairs
MOIS	Ministry of Intelligence and Security
PMOI	People's Mojahedin Organization of Iran
NCRI	National Council of Resistance of Iran
SAVAK	Persian name acronym for Shah's secret police
IRGC	Islamic Revolutionary Guards Corps
QUDS	The Quds Force division of the IRGC
SMS	Short Message Service
SNSC	Supreme National Security Council (Iranian regime)
TATP	Triacetone Triperoxide (Explosive's material)
VSSE	Belgian State Security Service

FOREWORD

When I began serving as Assistant to the President for Homeland Security in 2001 under the George W. Bush administration, America's attention had just been captured by the perverted interpretation of Islam that reared its ugly head to inspire the September 11 terrorist attack on the World Trade Center in New York City.

But that beast had already been out of the cage in Iran since 1979, slowly but surely killing and intimidating the Iranian people and causing greater oppression and suffering for them and other peoples in the region. It was Tehran's model of pseudo-religious, fascist state power that inspired the September 11 terrorists, to whom Tehran gave sanctuary, funds, and encouragement before and after the attacks, up to this day, as confirmed by former Secretary of State, Mike Pompeo.

This well researched book is about a foiled, state-instigated terrorist attack on the annual gathering of the National Council of Resistance of Iran (NCRI), on June 30, 2018, near Paris. I had personally attended the NCRI's annual gathering several times. The 2018 event was attended by almost 100,000 participants in the span of 10 hours, and hundreds of political dignitaries from around the world. Had the terrorist plot succeeded, it would have certainly been the deadliest terrorist incident in Europe. Despite the severity of the plot and the court's definitive conclusion that it was an act of state terrorism, Western governments, especially in Europe, failed to take appropriate political measures to punish and dissuade the actual decision-makers behind the crime. Even more disturbing is the decision by the government of Belgium in early 2022 to sign a treaty, clearly designed to justify releasing the ringleader of the terrorist plot, with those who ordered the bombing of the peaceful rally in Villepinte.

The struggle against terrorism emanating from Tehran's rulers, however, cannot be understood if the wider struggle for the heart of Islam and the larger political struggle between the ideas of the MEK and the regime, is not understood. Islam, like all great religions, has been abused by a caste of professional preachers and clerics who rode into power on the coattails of Ruhollah Khomeini and established a religious-fascistic state model that abuses popular rage against historic grievances and modern contradictions, while expanding control of all aspects of life under its rule through terror, intimidation, and coercion to remain in power, all while claiming religious piety. The emergence of Khomeini and his fundamentalist and clearly violent and backward brand of Islam is a direct consequence of the tyranny of the Pahlavi monarchy that ruled Iran for more than fifty years. The Shah systematically destroyed all democratic forces, executing and imprisoning many, including MEK founders and leaders. The resulting political vacuum gave Khomeini and his network of mullahs a path to hijack the essentially freedom-seeking movement, and to establish an extremist regime.

This struggle spearheaded by the MEK against the virulent and backward ideas of Khomeini and his successors defines the future of not only Shia Islam and Iran, but also of the terrorist threat that the Iranian regime perpetuates and nurtures against the West, and of course, its own people and the region.

To defeat Iranian state terrorism, we cannot but help to get to the crux of the matter, the heart of the octopus that beats in the halls of power in Tehran. Therein lies the engine for hate, terrorism, murder, and destruction that threatens our values of democracy, freedom, separation of church and state, gender equality, the sovereignty of free peoples, and the progress and prosperity that we in the West have so long enjoyed.

This book is an excellent study of one of the most intricate and sophisticated terrorist attacks by the Iranian regime that could have been one of the deadliest to date on European soil, against precisely that potent foe in the Iranian Resistance that spells its end.

I recommend this book to everyone interested in learning the depths to which the Iranian regime will go to extinguish the hope for change and freedom and modernity in Iran, and by extension to defeat the values for which modern humanity has fought so hard to enshrine in the Universal Declaration of Human Rights, our own US Constitution, and other modern instruments of human progress and prosperity.

We, freedom-loving peoples who cherish the human journey from coercion to liberty throughout human history, are in this together. We, who wish for the full blossoming of our potential to change the world for the better, should understand the enemies of our values and our freedoms. Today, there is no more dangerous enemy to human progress and liberty than the Iranian regime, with its malign and destructive role and the ideas that underpin it. This book on the most important terrorism case in Europe, hatched, directed, and carried out by the Iranian regime's senior leadership, will certainly help to further our understanding.

Finally, the terrorist plot against the MEK and NCRI in the heart of Europe demonstrates the extent to which the regime is terrified of the democratic alternative to its rule. This book is a reminder to all policymakers in Europe and North America that attention to the desire of the Iranian people and the organized resistance has been a missing factor in their policies vis-à-vis Iran for over four decades.

A new policy is long overdue.

Tom Ridge
First US Secretary of Homeland Security (2003 to 2005)
Erie, Pennsylvania, August 2022

PREFACE

When in July 2018, German security services and law enforcement agencies, in a joint operation with their Belgian and French counterparts, arrested a sitting Iranian diplomat serving in Vienna, enroute to Austria, for planning and directing the attempted bombing of a huge exposition hall in Villepinte, France, it immediately sent shock waves through the world. The target was the site of the annual Free Iran World Summit, which was attended by Maryam Rajavi, the President-elect of NCRI,[1] the principal opposition to the regime, hundreds of world political leaders and dignitaries, and a huge attendance of Iranian dissidents.

The Iranian regime's president and foreign minister denied culpability, but the trial and conviction of the Iranian regime's diplomat for plotting to commit terrorist murder proved beyond any reasonable doubt that Iran's Foreign Ministry, hand in glove with the Ministry of Intelligence and Security, had abused diplomatic cover to launch what could have been one of the deadliest attacks on European soil, targeting Mrs. Rajavi, and many other individuals in Villepinte.

This episode in the Iranian regime's desperate, four decades bid to shut down its formidable opposition brings to light all the varied elements of the ruling theocracy's extraterritorial terrorist operation, including decision making, targeting, tactics, funding, and spy craft.

This case is unique in that European security services were able to interdict and interrupt a very deadly terrorist operation. The successful investigation, trial, and conviction of the four terrorists, including the Vienna-based diplomat, brought to light many realities about how the regime uses terrorism, and how Europe's political leadership instead of building on the successes of its security and judicial services, squanders it by appeasing the rogue state sponsor of terrorism in Iran, thereby ensuring the perpetuation of Iran's state terrorism.

In preparing this book, a large portion of available pages of the Assadi case documents have been meticulously reviewed, thousands of pages of news have been analyzed, hundreds of interviews have been conducted, and all sources have been verified. However, many aspects of this and other instances of Iranian state terrorism against the opposition remain under-researched and uncovered.

This is demonstrated, for example, by the lack of sufficient attention and research into the decision to commit this terrorist crime at Iran's Supreme National Security Council (SNSC),[2] headed by Hassan Rouhani, the regime's president at the time, and his foreign minister, Javad Zarif, demonstrating the engagement of the entirety of the regime in such acts. This is attested to by the role and undertakings of Saeid Hashemi Moghadam. Hashemi Moghadam was a deputy to Iran's Intelligence Minister and a liaison with European intelligence services, well known to them. In the aftermath of the foiled Villepinte terrorist operation, he was named as the commander of the plot and was designated as a terrorist by the European Union.

Another important issue is the significant amount of information and intelligence leads gleaned from Assadi's documents and notebooks that showed the extent of the Iranian regime's terrorist network in Europe and its direct link to the regime's embassies. The court handling Assadi's case concluded that he had been running a network of agents in Europe. The evidence showed that such a network went far beyond the three agents arrested and convicted in this case. This information has not been publicly divulged and intelligence agents involved in this network have not been expelled or faced consequences, as called for by the Iranian Resistance. Who has replaced Assadi to run the network? Why have European governments kept silent on this issue? And many other lingering questions require political decisions to inform the public and to take necessary action.

Despite the outstanding questions, this book, focuses on a solid body of established facts to show the totality and anatomy of a horrific act of state terrorism by the Iranian regime.

We would like to acknowledge the selfless work of a network of Iranian MEK dissidents inside Iran who worked tirelessly in dangerous circumstances to corroborate the facts. We would also like to thank the Belgian, German, and French security services, law enforcement, and judiciary for their professional and diligent work to uncover and bring this case to trial and conviction. Were it not for their work, yet another terrorist plot by the Iranian regime would have been swept under the carpet by a political establishment that has appeased the religious dictatorship in Iran for far too long.

We hope that the publication of this book will enlighten students of Iranian affairs about the way in which the regime in Tehran uses every means at its disposal, including its diplomatic representatives, to carry out its terrorist missions abroad against Iranian dissidents and others.

Finally, we hope that this book will be a reminder to policymakers throughout the world that making concessions to the Iranian regime's state terrorism, or merely remaining silent on the topic, will only enable more of the same.

INTRODUCTION

Assadollah Assadi, became the first-ever serving Iranian diplomat to be detained, investigated, tried, convicted, and imprisoned, after he plotted to blow up thousands of participants in the Iranian Resistance's annual Free Iran World Summit in Villepinte, France, where Maryam Rajavi, the President-elect of the opposition National Council of Resistance of Iran was speaking, along with hundreds of political dignitaries from across the globe.

In late February 2022, authorities in Iran detained a Belgian aid worker, and this time, it was Belgium's turn to be blackmailed with yet another hostage taking by a regime that for over 40 years has taken advantage of Western appeasement to further its illegal and murderous ways. Hostages are the Iranian regime's leverage to set Assadi free and return him to Iran, from where he had set out in late June of 2018 with a highly sophisticated and lethal explosive device in his diplomatic pouch. Assadi and his paymasters in Iranian intelligence didn't think twice about moving the bomb to Vienna on a commercial passenger jet.

The fact that Assadi was under close surveillance and caught red-handed delivering the bomb to his accomplices in a Luxembourg Pizza Hut does not bother the Iranian regime. To them Assadi is a hero diplomat carrying out his "duties" albeit in direct contravention of the Vienna Convention on diplomatic relations and international law.

This case highlights the close cooperation between the Ministry of Foreign Affairs (MFA) and Ministry of Intelligence and Security (MOIS) in terrorist activities in Europe.

After the February hostage-taking of the Belgium national in Iran, the regime clearly communicated back-channel messages to

Belgium, and the two parties secretly signed a prisoner-exchange treaty on March 11.

The first public unveiling of this "pact with the devil"[3] came when Belgium's justice minister, Vincent Van Quickenborne, urgently presented a bill to the Belgian Parliament on June 29, which sought ratification for the treaty with Iran by sandwiching it between two other prisoner exchange treaties. He would later defend the unsavory bill by meekly offering, "Iran is a rogue state, but we don't choose to whom we talk." He emphasized that freeing the Belgian was "our priority."[4]

If Prime Minister Alexander De Croo and his justice minister had had their way, the bill would have been enacted four business days later.

But members of Parliament, including some in the government coalition, strongly criticized the treaty. Simultaneously, the Iranian Resistance, condemned the possibility of releasing Assadi back to Iran and called for action to prevent it. This call galvanized opposition to the shameful bill among Iranians, in the Belgium Parliament, in the press, and in the court of public opinion.

Those opponents argued that by backing down in the face of Iran's blackmail would endanger the security of European citizens and Iranian dissidents alike and embolden ever more hostage-taking and terrorism. This campaign led to the debate on the treaty that continued for over two more weeks.

The treaty's ratification was expected by July 4, but it was ultimately ratified over two weeks later, early on July 21. The NCRI, its president-elect, and a group of potential victims of Assadi's terrorist plot, however, have launched a legal challenge to the government's bid to free a convicted terrorist. That challenge has yet to be heard and settled. In the meantime, a court injunction is in place barring Assadi's release until the court decides on the case after hearing from the two parties.

INTRODUCTION

The first three chapters of this book cover, in minute detail, the hatching of the terrorist plot, its painstaking execution from Tehran to Vienna to Luxembourg to Belgium to France, the intelligence tip leading to the surveillance, the importance of the 2018 Free Iran World Summit as a target for Tehran, the consequence of an attack on the main protagonist, the four members of the terrorist cell, including the ringleader, the regime's "swallow"[5], the sleeper cell, and the mule.

Chapter four discusses Iran's state terrorism, and chapter five details its extensive terrorist network in Europe as revealed by Assadi's "green book". The judicial proceedings and court conviction of the terrorist ring is covered in chapter six, with the court judgement presented in chapter seven. In chapter eight we turn to the West's failing to politically address the Iranian regime's flagrant violation of EU and international law. Finally, chapter nine discusses, the Belgian treaty with the Iranian regime and the consequences of it paving the way for a convicted terrorist to be sent back to Iran.

CHAPTER 1

The Plot

On July 2, 2018, it took a few minutes to understand the meaning, importance, and consequences of the news that all major news media reported.

The State Security Service (VSSE) and the Federal Prosecutor's Office of Belgium issued a joint statement in Flemish, French, and English, announcing the foiling of a major terrorist plot against a summit organized by the NCRI in Villepinte, France.

Many questions were raised by the revelation of this threat to an annual event attended by a huge audience of Iranian dissidents and hundreds of senior political figures from all over the world: What would have happened had the terrorist plot not been foiled? What impact would it have had on the struggle in Iran? How would Western countries have reacted to the death and injury among dozens of their former officials?

The dimensions of Tehran's state-sponsored terrorist plot, directed by a sitting official diplomat, were surprising and shocking, marking a turning point in the Iranian regime's terrorist activities abroad. The statement by VSSE and the Belgian Federal Prosecutor's Office reads in part (Refer to Appendix D):

> *Federal Prosecutor's Office and Homeland Security Press Release*
>
> *Based on important information from the Belgian Federal Intelligence and Security Agency, a terrorism investigation was initiated by the Federal Public Prosecutor's Office.*
>
> *Within the framework of this investigation, an arrest warrant was issued today for Amir S., born on 26 April 1980, and his wife Nasimeh N, born on 20 September 1984, both of Belgian nationality*

but of Iranian origin, by an Antwerp Investigating Judge specialized in terrorism.

They were charged with attempted terrorist murder and the preparation of a terrorist offence.

Both are suspected of wanting to commit a bomb attack in Villepinte (France) on Saturday 30 June 2018 at a conference held there by the MEK, the People's Mojahedin of Iran. This organization is an Iranian opposition party that was founded in 1965 and outlawed by the Iranian Government in 1981… The arrested couple were intercepted, on board their Mercedes, by the special units of the police in Sint-Pieters-Woluwe.

During the search of that vehicle, approximately 500 grams of TATP and an ignition mechanism were found in a small toiletry bag. DOVO conducted a controlled detonation of this explosive.

At the request of the Investigating Judge, the Antwerp Federal Judicial Police carried out five house searches on Saturday in Wilrijk, Boom, Ukkel, Mons and Leuze-en-Hainaut. The results of these searches cannot be communicated for the time being.

At the same time, a suspected accomplice, Merhad A, born on 31 July 1963, was deprived of his liberty in France. Two other people were released in France after questioning.

A contact person of the couple, Assadollah A., born on 22 December 1971, of Iranian nationality, was also arrested in Germany. He is an Iranian diplomat at the Austrian Embassy in Vienna.

This operation was only possible because of the information position that the Belgian Federal Intelligence and Security Agency (VSSE) has built up in this file. In a short period of time, the VSSE has collected, exploited, and enriched essential information, also thanks to an excellent exchange with foreign intelligence services. Cooperation between the Federal Public Prosecutor's Office, the VSSE, the Antwerp Federal Judicial Police, DOVO and the French (DGSI) and German judicial authorities has made it possible to prevent a terrorist attack.

Initial information

Although the information in the above initial report is not complete, the basic information of the Villepinte bomb plot is mentioned in the announcement. The full names of the four people who were directly involved in this case are as follows:

- **Assadollah Assadi** was an officer of the Ministry of Intelligence of the Iranian regime, who had the official diplomatic position of the third secretary of the embassy in Vienna. He was arrested on the morning of Sunday, July 1, 2018, in southern Germany. Assadi was the commander of the operation.

- **Mehrdad Arefani**, a professional and experienced agent of the Ministry of Intelligence, who worked as a terrorist sleeper cell and was at the scene of the attempted terrorist operation as Assadi's "eyes and ears". He was arrested on the evening of June 30 at the summit venue in Villepinte.

- **Nasimeh Naami** and **Amir Saadouni**, a married couple, who after years of training and preparation were tasked with detonating the sophisticated bomb supplied to them by Assadi after carrying it to the conference location in Villepinte, were arrested at around noon of the day of the intended operation on June 30, 2018, in a Brussels suburb.

Figure 1 – Left to Right: Assadi, Arefani, Naami, Saadouni.

A Peaceful Summit

For more than 10 hours, on June 30, a massive gathering of Iranian dissidents and hundreds of political figures present at the Villepinte Hall in France listened to the speeches of political figures from 70 countries and watched cultural performances in complete peace and enjoyment. The summit received extensive media coverage and continued until the end of the program without any issues or incidents.

Mehrdad Arefani was arrested that evening in a special operation by the French police in the parking lot of the Villepinte Hall. But aside from that, everything moved smoothly. There was no hint of any terrorist plot, except that the police and even the French military had deployed a large force on location. Although this situation was different from previous years, it did not attract special attention at the time.

The Iranian regime had officially asked France to cancel this program,[6] but in response to a letter by members of France's National Assembly, the French government said that freedom of expression in France is guaranteed and rejected this demand. Therefore, it was normal and necessary to take security measures to prevent any possible incident.

Investigating Judge Orders Surveillance

Five days earlier, on June 25, 2018, the State Security Agency of Belgium, the country's highest security organization, announced that, based on reliable information, Amir Saadouni (born April 26, 1980) and Nasimeh Naami (born September 20, 1984) might engage in or initiate a violent act in France. Both lived in Antwerp. (Refer to Appendix C).

The next day, the investigation of this case was handed over to a judge in Antwerp.

On June 26, the investigating judge issued an order to control and record phones conversations of Saadouni and Naami.

On June 29, the investigating judge ordered the examination of the bank accounts and the collection of information about their bank transactions.

Mehrdad Arefani's phone was also wiretapped by the police on June 30.

Terrorist Plot Starts

The plan to blow up the Villepinte Hall was first raised in a meeting between the Naami-Saadouni couple and Assadollah Assadi (alias Daniel) in a train ride between Vienna and Salzburg in March 2018.

This matter is addressed in the text of the judgment of the Antwerp Court of Appeal in a detailed and technical manner:[7]

> *From the statements of the defendants Amir Saadouni and Nasimeh Naami, it appears that in March 2018, two meetings were held with Assadollah Assadi in Austria, in which Assadi discussed for the first time the placement of an explosive device during a gathering in Villepinte. Based on the traffic related to the mobile antenna tower and the invoice for a night's stay in a hotel in Vienna, it can be determined that these meetings took place on March 1, 2018 (on the train between Vienna and Salzburg, where the three got off on the way and went to a park) and on March 16-17, 2018 (in Austria). Also, on March 17, 2018, the new Austrian mobile phone number of Assadollah Assadi (436602227681) was activated. Two days later, on March 19, 2018, the new mobile phone number of the defendant Amir Saadouni (32485508387) was activated.*

> *From the email traffic of March 25, 2018, between Assadollah Assadi on the one hand and the couple Amir Saadouni-Nasimeh Naami on the other, it seems that the couple did not act overnight and thought*

carefully beforehand. For example, it was established that they gave their definitive consent only if a number of conditions were to be met, namely an increase in the monthly fee to the amount of €2,000, an additional fee for their part in placing the bomb, and a statement that in any case that fee should be taken into account because the accused Amir Saadouni had to buy a house.

Before the May 12, 2018, meeting in Austria, through letters between April 7, 2018, and May 7, 2018, it appears that the couple Amir Saadouni-Nasimeh Naami provided information about the MEK, especially about the annual gathering, to Assadi; the annual summit held on June 30, 2018, [see emails dated May 3, 2018, and May 7, 2018, from the defendant Amir Saadouni to Assadollah Assadi].

On May 25, 2018, the defendant Amir Saadouni sent an email in which Assadollah Assadi confirmed his agreement as follows:

Saeed and Monshi [Naami] have put a lot of thought into the card game for the wedding party and have decided that it has to be a very professional game to win the competition!

However, their cooperation is again subject to the adjustment of their wages. This was expressed using a coded language as follows: "Both agree, but if Mohsen promises that he can present a big surprise, so that Saeed's fatigue of the past years will be ameliorated" [May 25, 2018, letters from the accused Naami to Assadi].

Saadouni's Account of the Plot

In his first series of interrogations on July 2, 2018,[8] Saadouni explained the starting point of this plan, while attempting to downplay the importance and seriousness of the terrorist act that they were about to conduct.

Saadouni:

I have been in contact with Daniel [Assadi] since 2007. He was an employee of the Iranian embassy in Vienna. Daniel asked me to do something at the Paris conference three months ago. He told me he was going to provide me with a device that would only make noise and nothing else. He told me to leave it at parking lot, where there were no people. The participants would be in the hall. I received the device from Daniel in Luxembourg. It was a very small dark blue women's handbag. Daniel took it out of his backpack and handed it to us, my wife put it in her purse. I put the bag in a suitcase. Daniel instructed me to cover the bag with plastic wrap. When I took the bag from Daniel, I looked at it. Daniel said, 'the charger is connected' I had to charge it at night, which I did on the night of June 29-30. There was also a remote control. I don't think there is anything left (to say). My wife had nothing to do with it. Daniel paid me €1,000-1,500 per month from since 2015. The first year was a trial year to see if I could be trusted. The deal was for me to work for Assadi for four years. In 2012 or 2013 they paid me from Ahvaz in Iran. It became quite serious from 2015 onwards. Since 2010 I was in a contact with someone else in Brussels. I know that no one from the MEK was aware of my position.

Assadi's Keen Interest in MEK Meetings

The meeting between the Naami-Saadouni couple with Assadi (Daniel) was described as follows by Saadouni during his interrogation by the Belgian judicial police on November 23, 2018:

Q. When was the last time you met Daniel before he was arrested?

A. This was in Austria. Normally, we would fly to Salzburg by plane, but due to plane delays, we went to Vienna. Naami was also there. This was in March or April 2018.

I always had to book a ticket to Vienna and then take a train to Salzburg. We boarded the train and got off somewhere, I don't know where. I know we were on the train for an hour and a half before we got off. I know there is a very famous park in that city. In this meeting we talked about recording conversations. I always had to go to important meetings of the MEK. I went and then I had to record the issues discussed there. This was made very difficult because there was strict control [and bringing mobile phones into meetings] was usually prohibited. Daniel told me that I should give him the car key to install a recording device. Daniel said in one of his last messages that he made me a golden key, which he meant a car key. Daniel also asked Nasimeh for a key and took them both to Tehran to see if they could install recording devices in them. We gave these keys to Daniel, but we didn't get them back. We were supposed to receive these at the meeting in Luxembourg. Daniel said that his MOIS colleagues were going to install recorders in them, but he never mentioned a name. I don't know exactly either.... These keys were very important because they were used to record conferences. Daniel didn't trust me to tell the truth, so I had to give him the recordings, so he could know I was really there. Daniel considered the meeting in France very important. He was debating whether to come to France himself. Of course, he could not come to the meeting himself, but to get information as soon as possible, he wanted to come to France. It was about a meeting in May 2018, which was about the situation inside Iran. Daniel wanted to get this information as soon as possible. This was very important because there were international sanctions against Iran. It was very important for him to hear the conversations of the personalities, because the MEK were talking about this. The MEK have influence on senators and politicians, they have the support of Israel and Saudi Arabia. The appointment to work on this was in Salzburg...

Extensive Email Communications

In the period between March 1 and June 30, the parties continued to exchange emails and SMS intensively and transferred their content with the codes they had agreed upon. The email used by Naami, and Saadouni was mishoo_boonty84@yahoo.com. Assadi used jagerurban2016@yahoo.com in these communications.

In most of these email exchanges, Naami was the main party, and she addressed Assadi as "brother" or "uncle." Sometimes she addressed him in the third person. Most of these communications were about the bombing plot and the meeting they wanted to have to receive the explosive material. Ten days before this meeting, Assadi would go to Iran on June 18 to bring the manufactured and tested bomb with him.

Some of these emails exceptionally deal with other events related to the MEK. In all emails, correspondence is conducted in a coded language. Two detailed interrogations of Saadouni have been devoted to describing and deciphering these codes.

From Assadi to Saadouni, March 2, 2018

Every day that passes, I yearn to meet my dearest loved ones and hope that it will be fulfilled soon. Say hello to all the families and fill our place in your happiness. Thank you for the information about the party [the conference in Villepinte]. 9

... If a new chef [another person from the MOIS] wants to participate in this competition, Monshi's [Naami] father will do this with the coordination of director Mohsen [the MOIS contact inside Iran] and you should automatically know that this person is also approved by both her father and also Mohsen.10

The competition proceeds slowly without any rush. Feel free to give any information to Monshi's [Naami] father. Take care of your family. They have not entered the competition [the Saadouni family was not included in this mission]. Write me about your situation, what happened at work and when will you be released from class and school? What happened to the psychiatrist? Has Monshi's [Naami] house purchase been resolved? Also, please see what the price is, if possible, we can make an appointment for 17 cartons [17th day of the month]. If you want me to order, I will post a course [possible meeting place] for you.

From Assadi to Saadouni, March 13, 2018

Hello. Thank you for organizing the ceremony well. You were supposed to write to me about Zakia, but I didn't see anything. Did you send it, and it didn't arrive, or you didn't send it at all? You did not write anything about the order of 17 cartons [date of face-to-face meeting]. Please tell me if you received the two emails dated March 5 from me or not. Anyway, I am waiting for your news. Starting tomorrow, I have a shift every day in the boarding house that you used in the last course. Please let me know at 17:00. If you see those 17 cartons are not enough, please tell me how much I should order for you so that I can see whether I will get the money or not. [Coordinating the date and place of appointment]. I am proud of you from the bottom of my heart.

From Naami to Assadi, March 25, 2018

Greetings brother, God bless you, unfortunately we couldn't meet in person, but anyway, your greetings arrived, and I was very happy. Say hello to Mohsen [MOIS contact in Iran] and tell him that Saeed [Saadouni] has a lot of mental preoccupation and is worried about his family life and the future

1. The monthly loan [monthly salary] where he lives should be 2000 apples [Euro] to be sure that one day if for any reason there is no more hope... he has not lost anything, and his youthful corner and job position are now lost. And don't stress.

2. In addition to a monthly fixed deposit of 2000 apples [fixed salary], Mohsen [Ministry of Information] should accept the additional expenses of Saeed [Saadouni] who is engaged in activities.

3. To give Saeed [Saadouni] a complete loan without advance payment every season because another house will be bought soon, and the bank must be responsible. Saeed [Saadouni] is under too much work stress and is no longer able to respond to marginal problems.

I kiss you, brother, I hope God blesses you and your family with health and wellness in the new year. I am waiting for a letter to know what to do... God bless you.

From Assadi to the Couple, May 2, 2018

Greetings to you.

I am also happy that you are healthy and well. I hope that you will always be happy and cheerful and that expect for not seeing me, you would not feel sad.

If we're going to have a [face-to-face meeting], we have to have a party before Grandma's party [Villepinte Conference].

Just please see your itinerary and tell me how many cartons of fish you can order? [Which date is suitable]

Please visit the boarding house [email] once this next week to make sure that it is clean and tidy for the guests to have a good time.

...hoping to make you proud as much as possible

Naami's Response to Assadi, May 3, 2018

Hello brother, how are you? We are also good. Saeed also said hello, and he will be back on Monday....

All this time, both Monshi [Naami] and Saeed [Saadouni] followed new cooking and put it in the archive, according to the order of fish, which can be heated after June 6, but again, Saeed's opinion is important because he is busy with classes these days... BTW, tell Dani [Daniel, aka. Assadi] that the boarding house will be cleaned on Tuesday and Wednesday next week after 6 o'clock for sure!

[What they meant was that they were looking for information on the MEK and that they had kept it to give it to Assadi later. He suggests meeting after June 6 and to chat two days the following week]

BTW, tell Daniel [Assadi] to try to make an appointment in person when Mohsen [more senior than Assadi and the liaison to the Ministry of Intelligence inside Iran] has given him an additional deposit [incentive money]. Because Monshi [Naami] here alone is looking to buy a new house, but there are a lot of expenses ahead, and this is the reason for Saeed's [Saadouni] stress…

From Naami to Assadi, May 7, 2018

Hello brother, how are you?

We went to the Belgian office yesterday at 17:00… The main speaker was Firouz Mahvi, whose main topic was about the galaxy [the Paris conference], the uprising, and the fate of the regime, and… the last thing, he explained about a series of events in Albania that Mohsen's friends [people from the Iranian embassy] have caused the authorities [Albanian authorities] trouble again. It is not bad to listen and be able to plan more about Albania in the long term. Unfortunately, because he was a speaker for nearly three hours, the quality of the recording was very low, and the original version is kept for you in the Monshi's [Naami] archive. P.S., you had promised a gift for Saeed [Saadouni] that would order, so that he could send the original like in CD's. I hope you think about it and get it as soon as possible…

Clarification: In this email, in addition to the topic of the major Summit on June 30th, Naami also offers Assadi guidance for dealing with the MEK in Albania, the location of its headquarters and residence for over 3,000 members, Ashraf 3.

From Assadi to the Couple, May 8, 2018

Hello, don't be tired

Wednesday is ok, and if you like, you can buy 12 packages of fish [12 o'clock]. Please let me about it on Wednesday.

If for any reason Wednesday is not possible or if the boarding house is not arranged, let me know here, I will come tomorrow, I will visit, and we will coordinate when you can meet in person.

For now, with your permission, I leave you to God.

From Naami to Assadi, May 25, 2018

This exchange is notable in that the Naami-Saadouni couple announce their intent to proceed with the plot.

Hi, how are you? We are fine too, Saeed [Saadouni] is always asking how you are.

Saeed and Monshi [Saadouni and Naami] thought a lot about playing cards at the wedding [the operation plan at the event in Villepinte] and came to the conclusion that playing cards must be very professional to be able to win the competition.

Both agree, but if Mohsen promises to give a nice surprise, so that Saeed could overcome the fatigue of these several years!

Tell Daniel, if he also wants to participate in the wedding contest, Monshi [Naami] and Saeed [Saadouni] have only one chance to practice playing cards [to prepare for the operation], they can buy 8, 9, or 10 cards from Daniel!!! [Probably the suitable date for a face-to-face meeting].

From Naami to Assadi, June 2, 2018

Hello, are you well uncle?

I talked to Saeed [Saadouni], if the number of cards is 23 [June 23], it is very easy for Monshi [Naami] to order with Saeed [Saadouni], and say hi to Daniel [Assadi], tell me to order on [June 23] in Luxembourg, is it good? Hello, I am waiting for Daniel's answer to coordinate with Saeed [Saadouni] .

From Assadi to the Couple, June 2, 2018

Hello and thank you

Mohsen (MOIS liaison] also said hello and he would also like to participate in the competition [operational plan], perhaps his card will win.

Our effort is to provide a sufficient number of cards for the players, but you should pay attention to the important point that if we want high quality and excitement, these cards can reach the players from 22 numbers or more [after June 22].

Please look in your pocket and give me the number so that I know how many cards I can offer together.

Regarding sweets [money], don't worry, we reached an agreement with Mohsen....

From Assadi to Naami, June 9, 2018

Dearest of Uncle, hello to you

Very good, 23 cartons of luxury soap [Luxembourg]. Luxury soap [Luxembourg] is a very good soap and women can use it and be satisfied during the ceremony.

Daniel asked a lot about how you are and said to tell his niece: There is a 1% chance that Daniel [Assadi] will not be able to come to ceremony. Only 1%.

For this 1%, the only way is for the niece to pick up the car and take it to the first city of Kors Kors [Salzburg] from the side of the nail shop...

As I said, I have been involved in cleaning every day since the 18th. Except for one or two days when I visit Mohsen. [I am busy with emails every day at 18:00 hours, except for one or two days when I go to Iran].

Clarification: In this email, Assadi informs that there is a 1% chance that the meeting may have to be held somewhere other than in Luxembourg. In the next email, however, he changes this.

From Assadi to Naami, June 12, 2018

The good news is that 1% is no longer in play and Saeed [Saadouni] does not have to deal with the burden. God willing, everything will be done according to the routine.

Another news is that everything is ready for the celebration [for June 30 operation].

The only point is that I ordered good henna for the festival. [Explosive material suitable for the Paris meeting].

But I will probably have to order more than 23 cartons [after June 23].

That means maybe 24 cartons or more.

In short, I will definitely cancel the order of 23 cartons, and I am currently thinking about 24 cartons, and I hope your family will be successful as well.

Please, apart from the purchase offer, think about how many more are needed as spares to satisfy the guests.

Make sure to tell me. I go every day at the same time to clean the boarding house. Please come and help.

God bless you. Hoping for a wonderful celebration, God willing

From Naami to Assadi, June 13, 2018

Hello, are you well brother?

The Monshi [Naami] is waiting for the number of your henna order and agrees with the 24th [date for June 24th], just let Daniel [Assadi] know to make sure the party is in Lux [meeting in Luxembourg]

Saeed [Saadouni] cleans boarding house [email] every day. If you can, help out.

May God protect you, goodbye.

From Assadi, June 18, 2018

Hello, thank you very much for cleaning the guesthouse

It turned out very well and now Daniel [Assadi] can visit Mohsen [the liaison of the Ministry of Intelligence inside] and then prepare himself for applying the Henna [bomb].

I hope it will be a good celebration and everyone will be satisfied with this memorable celebration.

Daniel is going to see Mohsen today [Assadi is going to Iran today] so that he can succeed and come back happy.

Please, in the next week, try to ask this Daniel [Assadi] how he is doing every night so that he does not feel lonely.

Daniel's program is as follows:

From Saturday the 23rd to Monday the 25th, every day in the evening, the boarding house will be open 100% with Saeed [Saadouni].

Also, Daniel [Assadi] has been checking his email since Tuesday. But he's just visiting to see if there's a letter or not, please send a letter to Daniel [Assadi] from Tuesday only if it's necessary, otherwise there's no need.

It is likely that the price of henna per kilo will be around 14 Euros [time for the meeting]. As a result, you should be aware that if the price is lower, it will not increase.

I leave you to God

From Naami to Assadi, June 20, 2018

Hello brother, how are you?

Yesterday Saeed [Saadouni] was with Zakir [Brussels]. According to the latest figures, currently four buses have been booked for the Villepinte event, and Saeed [Saadouni] is supposed to bring a large, refrigerated truck from Paris to Brussels on 29 [June] to put sandwiches and soft drinks, which will leave at the same time as the buses the next day.

According to the mother's promise, we ordered 28 lux (Luxembourg) and we agreed on the price to buy a package of approximately 14 euros (14:00 hours).

I will clean the boarding house from Saturday... [I will check the email from Saturday].

With Saeed [Saadouni] not being here, you go to Iran every week [She says this because Assadi is in Iran on this date]

Take care of yourself, God willing, everything will be sold.

Assadi's Car Rental Three Months Prior

On March 28, 2018, three months before using it, Assadi signed a car rental agreement in Vienna to rent a vehicle from June 25, 2018, to July 2, 2018.

Regarding the decision to carry out the plan, the date of the car rental is very significant. On March 1, 2018, Saadouni and Naami received orders from Assadi to carry out the operation against the NCRI summit in Paris, on a train ride from Vienna to Salzburg. Because the explosive materials had to be tested, Assadi needed to consult with Tehran. From the examination of Assadi's passport, it has been determined that Assadi flew from Vienna to Tehran on March 28, 2018. On the same day, the rental contract is concluded online.

For this reason, it is believed that Assadi received the final order for the terrorist operation on March 28, 2018, in Tehran, and therefore, on March 28, he approved the rental contract online, probably from Tehran. Accommodations without exception were reserved through Booking.com.

Assadi took delivery of the car on June 25 at 5:41 pm with the odometer at 23,775 km. He put the car in the parking lot next to the car rental company and left with the car for Germany the next morning, June 26.

From then until the first day of July when he was arrested in Germany on the way back to Vienna, all his movements have been extracted by the police from the GPS of this rental car.

Although Assadi's identity was confirmed to the police after meeting Naami and Saadouni in the early afternoon of June 28 in Luxembourg, it seems that after that he was not yet put under special surveillance.

For this reason, his movements are recorded by only his two GPS devices: the rental car GPS, and his own TomTom mobile GPS.

The German police prepared a detailed report about Assadi's six-day trip from Vienna to Luxembourg, his departure to Liege, Belgium, after meeting in Luxembourg, and his return to Germany until his arrest in southern Germany. A summary of Assadi's six-day trip follows, based on the report of the German investigative police.

From Vienna to Luxembourg

Investigations show that Assadi and his family traveled from Vienna to Wiesent in Regensburg, Heidelberg on June 26, and from Cochem to Luxembourg City on June 28. They spent the night of June 26 at Gästehaus Rösch in Wiesent and spent the night of June 27 at Hotel Hieronimi in Cochem. On June 28 Assadi was in Luxembourg City from at least 1:09 pm to 3:45 pm. Police surveillance confirmed his presence in Luxembourg. According to the testimonies of Saadouni and Naami, the bomb was delivered in Luxembourg City. Assadi said in his interrogation that he was not in Luxembourg City at all. But his younger son, Ali, stated that his father met an old acquaintance in Luxembourg and took about one hour to 90 minutes to go and eat with him.

Bomb Delivery in Pizza Hut

The afternoon of June 28 is a turning point in the case. On that day, Assadi, who came to Luxembourg via Germany from Austria, was conclusively identified by Luxembourg police later in the day, after he met with the Naami-Saadouni couple who had gone there from Belgium. The couple received explosives and instructions from Assadi.[11] (Refer to Appendix G).

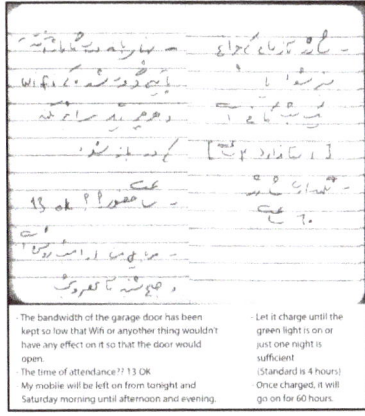

Figure 2 - Assadi's hand-written instruction about the bomb to the couple.

In this meeting, Assadi gave the couple a significant amount of cash (between €17,000 and €22,000).

The appointment was very important for them, and they had planned it weeks in advance and repeatedly exchanged dozens of coded emails and SMS about the day, time, and location of the appointment until finally deciding on June 28 at 2:00 pm in Luxembourg (city center).

Assadi had organized all his work in those days to make this meeting as normal and successful as possible. He left Vienna with his wife and two sons on June 26 and tried to make this dangerous trip appear as a family trip and visited several German cities on the 26th and 27th. He had also booked two hotels for two nights in the Netherlands to profess that they were going there for a family vacation.

However, the Naami-Saadouni couple had been under police surveillance by order of the Belgian judge since the previous day. Legally, the case was opened on June 25 against the Naami-Saadouni couple. On June 26, the Belgian State Security Service prepared a preliminary report, and subsequently, the Naami-Saadouni couple came under constant police surveillance.

On the morning of June 28, when they were leaving for Luxembourg, the Belgian police had them under constant surveillance until the border, and after crossing the border, through prior arrangement, Luxembourg police kept them under surveillance.

The couple went to Luxembourg with their own Mercedes and after reaching the city center, they first exchanged an "all clear" sign with someone and then parked their car and left for the location in the city's central square. After pausing shortly and walking around, they made contact with Assadi, whom they knew well. They met near Place d'Armes and Jan Palach squares and went to the Pizza Hut restaurant in the same area.

This meeting lasted about an hour and a half, during which time, Assadi put a small toiletry bag containing a bomb along with a detonator and a remote control in Naami's bag.

As it appears from Assadi's subsequent text messages to the couple, he was not satisfied with the atmosphere of the place where they met. He himself expressed this in coded language by saying: *"The food on that street was very dirty"*![12]

The phrase implies that he felt the place was under police surveillance. This is probably why he could not fully brief them on how to use the explosive device. Of course, it seems that they had already been briefed, but it may have been difficult to open the device and explain the details and how it would work in a public setting.

For this reason, he said: *"Look at the PlayStation 4 [bomb], if you have any questions, let me know."* **They answered:** *"We played, the Monshi [Naami] learned." Shall we leave?"* It means that Naami had mastered the bomb and they wanted to return to their house in Belgium. In return, Assadi answered: *"God be with you"*!

After this stage, the Naami-Saadouni couple again go to Alima Bourse, which is located nearby, and Assadi is also there, and they see each other for a few minutes.

The Luxembourg police still did not know Assadi's identity at this point, until he was stopped by police briefly later in the day, and for this reason, they refer to him as "T3" in their report. Assadi's two sons, Ali and Hossein, appeared to have the role of protecting their father, from afar.

Unexplained Move by Naami-Saadouni

The Naami-Saadouni couple did something that was not understandable to the police before leaving Luxembourg. The police report explains:

At 14:56, Saadouni and Naami got into their car. When Saadouni sat in the driver's seat, Naami gets into the right side of the car. After Saadouni closes the door on the left side of the car, he gets out a few seconds later and goes to the other side of the car. There he also closes the right door of the car. Then he returns to his place and closes the door. Two minutes later, around 14:58, Saadouni gets out of the car and bends the driver's seat forward so that Naami can get out of the back seat, who apparently had been there all this time. Until now, we don't know why Naami was sitting in the back seat of Mercedes-Benz for at least two minutes.

It later became clear that during this time the couple put the bomb in the compartment behind the driver's seat and Naami checked to make sure the bomb was in the right place before leaving. The report also indicates that Naami was responsible for this task and that is why the bomb was placed in her bag. After they separated from Assadi, they emphasized to him in an SMS message that Naami had learned to work with the device. In the reports of this case, there are dozens of facts that show that in this two-person team Naami-Saadouni, Naami is in charge. Although Saadouni was the front man in obtaining information (about the event), it was Naami who guided him.[13]

The Naami-Saadouni couple left the center of Luxembourg City at around 3:24 pm, heading towards Highway 4 in the direction of Belgium. They crossed the Luxembourg-Belgium border at 3:32 pm.

After less than two hours, some SMS messages were exchanged between them and Assadi, and at 5:15 pm they informed him that they had arrived near Naami's house. Here, the couple took the gift they got from Assadi to Naami's house. They returned home without any problems, although they were under surveillance all along. The situation was not the same for Assadi.

Assadi Touring the Luxembourg Market

Assadollah Assadi shows himself as a normal and simple tourist while strolling in the streets of Luxembourg City. He later wears a cap and sunglasses at a police checkpoint.

Figure 3 - Assadi walking through Luxembourg market area to meet with his accomplices.

Police Stop Assadi and his Family

Thirteen minutes after the Naami-Saadouni couple took the A4 and A6 highways back to Belgium, Assadi also took the same route with his family in the Ford with German vehicle license plate number EU-BI 3644 (D). Before crossing the border between Luxembourg and Belgium, the family's car was stopped by the police for control. The police stop lasted from 4:00 pm to 4:42 pm.

At 4:00 pm, Luxembourg police escorted the Ford S-Max towards the rest area of Aire de Capellen. At this point, the police took the passports and identity documents of all four passengers and identified them as such:

1. Assadollah Assadi, born on December 22, 1971, in Khorramabad, Iran. In his passport, it is noted in capital letters: third consul of Embassy of the Islamic Republic of Iran in Vienna.

2. Robabe Assadi, born on September 23, 1971, in Khorramabad, Iran. In her passport, it is noted in capital letters: wife of the third consul of the Embassy of the Islamic Republic of Iran in Vienna

3. Ali Assadi, born on May 28, 2001, in Khorramabad, Iran. In his passport, it is noted in capital letters: son of the third consul of the Embassy of the Islamic Republic of Iran in Vienna

4. Hossein Assadi, born on June 15, 1997, in Khorramabad, Iran.

Figure 4 - Assadi after leaving Luxembourg and during a police officer stop.

The Plot

Figure 5 - Police: "Suspect T3 [Assadi] in Alima Bourse [Luxembourg], near Saadouni-Naami. T3 seems to have hidden something under his T-shirt."

Assadi was not put under surveillance immediately after being identified, and his route, communications, and calls were not recorded. But after his arrest, the information about the routes he travelled on were extracted from his car and TomTom GPS unit.[14]

Assadi Goes to Belgium!

From Luxembourg, the Assadi family went to the city of Liege in Belgium. From 5:19 pm to 6:22 pm a break of about an hour is taken in a parking lot at the Belgian border. Assadi tried to communicate with Saadouni on June 28, between 5:09 pm and 5:12 pm. In total, three communications are stored in the recorded phone. But it was concluded that no conversation took place. But Assadi and Saadouni sent several SMS messages between 5:13 pm and 6:17 pm. A total of 29 SMS messages were exchanged. From the content of these messages, it can be seen that there is a conversation in coded language regarding the bombing operation at the NCRI meeting on June 30 in Villepinte, France. At the beginning of this conversation, Assadi asks Saadouni if he is okay and whether "they" had left. Assadi was worried that Saadouni and Naami might have been stopped by the police.

The reason for stopping during the route to Belgium for about an hour becomes clear. After the police surveillance in Luxembourg, which also lasted for an hour, he probably wanted to communicate with Saadouni to tell them in coded language what to do after being stopped by the police.

In Belgium, Assadi's family spent the night at the Ibis Budget Hotel in Liège.[15]

Recreational Trip after Delivering the Bomb!

The Assadi family's claim that they were on a holiday and recreational trip and specifically wanted to visit castles is not supported by the GPS data as most of the trip consisted of long drives with short stops at scenic locations. ...In Heidelberg only one stop of about half an hour was observed near the Heidelberger Schloss inside the city of Heidelberg. At 8:18 pm, they arrived at Cochem. The family probably left Cochem on June 28 between 10:09 am to 10:43 am and probably did not visit the Reischburg in Cochem, which according to its website is open from 9:00 am to 5:00 pm. On 28 June, apart from the 1:09 pm and 3:45 pm stops inside Luxembourg City, where the explosives were delivered, no stops of significant duration were made at tourist destinations. In Liège, the family arrived at the Ibis Hotel at 7:53 pm.

On June 29, Assadi traveled from Liège to Rheinbreitbach and stopped in Bonn. They spent the night in Rheinbreitbach at Haus Hillebrand. The next day, Assadi went to Cologne and spent the night at the Romantik Waldhotel Mangold in Bergisch Gladbach.

Notably, less than two days after the explosives were delivered to Saadouni and Naami, the Assadi family visited more tourist sites. In the early afternoon of June 29, the Assadi family did not leave Liège immediately, but instead visited a tourist center in Liège known as Montagne de Bueren. where they spent about 2 hours near the museum, La Boverie and Mediacite shopping center.

On June 30, they visited different sightseeing areas or shopping malls in the Cologne/Bonn area. Here, apart from visiting some stores on that day, there were also very long stops inside Bad Godesberg, de Bismarckturm in Bonn, near the Beethoven House, Cologne Zoo and within the city of Cologne and around the perfume shop, Dufthaus 4711. This shows that after the possible delivery of explosives to the suspects Saadouni and Naami on June 28 in Luxembourg City, Assadi was trying to make it appear that he was on vacation by visiting as many tourist centers as possible. However, these stops were all short. The claim that the Assadi family visited castles is only supported by a stop at Heidelberger Schloss.

Scrubbing Traces of Explosives in Car Wash

After receiving no confirmation or any news from Naami-Saadouni on June 30, Assadi decided to wash his rental car.

It would be very strange for someone to take a rental car to a carwash two days before handing it over, when it would have to travel another 900 km first. Because TATP explosives were possibly transported in the rented car, washing the car inside and out indicated that the possible traces of the bomb were being removed and destroyed. [16]

Scientific technical testing by forensics experts after Assadi's arrest did not show that there were any traces of TATP left behind. But the fact that a sniffer dog reacted to the car, during Assadi's arrest by German police on July 1, 2018, suggested that it had carried the explosives, and the carwash did not remove all traces of the explosives. The dog was more sensitive to the traces and had sensed them.

It is also notable that when returning from a carwash in Colone on the way to Bergisch Gladbach, Assadi stopped at a gas station to fill up his car, raising the question of why he had not done so at the carwash which also a gas pump. It seemed that Assadi was hurried and concerned during the carwash.

Assadi is Looking for News!

Between June 30 and July 1, Assadi visited several websites and read online articles related to the event at Villepinte. He visited the website of Fars news agency 12 times between June 29 and July 1. Assadi was probably looking for information about the NCRI summit in Villepinte from June 29 to July 1 on his iPad. Saadouni and Naami, under arrest at that time, did not provide any information about their whereabouts on June 30 and there had been no confirmation about the events in the news. This seems to have worried Assadi.

Arrest of Naami-Saadouni

The Naami-Saadouni couple, who left their house in a Mercedes Benz to participate in the Villepinte event, were arrested by the

Belgian police at 12:30 pm on Saturday, June 30, around Brussels, while they had the bomb in a toiletry bag inside a suitcase.

After the arrest, the couple was quickly transferred to the judicial police center and subjected to initial interrogations. In the evening of the same day, a police bomb squad acted to neutralize the explosives found in their car.

Belgian police report on arrest of the couple

At around 9:00 am two French police colleagues joined us as liaison officers, and at 9:45 am the prosecutor… arrived.

Verbal permission

At around 10:04 am the investigating judge gave us a verbal order over the phone to wiretap the phone number 32477262614 used by Mehrdad Arefani.

At around 11:07 am an incoming call is made from phone number 32487102001 to Saadouni's phone number.

Shortly after this call, our surveillance teams observe the subjects, Saadouni and Naami, leave the Boomsesteenweg 81 address at 11:14 am, get into their Mercedes vehicle, and drive away.

In consultation with our BTS officer, it was decided to intervene with the vehicle as soon as it became clear that they were driving in the direction of the French border. However, we note that the suspicious text messages between 11:31 am and 11:44 am between Saadouni (32485508387) and Austrian number (436602227681) are exchanged.

We will immediately report this to the investigating judge, and she will report the text messages that are verbally relevant. We are preparing a separate report on this matter. According to the developments, the investigating judge will also come to our office.

The translator gives us the translation. The translation is difficult to read because it is clear that both people are speaking in code.

However, we cannot ignore the idea that the conversation about "antenna" and "installed" may be relevant. They are also speaking of moving forward the game from 20:00 to 17:30. Saadouni deletes the SMS regularly from 2:00 to 5:30 pm

A decision will be made at 11:48 am in consultation with the investigating judge and the federal attorney general's office to intercept the vehicle at the first opportunity and depriving the occupants of their freedom.

We meet the BTS officer who informs us that it is difficult to follow the Saadouni vehicle as it constantly adjusts its speed from 130 km/h to 180 km/h and vice versa.

Arrest of Saadouni and Naami

At 12:27 pm, Saadouni's Mercedes-Benz leaves the Huart Lane exit and 61 rue de Hinnisdael in Woluwe-Saint-Pierre. Special units stop the Mercedes at around 12:30 pm and the arrest of passengers. Hinnisdale's wide street also helps create a spacious environment.

The investigating judge, present at our command headquarters, at 12:40 pm verbally confirms the arrest and orders the transfer of [both suspects] to our offices for questioning. The transfer is carried out by special units. We will then contact DOVO [Police Special Explosive Ordnance Unit] who will be at the scene and at 12.43 pm We will inform Officer [...]. We will keep them informed of ongoing operations and imminent DOVO intervention. The colleague said that we will take necessary measures to establish a safe environment (200 meters according to DOVO).

Assadi's Rush Back to Vienna

The claim that the Assadi family may have been on a holiday trip is highly questionable. After meeting Saadouni and Naami, as the couple were not able to go through with the planned operation on June 30, and as they did not make any further contact to come for a planned meeting on July 1. Assadi and his family left Bergisch Gladbach at 10:20 am on July 1 and headed straight south (Würzburg, Regensburg).

On this route, they only stopped for 20 minutes at the highway's service area. The distance from the location where they were arrested, the Spessart Süd service area, to their next reserved hotel in Regensburg is 258 kilometers. Assadi would have had to travel another 648 kilometers from the Spessart Süd service area to his residence in Vienna. He had planned to perhaps stop at the reserved accommodation in Regensburg on the night of July 1 to July 2. This all suggests that this was a quick, purposeful, and hastily arranged return trip to Vienna.[17]

Separate observations in the above report raise the suspicion that the family's purported vacation trip was just an excuse to hide its primary purpose: to deliver explosives to Saadouni and Naami.

According to Assadi's car rental agreement, when the car was picked up on June 25, 2018, the mileage was 23,755 km. After their arrest, it was established that they traveled 1,951 kilometers from June 26 to July 1. This distance is consistent with the travel reports in the above report. As such, it can be concluded that there was no other travel other than the one described above.

Assadi is Arrested in Southeast Germany

On July 1, Assadi headed towards Beieren via the A3 expressway from Bergisch Gladbach. Until the moment of his arrest at the Spessart Süd parking lot, he took an intermission only once for 20 minutes at the Weiskirchen Süd parking lot. In the meantime, the Am Peterstor hotel in Regensburg was booked by the Assadi family to spend the night from July 1 to July 2.

More than €10,000 in Cash

Bills found, e.g., for hotels, gas stations, and other purchases during the trip were without exception paid in cash. At the time of Assadi's arrest, a relatively large sum of €10,415 was seized. The purpose of that cash has not been established with certainty up to this point. The suspect had a booklet of receipts, only some of which were filled out. The receipts were for sums up to €5,000 that Assadi had dispersed. (Refer to Appendix H).

In Assadi's rental car, notes with summary statements of expenses were also found, which show that these statements were payments to an informant identified as Saeed, most likely referring to Saadouni. In his interrogation on June 30, Saadouni stated that he always received between €3,500 and €4,000 in cash for the information he gave to Assadi in meetings every three or four months. Previously, Saadouni had said that no compensation had been considered for the planned meeting in Cologne on July 1, because Assadi could not make this decision alone and had to consult with Tehran.

Under interrogation, Naami also stated that she received an amount of €35,000 from Assadi. Considering that Assadi's trip was coming to an end and based on the above observations, part of the €10,415 seized was probably intended as a reward for Saadouni and Naami or for other informants. The fact that Assadi had a pad of empty receipts and that suspects, Saadouni and Naami, admitted they had received compensation, makes this suspicion stronger.

Flexible Planning

It has been determined from the information of Booking.com that sometimes more hotels were booked than were needed for one night, which were then canceled ahead of time. What attracts attention is that the first hotels were booked in the period from June 7 to June 12, 2018, in connection with overnight stays in Regensburg, Heidelberg, Brussels and Cologne from June 21 to June 25, 2018. All these hotels were canceled on June 12, 2018, at 11:21 pm to 11:22 pm. From the reservation information, it can be concluded that Assadi probably planned the first trip for June 21 to June 25, 2018, and the overnight stay in the mentioned cities was considered, and there were also double reservations that were canceled before use. It should be added here that the suspect Assadi was probably in Tehran from June 19 to June 22, 2018, which explains the cancellation of hotel reservations for the period from June 21 to June 25. The initial trip from June 21 to June 25, when Assadi and Saadouni were scheduled to meet during this period, can also be explained from the coded conversation on the Nokia device. In the message of June 4, 2018, at 6:03 pm, Saadouni tells Assadi that he bought 23 playing cards and asks Assadi for the price. Assadi replies that he is ready to pay the price in the last week before (the big event in Paris). This is probably related to an appointment on June 23, which still has no specific time. On the night of June 13, between 6:52 pm and 7:18 pm, just one day before the reservations for the period of June 21 to June 25 were canceled, Assadi and Saadouni used coded language to set up a meeting at noon on June 28. Assadi first suggests June 25 or 26. In response, Saadouni says that June 28 at 12 o'clock is better for the secretary, a codeword for Naami. In the message of June 23, at 8:30 pm, Assadi asks again in coded language if 2:00 pm is also good. This is confirmed by Saadouni.

SMS Messages Exchanged

Some SMS messages between Assadi and Naami-Saadouni couple after meeting in Luxembourg follow:

June 28, 2018

Assadi: ... Look at the PS4 [bomb], tell me if you have any questions

Nasimeh: We played. Monshi [Naami] learned. Shall we leave?

Assadi: Did you leave?

Saadouni-Nasimeh: We are near the Monshi's office [Naami's house].

Assadi: Thank God, what time should we contact tomorrow?

June 29, 2018, 8:05 pm

Assadi: How are you? Is the game installed? [In order to install bomb components]

Saadouni: Yes, the game was installed, we won [we succeeded in the operation], we will play ball on Sunday morning

Assadi: God willing, I will only contact you tomorrow at 11:30 and 20:00 [I will contact you]. Let's play together. [show up on time]

Saadouni: I will definitely come and talk.

Saadouni: If the PS [PlayStation, the code name for the bomb] is not installed, shall we go back to the house [Belgium] or go for breakfast [in Germany].

Assadi: It will be known at 20:00 [at 20:00 Saturday night] when we have a game [communication], bye.

Saadouni: Okay, uncle

Assadi: If you want, let's move the game forward to 20

Saadouni: Yes, 17.30 is better

Assadi: Yes, 17:30 is good, your team will win, God willing

Saadouni: Ok. See you, bye [the time of the last SMS is at 20:25]

June 30, 2018, 11:31 am (Saadouni is driving)

Nasimeh: Hello, we set up the PS [bomb], we are going to win the cup [operation], uncle

Assadi: You are right. Is the TV plug connected or not? [He checks the connection of the bomb circuit]

Nasimeh: Yes, everything is fine

Assadi: Well done. Don't take the mobile phone with you, leave it in the dashboard [of the car], I will go cleanup [check the mobile phone] regularly from 2:00 pm until 5:30 pm

Nasimeh: Ok, I will come to the boarding house at 6:00 pm [to send SMS]. Pray for us.

Assadi: God's hand is with you!

June 30, 2018, 1:06 pm

[Assadi]: When in the playground [inside the hall], don't go to the boarding house in [do not communicate] After leaving [from the hall or Villepinte area], go, then later go to the boarding house [come to contact after leaving there].[18]

[Assadi]: How are you? are you safe?

... [Silence]

[Assadi]: How are you? are you safe?

... [Silence]

[Naami and Saadouni are arrested at 12:30 pm on Saturday, June 30]

Actions of Paris Prosecutor's Office

The significance of the Free Iran World Summit of 2018 was not lost on French authorities. They were aware of this large gathering's immense political, diplomatic, and security implications, in light of the event having been hosted in various Paris suburbs for nearly two decades. The Iranian regime's backchannel demands to cancel the event in 2018 were firmly rejected. Just before the event, President Emmanuele Macron's chief of staff responded formally to a letter by French political figures supporting the Resistance, declaring that freedom of expression in France was guaranteed.[19]

Therefore, as soon as French authorities learned about the possibility of a security threat to the summit from Belgian authorities and other intelligence sources, they sprang into action. The anti-terrorist department of the Paris Prosecutor's Office began a series of actions before the arrest of the Naami-Saadouni couple in Belgium based on information received from Belgian authorities on June 28.

The anti-terrorist department of the prosecutor's office respectfully informs that it has taken over the said issue and has handed over the investigations to you.

..... Please keep me updated on the progress of the investigations.

[name redacted], Deputy Prosecutor

Paris, June 28, 2018

On behalf of the Department of Internal Security

To Ms. [name redacted], Deputy Prosecutor at the Paris Provincial Court, Anti-Terrorism Section

Subject: Profile of a Belgian couple of Iranian origin living in Belgium who intended to commit violent acts on French soil.

I draw your attention to the following points.

Information obtained through international cooperation has been provided to the directorate indicates the planning of a violent act in France on Saturday, June 30, 2018.

The service has received two documents from Belgian judicial officials explaining the threat to carry out an act of violence on French soil. The two mentioned documents are attached.

The mentioned criminal project was supposed to be carried out by a Belgian couple of Iranian origin, Amir Saadouni and Nasimeh Naami. These two were married on December 14, 2005, in Iran. ... Saadouni and Naami are supposed to go to France next Saturday, June 30, to participate in the annual conference of the People's Mojahedin Organization, which will be held at the Villepinte Exhibition Park in 93 District.

In the past, the couple had participated in the annual conference that the Mojahedin Organization organizes every year in France.

...In light of the information provided by the Belgian authorities, our service fears that the couple will use the conference of the Mojahedin Organization in Villepinte, scheduled for June 30, in order to carry out this violent act.

Belgian officials have launched a judicial investigation into the matter, and investigations have been assigned to the Antwerp judicial police.

The couple is currently under legal control by the Belgian judicial police through physical and technical surveillance.

In the event that Amir Saadouni and Nasimeh Naami cross the border and enter France, we request the following measures:

Wiretapping and geographic coordinates

In this emergency situation, wiretapping the phones used by Amir Saadouni and Nasimeh Naami will allow their location to be determined and more information to be obtained about their criminal plan... (their telephone numbers are mentioned).

Also, if these mobile phones are used in France, we request permission to record and listen to outgoing and incoming conversations (voice, SMS, MMS, Internet, 3G and G4) on these phone lines and from their origin as well as their geographical location.

Requesting permission in relation to a device or technical system to collect technical connection information that allows the device or its owner's subscription number to be identified, as well as data related to the geographic location of a device used.

In this way, in the same emergency room and for the purposes of research, it is necessary to use the device or technical system to collect technical data connected to identify the device or its owner's subscription number, as well as the technical data of the location of the device used in the mentioned lines.

The report is given in order to assess the necessary follow-ups.

Arrest of Mehrdad Arefani

The French anti-terrorist police, upon receiving an order from the deputy public prosecutor of Paris, a specialist in counterterrorism, published information related to Mehrdad Arefani as follows:

Arefani was present at Villepinte. As he was leaving the venue just after 7pm, he was arrested by the police at the car park to the surprise of other Iranians from Belgium, who at first thought this must be a mistake. Unlike others who were questioning the motive of the police, Arefani, a well-trained agent, was unusually calm. The police confiscated a mobile Nokia phone from him with only one Austrian number in it, which later was revealed to belong to Assadi.

CHAPTER 2

The Target

The annual world summit of the Iranian Resistance was held near Paris on Saturday, June 30, 2018, with tens of thousands of opposition supporters, and hundreds of international dignitaries, senior former officials, lawmakers, and human rights activists, in attendance, to hear a keynote address from President-elect of the National Council of Resistance of Iran (NCRI), Maryam Rajavi, and solidarity speeches from the dignitaries present.

The venue was the huge Hall 5 complex of the Parc des Expositions de Villepinte, situated in the north of Paris. The venue hall was fitted with full seating and bleachers a huge attendance.

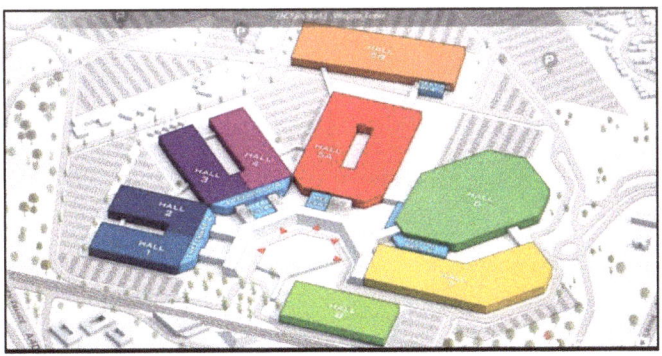

Figure 6 - Schematic of Paris Nord Villepinte.

As the huge gathering began, it was packed with attendees from all over the world. The annual event has been the premiere conference of the Iranian Resistance to underline its will to overthrow the religious dictatorship and bring about a free, democratic, secular, non-nuclear Iran. The NCRI political platform offers a transitional period after the regime's overthrow of six months, to hold a free election for the Iranian people to choose their own representatives to rule the country. A key issue in the discussion during the conference was support for Maryam Rajavi's Ten Point Plan for Future Iran[20]. The conference has been convened around the same time for nearly two decades, bigger in size, and with more prestigious political and human rights personalities in attendance, with each passing year.

Figure 7 – Huge attendance of Iranians at the Free Iran World Summit on June 30, 2018, at the Villepinte exhibition center, near Paris.

Speakers from dozens of countries from five continents emphasize the need to confront the Iranian regime's malign and terrorist activities outside Iran as well as its human rights abuses.

It was common knowledge that Mrs. Rajavi was the keynote speaker, and in June 2018, it was clear that she would attend and be present in the VIP section, seated with other dignitaries.

In one of several Fox News reports covering the event,[21] reporter Benjamin Hall said:

Iranians in exile and supporters from all over the world holding a massive rally in Paris today, calling for freedom in Iran after decades of oppression. Benjamin Hall has more from Paris: For the last 10 hours we have witnessed the largest ever gathering of Iranian opposition figures in the world. More significantly was the size of the US and international delegation here from both sides of the political aisle, all calling for regime change in the Islamic Republic. This event has taken place every year for 14 years, but it was bigger this year and, in many ways, very different...It's been more of a rock concert than it has been an opposition political rally with over 100,000 people attending. But what they're talking about is deadly serious human rights abuses in Iran, growing protests across that country, and now the very real possibility of regime change.

The US delegation was here in force, Rudy Giuliani, Newt Gingrich, Bill Richardson, as well as former heads of the FBI, and prime ministers, ambassadors, foreign ministers from across the world, all joining the growing chorus for democratic regime change under the NCRI, the National Council for the Resistance of Iran.

Dignitaries

Figure 8 - Dignitaries at Free Iran 2018 gathering that sat within range of explosion, had the bomb exploded.

The prominent personalities who addressed the rally included Louis Freeh, former Director of the FBI; and Gen. George Casey, former US Army Chief of Staff, from the United States; Stephen Harper and John Baird, former Prime Minister and Foreign Minister of Canada; Bernard Kouchner and Philippe Douste-

Blazy, former Foreign Ministers and Rama Yade former Minister of Human Rights of France; Ambassador Giulio Terzi, former Foreign Minister of Italy; Sid Ahmad Ghozali, former Prime Minister of Algeria; Eduard Lintner, former German Deputy Interior Minister; Rt Hon. Theresa Villiers, former Secretary of State for Northern Ireland; Michele de Vaucouleurs and Philippe Gosselin, French parliamentarians; Senator Roberto Rampi, representing the Italian delegation; Anna Fotyga, former Foreign Minister of Poland and Member of the European Parliament; Pandeli Majko, Minister of State and former Prime Minister of Albania; Ben-Oni Ardelean, Vice-chairman of the Chamber of Deputies of Romania; Saleh al-Qalab, former Publicity Minister of Jordan; and Nazir Hakim, General Director of the Syrian opposition coalition. Additionally, there were hundreds of political figures sitting in the VIP section.

Maryam Rajavi, Prime Target

Figure 9 - Mrs. Rajavi passing by the VIP section, where the bomb was due to be detonated.

Based on a statement made by one of the perpetrators, Assadi, as mastermind of the plot, was mainly interested in targeting Mrs. Rajavi, with the bomb plot.

This is not the first time the Iranian regime had tried to assassinate the President-elect of the NCRI.

The New York Times reported upon another assassination attempt in Dortmund, Germany, in an article entitled, *"US Asserts Iranians Plotted to Disrupt Rally in Germany."*[22] The piece, dated June 1995 noted:

> *Iranian diplomats working out of their embassy in Bonn plotted to disrupt a huge opposition rally in Germany last week, perhaps with the intention of assassinating a leading Iranian dissident (Mrs. Maryam Rajavi), American intelligence officials said today. At about the same time, Germany asked two Iranian intelligence officials to leave the country because of evidence that they were planning potentially lethal operations from German territory, the American officials said.*

The New York Times added:

> *The discovery by German intelligence that Iran's embassy in Bonn was assembling a team from the terrorist group the Party of God to violently disrupt the rally, and perhaps assassinate Mrs. Rajavi. Since Germany has led the Europeans in defending what it calls a 'critical dialogue' with Teheran that is based on high-level exchanges and efforts to boost trade, it is not surprising that German authorities have kept quiet about the alleged plot but have clung to the official line.* [23]

Hossein Mousavian, currently "a Middle East Security and Nuclear Policy Specialist at the Program on Science and Global Security" at Princeton University, was Iran's ambassador to Germany at the time. Mousavian is believed to have been involved in several terrorist attacks emanating from Tehran and implemented through its embassy in Germany at the time. [24]

Several months later, a statement by the Secretariat of the NCRI unveiled another terror conspiracy on Mrs. Rajavi's life. The statement dated May 13, 1996, states, *"The mullahs' Intelligence Ministry had a plan to attack the residence of Mrs. Maryam Rajavi, the Iranian Resistance's President-elect, in a Paris north suburb, Auvers-sur-Oise, using rockets and mortars, reports from within Iran say. The cargo of arms and ammunition discovered on the ship, called Kolahdooz,* at a Belgian port [Antwerp], was to be used in this terrorist scheme. The shipment on Kolahdooz contained a high-caliber mortar launcher with delayed-action mortar shells (320mm mortar launchers which use 125kg shells), packed in food containers and ostensibly destined for Munich. Despite the fact that the ship finally docked in the German port of Hamburg, the said cargo was unloaded in Belgium to facilitate its subsequent transfer." [25]

Focusing "on the intelligence services of the Islamic Republic of Iran," a 2021 report from the German Office for the Protection of the Constitution in Hamburg, wrote:

> The focus of the Iranian intelligence services is therefore on spying on and fighting opposition groups and individuals at home and abroad… The main focus of the MOIS in intelligence activities in western countries is on the 'People's Mojahedin Organization of Iran' (MEK) and its political arm, the 'National Council of Resistance of Iran' (NCRI)…In addition to the intelligence operations of the MOIS, various activities by the Quds Force in Germany have also been identified in recent years. This is a special intelligence unit of the Iranian Revolutionary Guards.

Foiled Terror Plot in Albania

In March 2018, Albanian authorities thwarted yet another attempt by Tehran to bomb an MEK venue during a Persian New Year celebration gathering near Tirana. Mrs. Rajavi was the keynote speaker in the event. The failed attempt led to the expulsion of the Iranian regime's ambassador and another senior Iranian diplomat from Albania. Two other diplomats were expelled in January 2020 [26] and an educational center run by the Iranian regime was shut down after it was revealed to be a cover for Tehran's espionage activities against the MEK.

Reuters wrote on October 23, 2019:

> *Albanian police foiled a number of planned attacks last year by Iranian agents against an exiled Iranian opposition group living in Albania, a senior officer said on Wednesday. General Police Director Ardi Veliu said an active cell of the foreign operations unit of the Iranian QUDS forces had been discovered by Albania's security institutions."* [27]

Shedding more light on the issue, the Voice of America reported from Albania on October 23, 2019:

> *In a press briefing attended by VOA Albanian in Tirana on Wednesday, Albanian Police Chief Ardi Veliu displayed photos of three Iranian men and one Turkish man suspected of involvement in the cell that he said was targeting the People's Mujahedeen of Iran group, also known as MEK….*

> *Veliu said the alleged cell leader's family name is Peyman and described him as an Iran-based operative of the Quds Force, the overseas wing of Iran's Islamic Revolutionary Guard Corps. He said Peyman had sent another Iranian cell member, Alireza Nagha-Shazadeh, identified as a former MEK member with an Austrian passport, to Albania several times to gather information for a planned attack on the group. The Albanian police chief named the third Iranian suspect as Abdolkhalegh Malek-Zadeh, who he said was based in Turkey and had been working for the past two years with a Turkish man named Abdulselam Turgut to plan terrorist attacks at the behest of Peyman and the Quds Force.*

> *… Veliu said the four suspects had plotted to attack high-level MEK members attending Persian New Year festivities in March 2018 but were prevented from doing so by Albanian police action. In a Wednesday tweet, Albanian Deputy Interior Minister Romina Kuko thanked her government's security agencies for having "successfully foiled" an attack by the alleged cell on MEK members in the country.* [28]

According to a report by the "International Institute for Counter-Terrorism," published on March 8, 2020:

> *On March 22, 2018, the Albanian State Intelligence Service (SHISH, Shërbimi Informativ Shtetëror) foiled a plot planned against a meeting of the MEK for the Nowruz (Iranian New Year). Two MOIS agents were arrested and expelled. Tehran dramatically increased its intelligence presence and operations in Albania after the government decided, in May 2013, to welcome around 3000 MEK members who were under attacks by Iranian proxies in Iraq.* [29]

Regime's Terrorism against MEK Continues

The Iranian regime's terror conspiracies against the opposition have continued. The annual World Summit of the NCRI was postponed on July 22, 2022, based on the Albanian Government's advice due to serious security threats by the Iranian regime.

Quoting the Associated Press, the Washington Times wrote on July 23, 2022:

> *A major gathering of Iranian dissidents in Albania opposed to the theocratic regime in Tehran this weekend has been abruptly called off owing to a terror threat, organizers said. US lawmakers and former government officials were set to be among those addressing the two-day "Free Iran World Summit" starting Saturday…*
>
> *The Iranian regime has long denounced the MEK, which has called for the overthrow of the government and has provided embarrassing scoops of Tehran's secret nuclear and military activities over the years. A top Iranian diplomat was convicted of participating in a 2018 thwarted plot to a previous gathering of the group in Paris.* [30]

In July 2022, following a warrant issued by the Special Court for Combating Corruption and Organized Crime in Albania, several individuals were subject of inspection and interrogation by the police, suspected of *"receiving money from Iran's secret services, the Qods Force and the IRGC to obtain information about the MEK in Albania."*

Mass Casualties Had the Bomb Exploded

Based on court reports, the explosives to be detonated inside the hall, was professionally made, very powerful, and capable of causing a catastrophe had the plot not been foiled by the police.

While the terrorists falsely claimed in trial that the bomb was merely meant to create some noise without any collateral damage, on December 9, 2021, two explosive experts shed light on the shocking scale of possible casualties, had the bomb exploded. A German expert, Mr. Ansgar Japes, appeared as a witness and underlined that the blast shockwave's radius depended on the bomb's weight and distance and noted that a policeman was injured when the bomb was remotely detonated, despite being 200 meters away, and outside the security cordon. The expert further stated that the professionally made bomb was designed to produce a large number of deadly shrapnel. According to Mr. Ansgar Japes:

> *Solid parts, especially metal parts such as the antenna base, could be accelerated by the explosion and then act as shrapnel. If the chairs were made of wood, they could tear decisively and with metal chairs, parts can be accelerated...shrapnel and fly away and it is simply decisive whether they hit someone or not."* He also emphasized that *"in a closed space the pressure wave can be reflected by the walls and all kinds of parts in the environment can be thrown off.*

Both in his report and during his court hearing, Mr. Gunther Backx (the other expert from Belgium who testified in the court) stated that the general structure of the IED should be regarded as very professional and shows a perception of possible trace investigations afterwards. It was pointed out that, for example, all parts of the IED were placed in direct contact with the explosive charge, which ensures maximum destruction of material afterwards. It was further stated that the RFT had a transmitting power of 28 dBm (approximately 0.7W), making transmission over several hundreds of meters without any problem.

The camera of the police "neutralization robot" used in defusing the bomb was destroyed, even though the robot was designed to resist explosions, according to the expert. One of the robot's handles was also damaged beyond repair. He emphasized that the bomb only "partially" exploded. Had it fully exploded, there could have been much more damage. The Belgian expert stated data and evidence led them to conclude that the bomb was professionally made. He said the materials used showed the designers knew what they were doing.

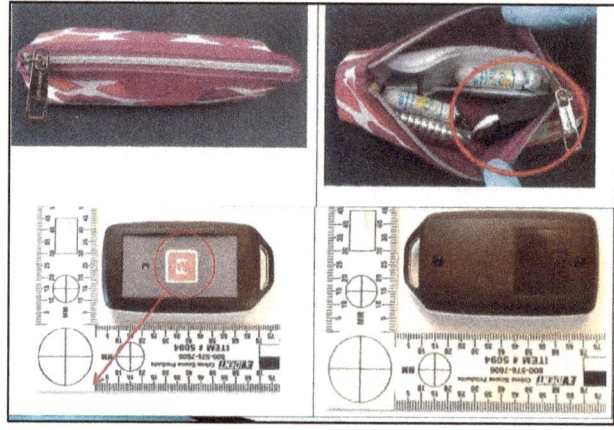

Figure 10 - Naami's toiletry bag containing bomb remote control.

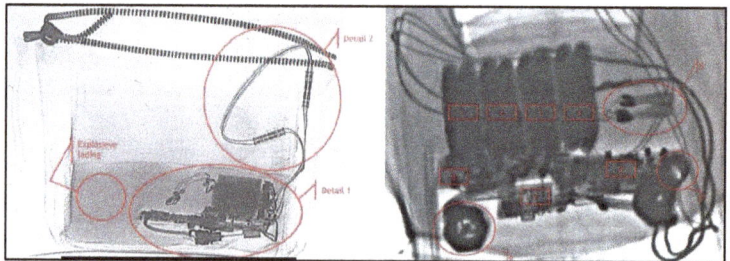

Figure 11 - X-ray of explosive device found in Naami's toiletry bag that was neutralized by a robot on June 30 in Woluwe-Saint-Pierre.

"The battery was placed in a specific way, so all components were together. They would have been destroyed during the explosion, and this

is another sign that the bomb was professionally made," the expert noted.

Finally, the Antwerp Court of Appeal, on May 10, 2022, concluded that. *"There is no doubt that the defendants acted with the intent to attack the MEK annual conference on June 30, 2018, in Villepinte, to kill with premeditation,"* the court quoted expert testimonies regarding the IED and underlines, that in its opinion there is no doubt that the explosive power of TATP *"should be regarded as large and very dangerous."*

Referring the TATP volume present in Naami's toiletry bag, the court says: *"Mr. Ansgar Japes stated in his report that the ignition of a quantity of 500 grams of TATP is based on a detonation conversion, considering in the case of a closed environment a very high potential possibility of fatal injuries to persons in the immediate environment. At the hearing on December 9, 2021, Mr. Ansgar Japes stated that TATP is an igniting explosive, which means that there will be a great danger to life from that substance in the immediate vicinity."*

When we look at the photos of the convention in Villepinte, we find that tens of thousands of people were packed in the large Expo Hall. A shock wave of more than 100 meters through this crowd would have had catastrophic consequences. If an armored explosive robot is damaged to such an extent that it is inoperative, one can imagine the consequences of such an explosion for the unprotected human body.

Stampede

While the defendants unsuccessfully tried to cover up the crime, the testimonies of explosives experts and their technical arguments showed the extent of the casualties which could have happened had they succeeded in their plan. However, in addition to the explosion, the bomb could have caused enough devastation to result in a stampede, causing many deaths or injuries in the crowd, including among small children. In a packed hall with tens of thousands of people of all ages, elderly men and women, children and even infants, the explosion would have caused many deaths and injuries.

A glance at other incidents leading to stampede demonstrates the severity of the outcome. The Hillsborough stampede in the UK during a football match in 1989 resulted to 97 deaths.[31]

In July 2010, 95 were killed and 500 injured in a stampede in Duisburg, Germany, during a music festival.[32]

In September 2015, in Mina, Saudi Arabia, more than 700 people taking part in the annual Hajj pilgrimage died in a stampede near Mecca. Another 863 people were injured in the incident, which occurred as two million pilgrims were taking part in the Hajj's last major rite, BBC reported. [33]

Another tragic incident happened in Baghdad, Iraq on August 31, 2005, when up to 1,000 Shia pilgrims were trampled to death or drowned in the Tigris River after rumors of a suicide bombing sparked panic. Many of the dead were women and children. [34]

There are other examples that underline the potential for the Villepinte bombing to result in a massacre.

Figure 12 – A huge attendance of Iranians at the Free Iran World Summit in Villepinte, June 30, 2018.

CHAPTER 3

The Terrorists

This chapter outlines information about the four individuals who played active roles in directing, controlling, and executing the terrorist plot to bomb the annual rally of the Iranian Resistance. It also highlights their mission and role in the terrorist plot, MOIS recruitment methods, intelligence methods, advanced equipment used by this network, the social covers used for secret meetings in different places and countries, as well as mechanisms and routes to Iran to obtain terrorist training and briefings.

Assadollah Assadi: Diplomat-Terrorist, Ringleader

At the time of his arrest on July 1, 2018, Assadollah Assadi, who was responsible for the execution of the terrorist plot of June 30, 2018, had a diplomatic passport and held the official position of the Iranian regime's third secretary at the embassy in Austria.

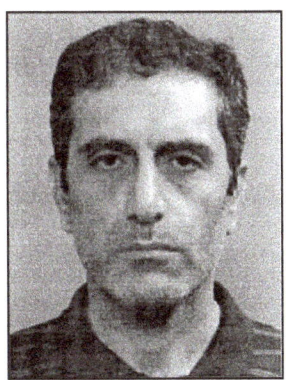

Figure 13 - Assadollah Assadi, diplomat-terrorist, ringleader of the terrorist plot.

It was of utmost necessity to the plotters for this terrorist plan to succeed, and so Assadi personally transported the bomb from Tehran to Vienna and handed it to the two intelligence agents, Saadouni and Naami, in Luxembourg, who were supposed to plant the bomb at the event venue.

According to information obtained by the Iranian Resistance, the regime's embassy in Vienna, oversaw the regime's intelligence agents across Europe. The intelligence hub was located on the third floor of the embassy. Assadollah Assadi, the head of the MOIS network in Europe, was the station chief.

On February 18, 2020, the Belgian intelligence agency, State Security Service (VSSE), delivered its assessment on Assadollah Assadi to the Belgian Federal Prosecutor, confirming that Assadi was a member of Section 312 of MOIS, which is designated as a terrorist organization by the European Union, and that he is an officer of this section that works with human resources, such as spies and mercenaries.

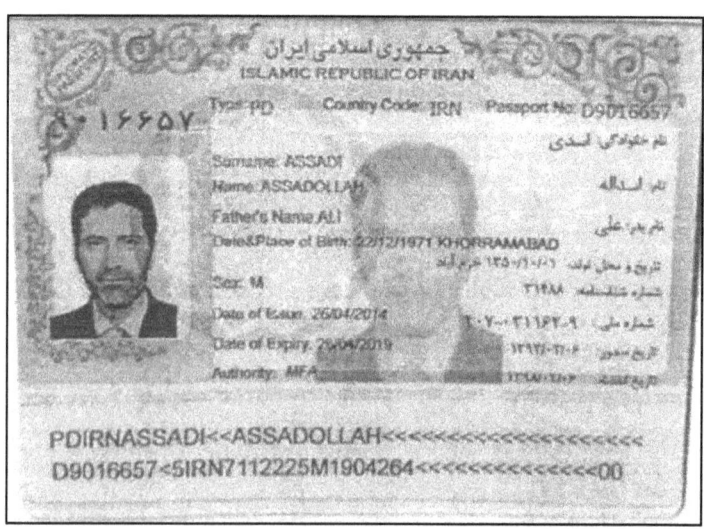

Figure 14 - Passport details of Assadi as confirmed by Belgian VSSE

Assadi's background

Assadollah Assadi was born on November 22, 1971, in Khorramabad city, capital of the western province of Lorestan. He joined the IRGC during the Iran-Iraq war in the 1980s. Since his father was the head of the war logistics headquarters in Khorramabad and trusted by the IRGC, Assadi received training in making explosives. [35]

After his arrest, the state-run newspaper Kayhan (the mouthpiece of the Supreme Leader Ali Khamenei) referred to his presence in the Iran-Iraq war in an article entitled, "What happened to the honor of the Iranian passport?"[36] The paper referred to Assadi as "Iranian diplomat Haj Assadollah Assadi, who is one of the veterans of the era of Holy Defense," the regime's term for the Iran-Iraq war. The daily added that Assadi participated in "neutralizing dozens of terrorist operations."

Following the end of the war, Assadi joined the MOIS in Lorestan province and was later transferred to MOIS headquarters in Tehran.

Assadi in IRGC and MOIS

As a senior Intelligence Ministry officer, Assadi operated under diplomatic cover for many years. He worked in an MOIS department that focuses on the activities of the PMOI/MEK.[37] The section is known as the "Hypocrisy" department, a reference to the regime's derogatory term for the MEK. According to Assadi's own admissions and case documents, his work targeted the MEK for over 30 years.[38]

After the invasion of Iraq by international coalition forces, Assadi was stationed at the embassy of the Iranian regime in Baghdad from 2005 to 2008 and was busy planning operations that included bombings and kidnappings against the MEK as well as bombings against American forces in that country.[39] Assadi was later transferred from Baghdad to Tehran and in June 2014, he was moved to Vienna.

Figure 15 - Document from Embassy of Iraq in Tehran attesting to Assadi's role in Iranian Embassy in Baghdad. Translated below.

    Embassy of Republic of Iraq – Tehran
    Ref number: 2032/4
    Date: 26/5/2008
    Foreign Affairs – Protocol

    The Foreign Ministry of Iran in a letter with ref number 721/84244 dated 2008/5/11 applied for a visa for the Third Secretary Mr. Kiomars Gholamali Reshadatmand, diplomatic passport number 9002641 to work in the Iranian Embassy in Baghdad replacing Mr. Assadollah Assadi.
    Please let us know if the requested visa would be issued.
    With thanks

    Enclosures:
    Copy of passport
    Visa application form
    Iraqi Embassy stamp in Tehran
    2008/05/26

Assadi, intelligence station head in Europe

Assadi was stationed in Vienna as the station chief for Intelligence Ministry in Europe (under the diplomatic cover of the third secretary) and advanced the regime's terrorist and espionage plots in Europe. Beginning in August 2015, he was in direct contact with the Saadouni-Naami couple and oversaw this terrorist cell.

Evidence obtained from Assadi's car

The documentary evidence obtained from Assadi's car shed light on a small part of his role in organizing and leading terrorist activities in Europe. The police registered about 120 items, of which more than 40 documents contained detailed information. The collection of information obtained from his phones, computers, hard drives, and USB drives amount to thousands of pages, a treasure trove of evidence that highlight an organized terrorist enterprise run by the Iranian regime in Europe.

Assadi claimed to have been on a family trip. However, he was carrying six phones (smart phones and feature phones) that had separate SIM cards (separate from his wife's and sons' phones), in addition to two extra SIM cards, two external hard drives, four USB flash drives, all containing information that was seized by the police, two SD cards, a laptop, a prayer book, and a series of notes as well as two notebooks that contained bomb specifics, and information about European countries, receipts for payment of money to spies for the regime, and numerous sheets of paper containing miscellaneous information. It appears that in the context of this mission, his immediate family members were acting both as a cover for Assadi's mission to deliver the bomb to his agents, and as a protective unit for him personally.

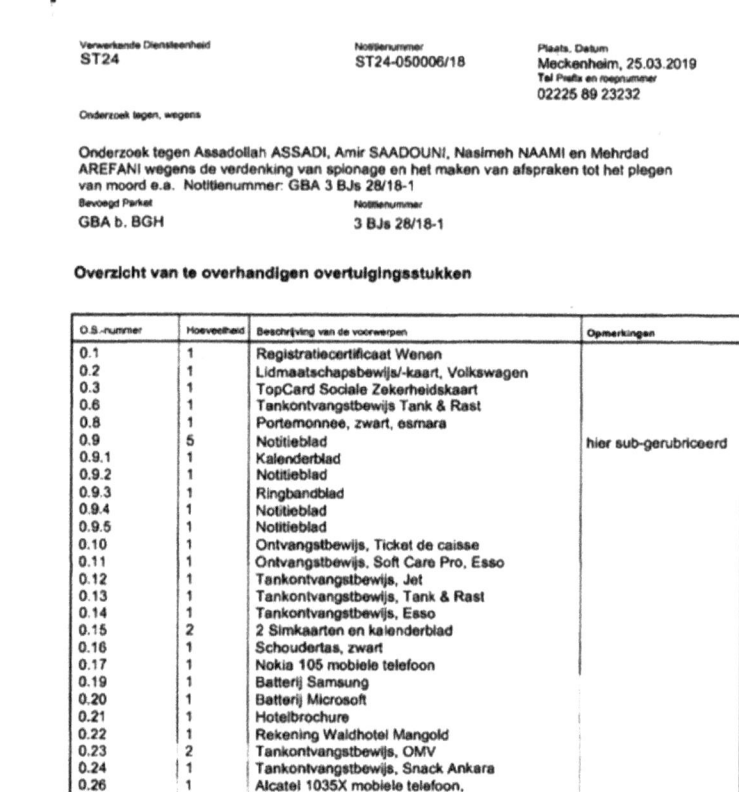

Figure 16 - A page of police report listing evidence in Assadi's car.

Documents found in Assadi's car:

- **Red notebook:**[40] In this notebook, Assadi wrote down instructions for setting off the bomb, as well as code words used in communications with Saadouni and Naami.

- **Green notebook:**[41] In this 200-page notebook, 101 pages contain about 289 addresses in 11 European countries, which reveal Assadi's travel routes in European countries.

- **Special telephones for communication with agents:** Assadi had allocated two phones for communicating with three the MOIS agents (Arefani and the Naami-Saadouni couple) inside the exposition hall in Villepinte. Each phone had only one Austrian phone number recorded in them. These phones were discovered by the police during the inspection of Assadi's car, and they represent undeniable evidence about communications by the operational command of the terrorist cell.

The technical details of each phone have been carefully examined by the judicial police:

Assadi used a Nokia 105 phone to communicate with Arefani.

He used a Nokia 105 phone,[42] to communicate with Naami and Saadouni. According to the police report, Hossein Assadi, Assadi's son, tried to hide this phone from the police at the time of his arrest.

An Alcatel phone and its SIM card belonged to Assadi.[43] In this phone, there is only one phone number with the name A, which refers to Amir Saadouni. This was likely to be used to check on the operation's execution. There are about 50 photos in this phone that are related to Iranian regime officials and Assadi's friends.[44]

- **Apple iPad**[45] containing information on the Resistance's annual gathering: This device contained information on hotels used by Assadi, as well as travel tickets that he had purchased. Information regarding wireless networks in hotels and places where Assadi was located were also found in this device. Assadi closely followed and recorded time-stamped images of the live 2018 Villepinte summit.

- **USB drive containing the final compiled information:** In the last meeting of Assadi with the Naami-Saadouni couple, they handed over a USB drive[46] to Assadi which contained the last batch of information they had collected. Information transfers via USB were a known method of exchange for Assadi and his agents.

- **Laptop containing training pamphlets for surveillance devices:** There were six training pamphlets for espionage devices in an Asus laptop[47] that was inside Assadi's car. One of these pamphlets contained instructions on installing and using a microphone in the keys of a car. According to documents, some time before his arrest, Assadi had taken the remote-control opener for Naami's garage door to install a microphone inside it. Naami had followed up with him several times to have the remote control returned to her. One of the documents is pictured below as an example.

The Terrorists

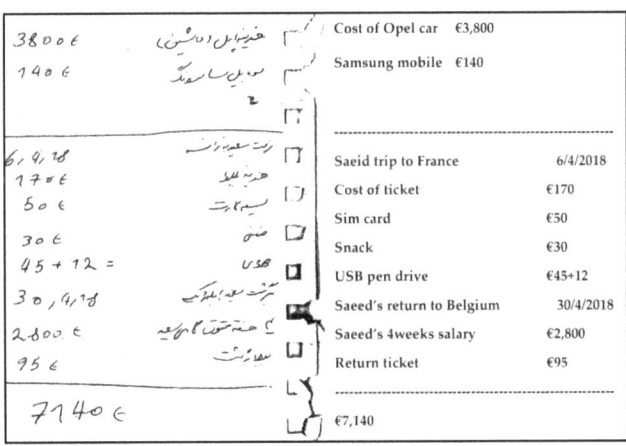

Figure 17 - Sheets of paper containing monetary requests from the Naami-Saadouni couple.

- **Sheets of paper containing monetary requests from the Naami-Saadouni couple:** Assadi[48] also carried papers that contained notes of monetary requests for the intelligence missions by the Naami-Saadouni couple. They asked Assadi to pay for their travel to Luxembourg, among other things.

- **Amounts of cash:** At the time of arrest,[49] Assadi had a brown bag that contained €10,450 in cash. The evidence was registered as number 0.51 by the German police.

Assadi's intelligence objectives

According to the judgment of the appeals court, Assadi assigned the Naami-Saadouni couple to collect the following intelligence:

Identifying the organizational structure of the MEK's branches in the Netherlands, Belgium, and France;

The funding methods of the MEK;

Identification of their managers;

Channels and communications - both personal and organizational - among various branches of the MEK;

The presence of national (and international) figures in the activities of the NCRI; at the annual summit on the occasion of International Women's Day and the Congress of the NCRI;...

Internal activities of MEK, such as organizing seminars about the situation in Iran.

There is no doubt that Saadouni and Naami sent their compiled information via email. Larger files, such as audio and video recordings, were stored on a CD-ROM or USB stick and handed over to Assadi during meetings.

Assadi's trips to Iran

Assadi travelled to Austria on June 23, 2014, to start his assignment.[50] He made one trip from Austria to Iran in 2014, three trips in 2015, three trips in 2016, six trips in 2017, and six trips in the first six months of 2018. As assessed by the police, the number of Assadi's trips to Iran increased during 2017, and in 2018, the high frequency of his trips to Iran was unusual.

Amir Saadouni: Infiltrator, Bomber

Amir Saadouni was a gullible sympathizer of the MEK in Belgium, who was recruited by the MOIS via Naami. He attended MEK events and activities, collecting information for the MOIS. He was an underling tasked with obtaining information and directed by his wife Naami on behalf of the MOIS.

Figure 18 - Amir Saadouni in prison.

The judgment of the appeals court clearly talks about the role of Saadouni and Naami in the terrorist plot:

Observations about ordered activities make it clear that Saadouni and Naami met Assadi on June 28, 2018, in Luxembourg. In this meeting, a USB, an envelope containing 18,000 euros, a new mobile phone number for the operation and a women's handbag containing an IED (improvised bomb) were handed over.

Two days later, on June 30, 2018, Saadouni and Naami were arrested in St. Peters-_____. While traveling in their Mercedes, they received some suspicious text messages from an Austrian phone number, in which coded language was used. There was talk of a "remote" to be installed and "move the time forward from 8pm to 5.30pm". Naami also referred to "going from 2 to 17:30" and "regimented cleaning". While tracking the car, it was found that Saadouni was implementing anti-pursuit techniques by constantly changing his speed from 130 kilometers per hour to 180 kilometers per hour, making it difficult to tail the car.

In their Mercedes-Benz vehicle, a cosmetic bag was found in a suitcase that contained an explosive device as well as a substance identified as TATP, which was subsequently detonated by DOVO explosives expert police during the neutralization process.

In addition, a yellow and gold notebook and a cell phone with only one contact, namely an Austrian number under the name "Daniel" were discovered, which subsequent investigations showed is referring to Assadi.

Various house searches were also carried out, including at the residence of the defendants Saadouni and Naami in Wilrijk, where three envelopes in a suitcase containing a total of €35,690 in cash were discovered.

Amir Saadouni, background, recruitment

Saadouni was born on April 26, 1980, in Abadan, southwestern province of Khuzestan. He traveled to Belgium on May 27, 2003, and requested political asylum.

He participated in the activities of MEK supporters in Belgium beginning in 2004. According to their own statements, Saadouni met Naami through the Internet in 2004. They married long distance in the winter of 2005. According to Saadouni's interrogations, he started cooperating with the Ministry of Intelligence in 2007. After obtaining an Iranian passport from the regime's embassy in Belgium, he made at least six trips to Iran from 2010 to 2018, five of them were together with Naami. He had been in direct contact with Assadi abroad, whom he knew by the nickname Daniel since August 2015. He had been supervised by Assadi to obtain organized information about the activities of the MEK, especially in relation to their headquarters in France, and to participate in the terrorist plot in June 2018.

Naami-Saadouni, espionage for money

The appeals court verdict says the following about the amounts received by Saadouni and Naami:

Financial investigations have shown that between March 2008 and June 2018, the amount of €123855.81 euros was deposited in various bank accounts for defendant Amir Saadouni. In the case of defendant Nasimeh Naami, the amount of €106495.57 euros has been kept as a cash deposit for the period of December 2010 to June 2018...

In addition, two other deposits of cash were discovered in their shared residence in the Wilrijk neighborhood, one amount of money worth about €35,700 euros and the other €98.00 euros. The defendants cannot provide an acceptable explanation in this regard.

Nasimeh Naami, Swallow, Infiltrator, Bomber

Nasimeh Naami was the main figure on the ground for the terrorist plot and effectively supervised Saadouni. The MOIS had trained Naami, and some members of her family also worked with the MOIS. The MOIS placed her as a "bait" or swallow[51] (*parastoo*) on Saadouni's path, and her marriage with Saadouni was part of the MOIS's plan.

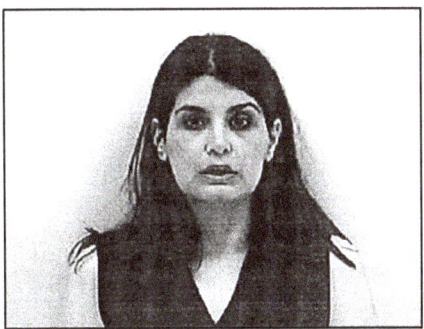

Figure 19 – Nasimeh Naami in prison.

The MOIS advanced its "sleeper terrorist cell" plot with the leadership of Naami and in active communication with the liaison officer of the MOIS. She had the role of logistics, communications, and management in the operational team of Naami-Saadouni.

Naami received the explosive material from Assadi in Luxembourg, who placed it in her bag. She learned how to set off a bomb and declared her technical readiness.

In order to conceal the mission and gain others' trust, Naami presented herself as a modern woman in social and business relationships to remove any suspicions about her MOIS affiliation. Her lawyer also used her public cover to unsuccessfully argue for her acquittal, suggesting that she cannot be an agent of the fundamentalist regime ruling Iran.

Nasimeh Naami: background, recruitment

Naami was born on September 20, 1984, in Ahvaz, the capital of the southwestern province of Khuzestan. She met Saadouni online while she was in Iran in 2004, and the following year they married remotely with the guidance of the MOIS. She went to the Netherlands in February 2007 with her Iranian passport and applied for asylum. With the help of Saadouni, she left the refugee camp in the Netherlands and applied for asylum in Belgium in March 2007. Following her travel to Belgium in 2007, the MOIS contacted Saadouni and the Naami-Saadouni couple started collaborating with the MOIS. In June 2010, Naami and Saadouni received Iranian passports from the regime's embassy in Belgium. The couple went to Iran in September 2010 on the orders of the MOIS and were directly briefed by the MOIS against the PMOI. Naami has made at least 12 trips to Iran from 2010 to 2018, during which she was trained and briefed by the officials of the MOIS.

Court documents show that after receiving an Iranian passport from the regime's embassy in Belgium in 2010, Naami made several trips to Iran between 2010 and 2018 to receive direct instructions from the MOIS and to attend intelligence-terrorist training courses.

Some of these trips are registered with her Iranian passport and some are not. According to the documents, from 2010 to 2018, she made at least 12 trips to Iran. She made two trips in 2010, one trip in 2011, four trips for a total of 132 days stay in 2013, one trip in 2014, two trips in 2015, two trips in 2017 and one trip in 2018.

There are many convincing indicators that Naami made more visits to Iran. Saadouni accompanied her during five of her known visits to Iran.

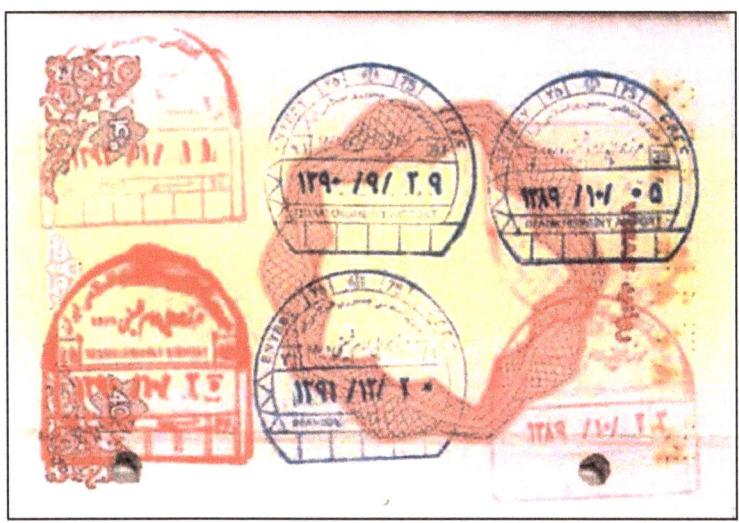

Figure 20: Naami's Iranian passport showing the number of her trips to Iran.

Search of Naami's house

Naami's house was searched, once on June 30, 2018, and again a few days later. A total of 88 items were seized. These included five passports, two of which were in hers and Saadouni's real names, and the other three were Iranian passports. It should be noted that the Iranian passports were issued when the Naami-Saadouni couple were still refugees in Belgium, and the basis of their refugee claim was that they could not return to Iran for fear of their lives. There were also 11 phones, a Dictaphone, two computers, six USB drives, two SIM cards and several telephone boxes. Naami herself had two Iranian passports and one Belgian passport. Naami has been sentenced to 18 years in prison.

Figure 21: Naami in Brussels, Belgium.

Mehrdad Arefani: Sleeper Cell, Lookout

According to the indictment, Mehrdad Arefani was the main person on the ground who had been instructed by Assadi to stay until the conclusion of the gathering and to ensure that Naami and Saadouni were doing their job well. Assadi was waiting for Arefani to inform him about the final outcome.

Figure 22 - Mehrdad Arefani

A Nokia phone with an Austrian SIM card was seized from Arefani, which contained Assadi's phone number. This phone was seized when Assadi was arrested. It was set up for special communications on the day of the expected explosion.

On the day of the plot, Arefani was sitting somewhere at the end of the exposition hall. According to eyewitness reports, he looked distressed during the event. His position in the venue was unusual because, according to Arefani's own statements under interrogation, he had a VIP card. Thus, the fact that he had moved all the way to the end of the hall indicated that he knew about the plan and had a mission on the day of the operation and was deliberately remaining as far away from the VIP section to avoid injury and to monitor the operation at a distance.

Arefani was ordered to do this and to deny such communications in potential interrogations and court hearings. But despite all these efforts, the documents and evidence were ultimately uncovered, and the prosecutor's indictment exposed the relevant communications.

Searches of Arefani's house, on June 30 and afterward, turned up a large set of equipment for spying against the MEK.

Arefani had bought a ticket to Turkey before the Villepinte event. He was supposed to leave for Turkey, and travel from there to Iran, two days after the gathering. The MOIS and Assadi, had tried their hardest to hide Arefani's connections with the MOIS and Assadi.

Mehrdad Arefani, background, recruitment

Arefani was born in Tonkabon city (formerly Shahsavar) in the northern province of Mazandaran on July 27, 1963. He traveled to Belgium in October 2000 and became a political refugee. He was an MEK supporter in Tonkabon city, who was arrested and imprisoned from 1981 to 1984. But he started to collaborate in prison with the MOIS while he was still in Iran, which continued after his release, according to reports.

The moment he arrived in Belgium, he claimed to be a sympathizer of the MEK and started collecting information about MEK supporters and other political groups abroad for the MOIS. To cover up his affiliation with the regime, he introduced himself as a secularist and an atheist poet.

According to court documents, Arefani had been collaborating with Assadi in the formation of the terrorist cell. He had face-to-face, e-mail and telephone communications with Assadi and was supposed to report on the execution of the terrorist plan to Assadi by being present at the Villepinte exposition hall.

Items found in Mehrdad Arefani's house

During the search of Mehrdad Arefani's house, in addition to several computers, three external hard disks were found, along with more than 10 USB drives and SD cards, several cameras and related accessories, €1,500 euros in cash (inside an envelope), a USB drive with a microphone, and a pair of glasses capable of recording and storing high-definition video.

A few of the items seized at Arefani's house are as follows:

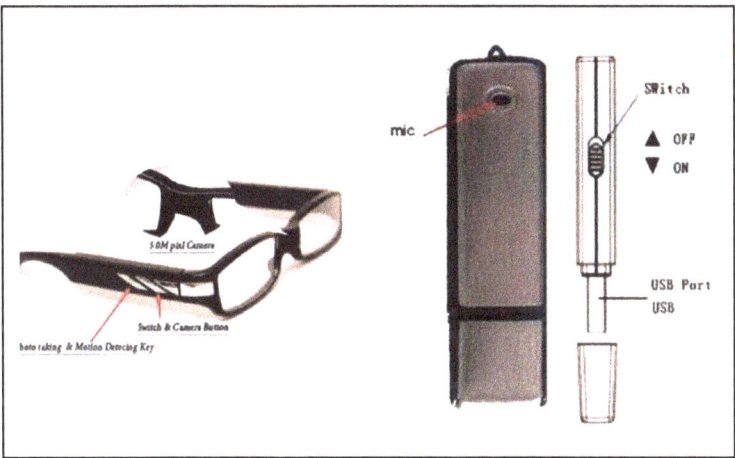

Figure 23 - A 1080p HD glasses with camera, and a USB flash drive with audio recording capability (evidence no. 158).

Large sums of money

From 2008 to 2018, amounts totaling €226,084.50 in cash were deposited into Arefani's bank account. The equivalent of more than €20,000 a year.

Any money he received as a refugee from the Belgian government would not have been in cash. Arefani used the cash he received from the MOIS to pay for his ongoing expenses and deposited the rest into his account.

Arefani's trip to Albania

In 2017, Arefani managed to travel to Albania along with the mother of MEK martyrs, whose brother resided in Albania. During this trip, he tried to provide several smart phones to the MEK while attempting to identify MEK centers and locations. On July 10, 2018, the Security and Counterterrorism Committee of the National Council of Resistance of Iran made revelations about this issue to the investigation branch of the Paris Court, which was planning to extradite Arefani to Belgium.

Communications with Assadollah Assadi

At the time of his arrest on June 30, 2018, in the parking lot of the Villepinte exhibition hall, Arefani had a Nokia 105 phone with an Austrian SIM card with the number 436543591456. There was only one Austrian number recorded in the phone under the name "Dady" with the number 436643691475.

In this phone, only one word "OK" was written as an SMS message, but it was not sent.

At the time of Assadi's arrest in Germany on July 1, 2018, he had a Nokia 105 phone with an Austrian SIM card with the number 00436643691475, which is the same number that was on Arefani's phone. In this phone, there was only one contact named "A. HOD" with phone number 00 436543591456, which was the same Austrian phone number as Arefani at the time of the latter's arrest. These two phones had been obtained and set up for the purpose of special communications about the anticipated explosion at Villepinte.

Saadouni has said that similar Austrian-number phones and SIM cards were also provided to him by Assadi. In this way, both the Nokia 105 and the Austrian SIM card inside it were obtained by Assadi and handed over to Arefani.

In its indictment, presented on November 27, 2020, the Belgian prosecutor's office referred to Arefani's role in the plot as follows:

> ... Arefani was supposed to watch whether Naami and Saadouni were doing their job well or not. The main person on the ground who stayed until the end of the program was Mehrdad Arefani and Assadi was waiting for Arefani to inform him about the results of the efforts.

> In addition to a Nokia 105, an Alcatel phone was also seized from Mehrdad Arefani's house, which he used to communicate with Assadollah Assadi. A review of the contents of the device shows that this device has a SIM card with a UK phone number of 447930124761. ... In the memory of this device, the Austrian phone number 4367761797619 was stored under the name 'dadash'.

In Arefani's house, several notes in his own handwriting were seized, in which the Austrian phone number of Assadi with the number 004367761797619 is registered. This is the same phone number that was also recorded in Arefani's Alcatel phone.

In these documents, there are also English phone numbers that Arefani used. He deliberately used British SIM cards, which, unlike other European countries, do not require an identification card for purchase, and are not registered with the identity of the SIM card holder. The methods for coding phone numbers used by Arefani were the same methods used by Saadouni and Naami.

Arefani's special skills

While in Iran, Arefani had received training in some professional skills as part of his training for his missions. He was a construction worker, had special computer expertise, was a poet, writer, and a purported human rights activist.[52]

He thus had various opportunities to gain information about people's lives (as a contractor). He could also obtain information by building websites, etc.

At the same time, to cover up the nature of his work with the regime, he was active in the field of human rights. In Vienna, he had established a non-governmental human rights organization called SOS Iran as a cover for his trips to Vienna and for his meetings with the intelligence officer at the Iranian regime embassy.[53]

He had also issued a statement condemning those who have refugee status abroad but still travel back to Iran.[54]

CHAPTER 4

State Terrorism

For many years, the MOIS branch at the embassy in Vienna, has been responsible for supervising the activities of MOIS branches and agents across Europe.[55] As a senior Intelligence Ministry officer, Assadi took over the post of MOIS European station chief, from Mostafa Rudaki, who was the highest MOIS officer in Europe, supervising its activities across the continent.[56] After moving to Tehran in 2017, and once several thousand members of the MEK were transferred from Ashraf in Iraq to Albania, Rudaki became the head of the MOIS branch at the embassy in Tirana, Albania. He was the mastermind of the foiled bomb plot against the MEK in that country in March 2018. Along with the regime's ambassador in Albania, Rudaki was expelled from that country in December 2018 due to his role in this terrorist plot.[57]

Belgian police investigations confirm Assadi's role and function as an intelligence officer working under diplomatic cover. On February 18, 2020, the Belgian intelligence agency, VSSE, submitted a report about Assadi to the Belgian Federal Prosecutor.[58] It states: (Refer to Appendix M).

> *Assadi is an officer of the Ministry of Intelligence and Security of Iran and worked under a diplomatic cover at the Embassy of the Islamic Republic of Iran in Vienna.*
>
> *Assadi is affiliated with Section 312 of the Ministry of Intelligence and Security of Iran (Section 312 of the MOIS is designated as a terrorist organization by the European Union[59]). He is an officer who works with human assets (spies and mercenaries).*
>
> - *Assadi was the special operational commander of the attack plot against the annual conference of the People's Mojahedin Organization of Iran (PMOI/MEK) in Villepinte (France).*

- *In the context of the preparation activities for the attack on Villepinte, Assadi acted as the managing officer for Amir Saadouni (26-04-1980) and Nasimeh Naami (20-09-1984). Two days before the attempted attack, Assadi handed them an explosive device containing the lethal substance TATP.*
- *The attack plot was hatched on behalf of and under the pressure of Iran. This was not a personal initiative on Assadi's part.*

Assadi Brings Bomb from Tehran to Vienna

After the bomb was discovered and neutralized in Brussels on June 30, authorities soon proved that it was made in Tehran. Assadi, who left Vienna for Tehran for a final operational check on June 19, 2018, personally received the bomb in Tehran. When he left Tehran on June 22,[60] he placed the bomb in his diplomatic pouch and took it to Europe via a passenger airliner.

In a document submitted to the federal prosecutor, the investigators stated, *"Iranian intelligence officer Assadollah Assadi took the bomb to be used for the attack with him on a passenger flight from Tehran to Austria"*.[61] (Refer to Appendix E).

At 6:05 am on June 22, with the bomb in his briefcase, Assadi boarded Austrian Airlines Flight 872 in Tehran, an Airbus A320[62] with a capacity of 180 passengers, destined for Vienna.[63]

The Anti-Terrorism Service of Austria, which became aware of Assadi's numerous trips to Iran, activated code 43 on the border control's computer system,[64] so that even when the advanced explosive detection devices' sensors detected a bomb as Assadi passed through the gates, the agents avoided apprehending him on the scene. The goal was to find out exactly what Assadi was planning to do after he entered Vienna.

On the second day of Assadi's trial on November 27, 2020, the prosecutor said that security authorities confirmed that there were unknown substances in Assadi's bag on June 22.[65]

On June 30, mid-day, after the discovery and partial neutralization of the bomb, it was found that the unknown substance was an explosive device consisting of about 500 grams of TATP. The expert assessment of DOVO[66] (explosive neutralization and disposal organization of the Belgian army) was that the bomb was produced by professionals.[67]

Planning Began a Year Prior

Almost exactly one year before his arrest, Assadi drove to Paris from Vienna in a rented car. The ten-day trip occurred in late June, and he returned to Vienna in early July. During this trip, Assadi spent June 26 to 29 in Paris. The purpose of the trip was to obtain an accurate assessment of how the Resistance's annual summit was to be organized in Paris.[68]

Figure 24- Mohammad Reza Zaeri visiting Khamenei.

According to information obtained from Assadi's GPS, during the three days, Assadi took photos and video of the Villepinte complex known as "Parc des Expositions", the hotel where international dignitaries participating in the annual meeting in support of the Iranian Resistance were staying, and particularly the Villepinte hall where the meeting was to be held.[69]

He was not alone in this surveillance mission. Accompanying him was Mohammad Reza Zaeri, one of the clerics close to Ali Khamenei, the regime's Supreme Leader. Assadi and Zaeri had travelled to France in a rented Skoda car, that Zaeri had rented for this mission.[70] They drove a total of 2,853 kilometers together, including the round trip from Vienna to Paris.

Born in 1970, Mohammad Reza Zaeri, is the son of Gholam Abbas. Zaeri senior is a former deputy in the Islamic Consultative Assembly (parliament) from Bandar Abbas city as well as a former governor of Hormozgan. He is currently a member of the Inspector General's department at the Supreme Leader (Ali Khamenei) office. He is extremely hostile to the MEK. Some of this animosity can be seen in Zaeri's Twitter and Facebook posts.

Figure 25 - Zaeri with regime's diplomacy cheif Mohammad Javad Zarif.

Zaeri was one of the few people who visited Khamenei in hospital in 2014. The photo of this visit was published by the public relations office of the organization responsible for preserving Khamenei's publications and was also featured on Khamenei's own official website.[71] The fact that a cleric close to Khamenei travelled all the way from Tehran for this mission carried a noteworthy message: Tehran attached special significance to the operation.

The number and frequency of Assadi's visits to Iran in 2018 showed that something out of the ordinary was happening. According to the case documents, Assadi made six trips to Tehran in only six months in 2018. Therefore, he essentially visited Tehran every month.[72]

Naami's last trip to Iran was on April 6, 2018, which is after the bombing mission was assigned to her and Saadouni. Two other features distinguished this trip. Unusually, she did not travel directly to Iran. She went to Kuwait on an urgent trip, and from there she apparently went to Abadan in the south of Iran with her Iranian passport and then returned on April 10.[73] This coincided with Assadi's longest visit to Iran in 2018. Assadi was in Tehran for 25 days from March 28 to April 21.[74]

Prime Example of State Terrorism

There is no universal definition of terrorism as such. By some accounts, there are at least 250 definitions of terrorism in academic literature, and governmental and inter-governmental sources, some of which include descriptions of state terrorism and state-sponsored terrorism.[75]

According to the Britannica encyclopedia, "Establishment terrorism, often called state or state-sponsored terrorism, is employed by governments … against that government's citizens, against factions within the government, or against foreign governments or groups".⁷⁶

But Miriam Webster's dictionary defines state terrorism a lot more succinctly, saying "State terrorism = Terrorism by a government".⁷⁷

In view of these descriptions, the Villepinte terror plot is a clear example of state terrorism, and this is exactly the conclusion reached by the investigators, prosecutors, courts, the US State Department, and European countries.

The Belgian State Security Service (VSSE) announced in a report signed by the Director General of this organization,⁷⁸ on February 18, 2020: "The attack plot was hatched on behalf of Iran and under the pressure of Iran. This was not a personal initiative on Assadi's part."⁷⁹

In the afternoon session of the second day of Assadi's trial on November 27, 2020, the prosecutor said, among other things, that since the Iranian government did not allow Assadi to appear at the trial, or to cooperate and answer questions, and considering that Assadi was working with the MOIS, this confirms that the Iranian regime was behind the plot. Therefore, it cannot be said that this was a personally motivated attack, but rather, the entire [Iranian] government is involved in this matter and contributed to it.⁸⁰

On February 4, 2021, the Belgian judges declared the fact that this was a government conspiracy. Paragraph 4.6.30. of the ruling states: *"It cannot be doubted that Section 312 within the Ministry of Intelligence was a group consisting of at least more than two people, which due to its size and hierarchical structure, had the required characteristics of a structured organization, with several people under the supervision of intelligence officers being managed in a coordinated way to obtain information and commit terrorist crimes in the framework of fighting and destabilizing the People's Mojahedin group/National Council of Resistance inside and outside the country".*⁸¹

This verdict adds that in the opinion of the court, *"There is no doubt that Assadollah Assadi and the aforementioned defendants have been actively working with the Ministry of Intelligence and especially Section 312 for a long time. It is certain that Assadollah Assadi entered the story as an intelligence officer related to the Ministry of Intelligence and the 312 Department in 2015 and was the operational commander of the planned attack against the annual conference of the People's Mojahedin in Villepinte since March 2018."*[82]

Two MOIS Officials Oversaw the Operation

The NCRI disclosed on August 8, 2018, that MOIS branches in the regime's embassies are controlled and commanded by the MOIS' "Organization of Intelligence and Foreign Movements", and the head of "Intelligence and Foreign Movements" is an MOIS deputy named Reza Amiri Moghadam, who was in direct contact with then Minister of Intelligence Mahmoud Alavi. Assadi implemented the terrorist operation against the Paris summit under the supervision of Amiri Moghadam.[83]

In 2007, on behalf of the regime's SNSC, Amiri Moghadam, who is considered to be one of the highest security officials of the regime, participated in negotiations with American forces in Iraq. Brig. Gen. Kazemi Qomi, the regime ambassador to Iraq, and Amir Hossein Abdollahian, then representative of the Ministry of Foreign Affairs and now the Foreign Minister, were also in those discussions.[84] Amiri Moghadam chaired the regime's delegations during the third round of negotiations with the US in April 2008. Ryan Crocker, the US Ambassador to Iraq, also attended those talks.

The terrorist plot to bomb the MEK's Persian New Year ceremony in Albania in March 2018 was also commanded by Amiri Moghadam. The plot was to be carried out using a truck bomb.

French officials said on October 2, 2018, "There was no doubt Iran's intelligence ministry was behind a June plot to attack an exiled opposition group's rally outside Paris and [France] seized assets belonging to Tehran's intelligence services and two Iranian nationals".[85]

The two I"anians mentioned above were Assadollah Assadi and Saeid Hashemi Moghadam. A French diplomatic source identified Hashemi Moghadam as the "head of operations at the intelligence ministry".[86] Hashemi Moghadam has also been the intelligence liaison with some of the European countries.

In a rare joint statement, the Ministers of the Interior, Foreign Affairs and Economy of France announced, *"This extremely serious act envisaged on our territory could not go without a response".*[87] (Refer to Appendix S).

As reported by the New York Times, on January 8, 2019, the European Union placed Hashemi Moghadam and Assadi on its sanctions list.[88] On the same day, the ambassadors of Belgium, England, Denmark, France, Germany and the Netherlands jointly went to Iran's Ministry of Foreign Affairs in Tehran to express their serious concerns about the regime's actions.

The Belgian judges referred to "Council of Europe Resolution 2001/931/CFSP on the application of specific measures to combat terrorism and Council Regulation (EC) No. 2580/2001 on specific restrictive measures against certain individuals and entities with the aim of combating terrorism" and said, *"It was also decided that there are sufficient reasons for the inclusion of Assadollah Assadi and Saeid Hashemi Moghadam on this list as people who are involved in 'terrorist acts within the context of GS 931'."* It added that Section 312 of the MOIS, *"the Department of Internal Security has provided the necessary financial and material support for the implementation of this plot".*

In the end, regarding Saeid Hashemi Moghadam, the ruling stated:

Saeid Hashemi Moghadam, the Deputy Minister of Intelligence for Internal Security Affairs of the Ministry of Intelligence and Security of Iran, is the hierarchical superior of Assadollah Assadi, the officer of this general administration, who arranged this foiled attack. In view of the function of the Internal Security Organization of the Ministry of Intelligence and considering his hierarchical rank, Saeid Hashemi Moghadam personally approved the foiled attack of June 30, 2018. (Refer to parts 3, 4, and 5 of the Prosecutor General's case file).89

The US State Department also blamed the Iranian regime and specifically its diplomatic apparatus. In a special briefing on July 10, 2018, a senior official of the State Department said clearly that "we blame Iran"90 for the Paris plot. He salso connected it to the broader Iranian trend of using its embassies for terrorist conspiracies.

The most recent example is the plot that the Belgians foiled, and we had an Iranian diplomat out of the Austrian embassy as part of the plot to bomb a meeting of Iranian opposition leaders in Paris. And the United States is urging all nations to carefully examine diplomats in Iranian embassies to ensure their countries' own security. If Iran can plot bomb attacks in Paris, they can plot attacks anywhere in the world, and we urge all nations to be vigilant about Iran using embassies as diplomatic cover to plot terrorist attacks. We are working very closely with the Belgians and the Austrians and the Germans to get to the bottom of this plot to conduct a bomb attack in Paris....91

Mike Pompeo, the US Secretary of State at the time, said in a speech entitled "Supporting Iranian Voices" on July 22, 2018:

Just earlier this month, an Iranian 'diplomat' based in Vienna was arrested and charged with supplying explosives for a terrorist bomb scheduled to bomb a political rally in France. This tells you everything you need to know about the regime.92

In a speech at the UN Security Council on November 19, 2018, US ambassador to the United Nations Nikki Haley reviewed the details of the terrorist plan and Assadi's role, and stated, *"These* *attempts to murder their political opponents on foreign soil reflect the true nature of the Iranian regime".*⁹³

Belgian Conclusions Based on Naami-Saadouni Statement

On May 20, 2019, the judicial police officers who were in charge of the investigation presented their conclusions about Naami's and Saadouni's statements under interrogation, in a section of their report:

Judging by several statements provided by Amir Saadouni and Nasimeh Naami, it is possible to extract a number of elements that indicate the possible involvement of Iran's intelligence in particular or Iran [regime] as a whole." This section of the report was entitled *"Indicators of potential involvement of the MOIS or Iran.*⁹⁴

This report includes the following assertions:

We refer to the following interrogations, namely:

In the interrogation No. 516236/2018, the suspect Amir Saadouni stated:

- *that he met a man in Luxembourg whom he knows as Daniel.*
- *that Daniel works as a servant at the Iranian embassy in Austria, but his real job is in intelligence*
- *That he [Saadouni] had the first meeting with an intermediary from the Ministry of Intelligence in Tehran*
- *that Daniel has a green diplomatic passport*
- *that he has had meetings with Daniel in Salzburg, Vienna, Milan, Venice and Luxembourg*
- *that depending on the type of information he provided, he sometimes received 3500 euros to 4000 euros from Daniel*

- that he received from Daniel in Luxembourg a device that produces a lot of noise, in addition to a mobile phone
- that Daniel talked three months ago about a meeting in Paris and that they should do something with that device there, and that he should first consult with Tehran because the device should be tested first
- that Daniel told them in 2015 that they should go to Iran and that they saw Daniel in a hotel in Tehran
- that he went to Iran and specifically to Ahvaz in 2013 at Daniel's request
- that Daniel was supposed to send a message to coordinate the place and time of the meeting for tomorrow. If he finds out now, it will end very badly for us. They will put pressure on everyone in Iran.

In the interrogation No. 516238/2018, the suspect Nasimeh Naami states:

- that she had promised Daniel that she would send a text message (using a mobile phone) at 17:30 regarding a celebration with fireworks that they were responsible for.
- that at that time, she asked if this could harm people or cause casualties. But they told us that doctors in Iran had tested the device and it was only supposed to cause a lot of noise. We were not allowed to stand near the fire with that bag. But otherwise, it does not harm people. Daniel gave us this bag in Luxembourg on Thursday
- that she doesn't know Daniel's number and that they changed their numbers regularly
- that Daniel works for the Iranian regime
- that they have passed on information about the PMOI, which is active in Europe, to Daniel

- that they met Daniel on Thursday in Luxembourg and that they usually met him in Vienna, Austria
- that they met Daniel for the first time at a hotel in Tehran and they were not allowed to leave that hotel
- that this organization [Ministry of Intelligence] was aware of the health condition of her father (Nasimeh's father), who is very sick. As a result, they could put pressure on them regarding this issue. This organization belongs to the Iranian regime and is the Intelligence Organization
- that Daniel said he speaks to many others. Amir Saadouni stated in the interrogation conducted by the investigative judge Van Hoy Landt that he received amounts of money transferred from Ahvaz, Iran, in 2012 or 2013. This continued until 2015 (it was constant).

In the interrogation No. 517493/2018, the suspect Amir Saadouni stated:

- that Daniel intended to inform the Ministry of Intelligence that he had accepted this mission
- that Daniel stated in the first meeting with him in Munich that he will work for the Ministry of Intelligence of Iran.
- In the interrogation No. 519585/2018, the suspect Amir Saadouni states:
- that Daniel said that he received the package from his colleagues
- that Daniel had to constantly consult with Iran. He did not pay the money from his own pocket.

Decision

In view of the above-mentioned items, we can infer that the suspects Amir Saadouni and Nasimeh Naami know the suspect Assadollah

Assadi as an Iranian diplomat with the nickname Daniel, who works with Iran's intelligence service, and that they provided him information in exchange for payment, whether monetary or otherwise, including trips to Iran.

In addition, it can be understood that there were very close consultations between Assadollah Assadi and Iran for preparing to place or throw the package.

MOIS Officials Meet Assadi in Prison

The highest officials of the regime met regularly with Assadi even while he was in prison.

The Iranian ambassador and the consul general of the Iranian embassy in Belgium were among those visitors.

But one visit from Tehran carried special significance.

According to the documents of the case, on August 13, 2019, a high-ranking delegation from Tehran visited Assadi. A large delegation of embassy officials, including Payman Saadat, the regime's ambassador to Belgium, accompanied them in this meeting.[95]

This five-member delegation was officially from the Ministry of Foreign Affairs, and the members of the delegation had provided information about their formal positions in the Ministry to Belgian authorities. (Refer to Appendix N).

In a report submitted by Belgian authorities about the delegation and the meeting, it was stated that they could not verify the identities of three members of the team that visited from Tehran for the meeting, and it is not clear to them whether the declared position titles were real or not.

One of these three people mentioned was Gholamreza (Reza) Lotfi, born in 1963, who had traveled to Belgium for this meeting as "consultant for the Ministry of Foreign Affairs".

Investigations carried out by the Iranian Resistance and conducted from its sources inside the regime in Iran reveal that this individual, Lotfi, is one of the most senior officials of the MOIS. Lotfi's identity was revealed at a press conference organized by the NCRI in Brussels on August 8, 2018.

Lotfi is the head of the Intelligence Department of the Ministry of Foreign Affairs, whose responsibility is to supervise the operations of MOIS stations in embassies as well as MOIS officers who operate under the cover of the Ministry. At the time of the terrorist plot, he simultaneously reported to Mahmoud Alavi and Javad Zarif, Ministers of Intelligence and Foreign Affairs, respectively, in then President Rouhani's cabinet.

The fact that one of the regime's highest-ranking intelligence officials, among the key people involved in the coordination of activities between the Ministry of Foreign Affairs and the MOIS, personally traveled from Tehran to Belgium to meet with Assadi, indicated that Tehran was keenly pursuing Assadi's case and that Assadi himself was still in contact with Tehran.

Role of MFA in State Terrorism

As some of the most well-known terrorism experts have emphasized, *"For decades, Tehran has been dispatching operatives to Europe to carry out assassinations and other acts of terrorism"*.[96]

This was not the first time that an Iranian official was directly involved in assassinations. On July 13, 1989, Abdul Rahman Ghassemlou, the Secretary-General of the Democratic Party of Iranian Kurdistan at the time, was assassinated in the middle of negotiations, by the very same delegation that had traveled to

Vienna from Tehran. It is very telling that the main figure in this assassination, Mohammad Ali Jafari Sahra Roudi, who was one of the senior commanders of the Islamic Revolutionary Guard Corps (IRGC), was injured during the assassination and was immediately hospitalized in Vienna. But Austria ultimately succumbed to the threats of the Iranian regime and sent Sahra Roudi to the airport on July 22, 1989, inside the vehicles of the Iranian Embassy that had a police escort. Sahra Roudi returned to Tehran on an Iran Air flight.[97] He later obtained senior posts, including the deputy head of internal security for the SNSC and subsequently the chief of staff for former Parliamentary Speaker Ali Larijani.

Another member of the assassination squad that killed Ghassemlou and his two companions was Amir Mansour Bozorgian, an alias for General Ghafour Darjezi. He was also arrested by the Austrian police following the assassination of the Kurdish leaders, but after some time he was able to go to the Iranian embassy in Vienna from the detention center. The police surrounded the embassy for months, but in the end, the officials of the Iranian Foreign Ministry were able to send the second member of the assassination team to Iran because of informal agreements.

Only four years later, in March 1993, Ghafour Darjezi led the assassination squad that killed Mohammad Hossein Naqdi, the representative of the NCRI in Italy. There, too, Darjezi was able to escape from the scene under a diplomatic cover.

Darjezi later changed his name in Iran and obtained significant governmental and quasi-governmental positions. For some time, he was in charge of the security of the country's radio and television. Later, he became the president of SAIPA sports club, but, he was now known by the name of Mostafa Modabber. Two years ago, his identity and some of his past record were revealed by a famous Iranian soccer player in the context of the regime's internal feuds.

Two Wings of Regime's Foreign Policy

Never has an accredited diplomat of the regime been arrested in the course of a terrorist operation under the regime's supervision. The dimensions of the conspiracy and terrorist act were unprecedented in every respect, because it was not about the assassination of a few people. Rather it was about an unprecedented terrorist act that could result in unimaginable casualties and one that had progressed to the final stages of its implementation.

Assadi's case represents a clear example of the close relationship between the MFA and the IRGC Qods Force (part of Tehran's security-terrorist apparatus).

The MFA in general and the regime's embassies in particular have played a key and sometimes decisive role in the regime's terrorist plots over the past 40 years. NCRI research regarding the regime's major terrorist operations in Europe over the last four decades has revealed that during this time, the embassies of the regime in almost all the main European countries, including France, Germany, Italy, Switzerland, the Netherlands, Sweden, Denmark, and Norway, have all been directly involved in terrorist plots, and that there was virtually no regime embassy that stood out as an exception to this rule.[98] In many cases, the regime's operations would have been practically impossible to carry out without the direct intervention and provision of resources by its embassies.

Javad Zarif, the regime's foreign minister for eight years during Rouhani's tenure, unwittingly provided an apt description about this particular function of the Ministry of Foreign Affairs.

On April 28, 2021, he released a video on his Instagram account showing his presence at a site near Baghdad International Airport where Qassem Soleimani, the former commander of IRGC Quds Force, was eliminated. In the same post, he described the regime's diplomatic arm and its on-the-ground presence (*"Meydan"*) as *"the two wings projecting the external power of the Islamic Republic of Iran".* He added that these are *"fundamental and complementary,"* and emphasized *"the imperative for the intelligent coordination of relations between these two wings, while priorities are determined by legal structures under the high-level supervision of the Supreme Leader".*[99]

On February 24, 2021, in a now famous interview that lasted for three hours and 11 minutes, Zarif sat down to talk with a regime political activist as part of an oral history project about Rouhani's government. The interview was released on April 25, 2021, and clarified what Zarif meant by the term *"Meydan"*. He explained that *"Meydan"* refers to the role and advancement of the objectives of the IRGC Quds Force in the Iranian regime's foreign policy.[100]

In the same interview, Zarif stated that the agenda of the Ministry of Foreign Affairs was essentially security-focused. He added:

> *There has never been an economic agenda set for the Ministry of Foreign Affairs. That's why at the start of the Ministry of Foreign Affairs in the 1980s, they closed down the economic directorate and in place of it, they created directorates for the region, which had a more acute political and security orientation.*[101]

In the hours immediately following Assadi's arrest and before the slightest details were publicized, Zarif described it as a false flag operation organized by the regime's opposition. Zarif likely had prior knowledge about the plot, since Assadi was officially part of the MFA.

More interestingly, Zarif denied the regime's responsibility at the Munich Security Conference on February 20, 2019, by suggesting if the bomb plot had been the work of Tehran, it would not have been scheduled for the day of Rouhani's trip to Europe but would have been carried out at least a day earlier or a day later.[102]

Of course, this is nonsense because the operation could only have taken place on the day the Iranian Resistance held the target gathering.

Decisions Made at Highest Levels

According to information that the Iranian Resistance has verified from multiple sources within the regime, the bomb plot was decided at the highest levels of the theocracy.

Maryam Rajavi, being the main target of the plot and one of the private plaintiffs in the court case, testified for seven hours in October 2019 in front of the relevant judicial authorities. During her testimony, she stated that the Iranian Resistance had obtained precise information from inside the regime, which showed that the bomb plot was approved by the SNSC chaired by then-President Hassan Rouhani. The responsibility for its execution was assigned to the Ministry of Intelligence and the Ministry of Foreign Affairs, specifically to Mahmoud Alavi, the Minister of Intelligence, and Javad Zarif, the Minister of Foreign Affairs.

According to this information, after the plot was decided by the SNSC, it was verified and approved by Khamenei himself, triggering its operational launch.

Mrs. Rajavi also provided to the judicial authorities diagrams and charts about the decision making process and the officials who were active in the impacted organs.[103]

It was revealed in the investigation documents that Assadi told Saadouni, *"If [the explosion] takes place inside [the exposition hall], he will personally go to the Master [Khamenei]... and I will make requests for his speech on your behalf [to mention you in his speech]."* This clearly confirms the fact that Khamenei was aware of the plot and that the plan was approved by him. (Refer to Appendix O for SMS text document).

Statements by Regime Authorities

Since the eruption of major anti-regime uprisings in December 2017-January 2018 and when the role of the PMOI/MEK became evident in these protests, the highest officials of the regime have publicly stated that dealing a fatal blow to the Iranian Resistance has been high on Tehran's agenda.

On January 9, 2018, Ali Khamenei, the regime's Supreme Leader, stressed that the uprising was organized by the MEK and that it had been planned for months. He threatened that *"this deed will not go unpunished"*, **adding,** *"Those who entered the scene out of excitement, whether they be university students or not, must be talked to and they should be educated. But the MEK's case is different".*[104]

On January 1, 2018, at the height of the uprisings in Iran, Ali Shamkhani, the Secretary of the regime's SNSC, told the regime's Arabic-language TV Al-Mayadeen in an interview, *"The Hypocrites (MEK) ... will get an appropriate response from Iran from a source that they do not expect."*[105]

On January 16, 2018, Mahmoud Alavi, the-then Minister of Intelligence, emphasized: *"The unknown soldiers of Imam Zaman (the term used by the regime to refer to MOIS agents) will soon give a crushing response to the terrorist and anti-revolutionary groups in the region."* [106]

On February 11, 2018, Hossein Ta'eb, then-head of the IRGC Intelligence Organization, said:

> *Our knowledge reveals that in recent events as well the notorious groups led by the main enemies of the nation exploited the legitimate economic demands of the people and tried to divert the people's demands by creating insecurity. ... Of course, their deeds will not go unanswered, and we will slap them in the face at the appropriate time.*[107]

Hesamoddin Ashna, a Rouhani adviser and the head of the presidential strategic research center, who also worked as a deputy to the Minister of Intelligence in the past, wrote in a tweet on June 18, 2018: *"Those who are looking for hot summers should not forget the Majaray-e Nimrooz"*. (*Majaray-e Nimrooz* or "Mid-day Event" is the title of a movie made by the MOIS about the February 8, 1982 attack on MEK senior leadership in Tehran. It was released on March 15, 2017. It was lauded by Khamenei himself and received several major awards from the regime).

Two days before the Resistance's gathering in Paris, the regime's Student News Network affiliated with the IRGC Intelligence mentioned the role of the MEK in starting the uprisings of the Iranian people, and while disseminating lies about the MEK, referred to a "bloodbath".

Investigation Confirmed State Terrorism

While the investigation by relevant Belgian agencies was purely focused on the facts related to the four culprits, and the court was to decide on their role accordingly, however, it became crystal clear that the terrorist plot in Villepinte was not the initiative of a few rogue elements within the regime but was rather a state decision taken at the highest level of the Iranian regime.

Based on available evidence the court concluded that *"there exists a group within the department 312 of the intelligence service MOIS, which was engaged in gathering information on the MEK/NCRI and used this information to select targets and ultimately to organize an attack on a convention of these Iranian opposition parties."* The court further concluded that the four perpetrators, together with other MOIS agents, constitute a terrorist group.

CHAPTER 5

The Modus Operandi

According to the documents obtained in the case file, it has become clear that in addition to the managing the terrorist network involved the terrorist plot against the NCRI summit in Villepinte, Assadi, as the MOIS station chief in Europe, was handling a network of intelligence agents all across the continent. This chapter deals with the extensive network of intelligence agents in Europe and also some aspects of the modus operandi of the MOIS network in the continent.

Network of Intelligence Agents in Europe

Numerous documents obtained from Assadi's car show that he was in contact with a large network of intelligence agents in Europe. A green notebook seized during the search of his car contained among other things, 289 addresses in 11 different European countries.

The police's summary of this notebook states:

Regarding the geographical spread, it should be noted that these notes refer to 11 European countries in total. However, there are no notes on non-European countries (with the possible exception of "unknown"). Most notes refer to a connection with Germany, as 114 contacts out of the 289, or 39 percent, were located in that country. There are also countless notes about France and Austria, comprising14 percent and 13 percent of his contacts.

Also, in the payment receipt sheets found inside the green notebook, there are official payment documents in Farsi language for three intelligence agents with pseudonyms whose real identities have not yet been established. Assadi met with and paid these agents in between the time when he returned from Tehran to Vienna on June 22 until his arrest, which explains why these sheets were inside Assadi's green notebook.

On June 23, 2018, Assadi paid the salary for the first quarter of 2018 of an agent with the pseudonym Kazemi. In the second document, he loaned €2,500 to the same person. In the third document, he gave that person €5,000 for the expenses of the first quarter of the year. (These payments are similar to the payment to Amir Saadouni, calculated separately from the expenses, and it is clear that the amount of €5,000 was the cost of this person's missions during the first quarter of the year). Altogether he paid a total of €9,900 to this person, from which €900 were deducted for a previous loan.

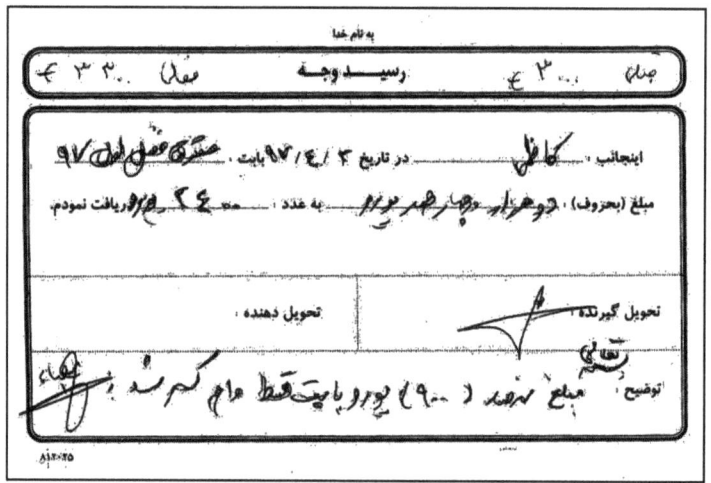

Figure 26- Receipt of a €2,400 salary of €2,400 paid to an agent with pseudonym Kazemi. It also mentions €900 been deducted for a previous loan.

The next three documents are related to an agent named "Bagherzadeh" who received €1,800 on June 23, 2018, for the first quarter of 2018. He also borrowed €2,500 and received €5,000 for expenses during the same period. In other words, this agent received a total of €9,000, of which €900 were deducted for a previous loan.

According to the next two documents, an agent named "Navid" received €1,600 for his expenses for the first quarter of 2018 and a laptop from Assadi. Some €200 were for transportation, €300 as salary increase, and €1,100 as financial assistance. A loan of €900 had already been given to this agent, bringing the total payments to €2,000. The documents do not specify the amount of the fixed salary of this agent, nor the date of the payment, which based on existing evidence, is assessed to be in the same time frame as the previous documents.

These documents make it abundantly clear that the three agents, Kazemi, Bagherzadeh and Navid, were in direct contact with Assadi, who met and paid them a week before his arrest. Their real identities, however, were not specified in the case.

MOIS Albania Based Network

Assadi also supervised a network of intelligence agents in Albania, where thousands of MEK members reside. Due to the importance of Albania, the MOIS sent Mustafa Rudaki, its former European station chief, from Tehran to Albania in December 2017 to manage the network of agents in that country. Assadi had replaced Rudaki in Vienna in 2014.

Hadi Thani Khani, one of the agents recruited by the intelligence station at the regime's embassy in Albania, wrote a letter to the United Nations Secretary General António Guterres, on February 14, 2021, and disclosed details on how these agents in Albania worked. Thani Khani was a member of this network for four years. He elaborated on how the MOIS recruited, funded, trained, and directed MEK dropouts who had come into the service of the MOIS to conduct espionage and engage in a demonization campaign against the MEK to set the stage for subsequent terrorist attacks.

This was not the only such case. On July 16, 2022, Albanian media reported that the country's Special Structure for Combatting Corruption and Organized Crime (SPAK), acting on the request of the Special Prosecutor's Office, had detained and interrogated 11 Iranians for espionage in the service of the Iranian regime on July 12, 2022. Albanian Police raided eight apartments, four offices, and several buildings where they stayed and conducted prohibited activities. The premises of the ASILA Association was also searched. ASILA is a front association affiliated with the MOIS purporting to provide assistance to Iranians in Albania.

According to the Albanian Police, these individuals had been under investigation for four years. They were suspected of carrying out espionage activities on Albanian territory on behalf of the IRGC, an entity designated by the United States as a Foreign Terrorist Organization (FTO), and the MOIS, EuroNews Albania reported.

According to the court order, these activities were carried out to prevent *"any possible terrorist attack."* The order further stipulated that these persons are accused of *"receiving money from Iran's secret services, the Qods Force and the IRGC to obtain information about the MEK in Albania."*

In a press conference on November 1, 2018, the Director General of the Albanian Police unveiled another case of MOIS operatives who had engaged in espionage against the MEK, with the intention to carry out terror attacks against the group. He identified Alireza Naqashzadeh, who had been working under the orders of an agent of the Quds Terrorist Force nicknamed "Paiman" in Tehran. The latter had also hired an operative named Abdul Khaliq Malekzadeh (alias Farhat) along with a professional killer named Abdus Salam Turgut in Turkey to carry out terrorist operations.

As such, it becomes clear that the espionage and terrorist network set up by Assadi and his associates remains to be active in Europe and is planning to carry out more operations.

Hiring Agents and Illegal Money Transfers

The ruling of the Belgian appeals court deals with the outcome of investigations into the financial activities of the three Assadi collaborators, which make it clear the MOIS offered financial incentives to these agents to carry out the plot.

Section 4.7.8 of the ruling states:

The elements of the criminal case, including the defendants' remarks, the results of the inspections and financial investigations, show without a doubt that the defendants Amir Saadouni, Nasimeh Naami, and Mehrdad Arefani have made great financial gains based on the events contained in the indictment D. It is certain that they were involved in a terrorist group between January 1, 2015, and June 30, 2018, and regularly received funds for the services they provided.

Section 4.7.9. adds:

Financial investigations showed that between March 2008 and June 2018, the €123,855.81 were deposited in various bank accounts for the defendant Amir Saadouni. In the case of the defendant Nasimeh Naami, €106,495.57 had been kept as a cash deposit for the period of December 2010 to June 2018.

It is noteworthy the largest cash deposits of huge sums that were deposited into the ING bank accounts of the accused Saadouni and Naami, were made in the days before the thwarted attack on June 30, 2018. Financial reviews have also shown that some cash deposits were paid on the spot. Successive deposits were made in the two separate ING accounts of each of the defendants, indicating that they had large sums of money which they deposited into their checking accounts at approximately the same time. On June 26 and 27 alone, a total of €16,750.00 cash was deposited into their account.

Further investigation of their assets shows that these cash flows, for which the defendants did not provide a justifiable explanation, were in no way proportionate to the lawful income of the defendants.

In addition, two other amounts of money were discovered in the shared house in the neighborhood of Villerique, one of which was around €35,700 euros and the other of €98.00 euros. The defendants could provide no acceptable explanation in this regard.

Section 4.7.10. of the verdict states:

On September 25, 2018, and December 19, 2018, defendant Amir Saadouni clearly stated that he received €17,000.00 euros for half a year of work from "Daniel" [Assadi] and that it was always paid in cash during their meetings. He received a salary of between €1,500 to €1,700.

Nevertheless, when calculating financial gains, police services have assumed that any cash deposits were in return for services rendered in connection with Saadouni's involvement in the terrorist group.

Also, it is clear from the conversations between Naami and Saadouni that they had acted for financial gains. For example, they talked about getting "a lot of cash." It is also clear that Naami actively negotiated with Assadi about the amount of money (they should receive).

Section 4.7.13. of the ruling deal with the financial status of Arefani. It concludes: *"Financial investigations show that between January 2008 and June 2018, the defendant Mehrdad Arefani deposited €226,084.50 in cash in various bank accounts. Also, the examination of the assets shows that these cash flows, for which the defendant did not provide a correct explanation, were disproportionate to his lawful income... An amount of €1,500 was discovered from his home."*

Money Transfer Methods

As stated in numerous documents of the case, Assadi generally transferred money to the network of his intelligence agents by paying in cash. Also, the MOIS used a money exchange to transfer money from Iran to Naami's account, so that the transfer of money would not be registered (and therefore not detected).

Documents below are examples of a May 2018 money transfer through an exchange from the city of Ahvaz in Iran to an exchange in the city of Brussels in Belgium for the transfer of money to Naami.

Two amounts of one billion rials and 1.1 billion rials were deposited from Iran into an exchange account in Brussels at the end of May 2018. The sum of these two amounts, 2.1 billion rials, equivalent to €27,500 euros at the daily exchange rate, were received by Naami from the Brussels exchange.

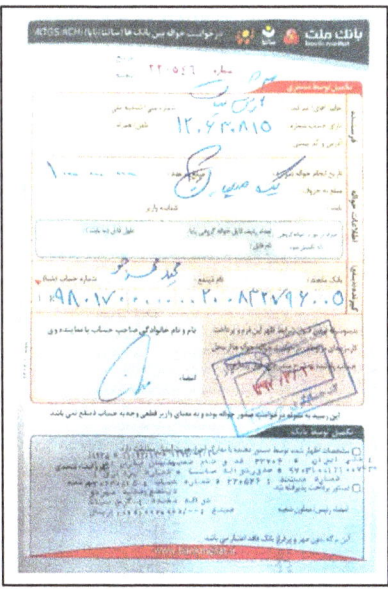

Figure 27 – Money transfer document.

Recruitment of Agents via Honey Trap

One of primary methods with which the Intelligence Ministry recruits agents is through training of female agents in sexpionage, to lay a honey trap, i.e., luring vulnerable men via female intelligence agents. In the mullahs' lexicon, these agents are dubbed "Swallows"[108] (*parastoo*).

This is how the regime secured the cooperation of Amir Saadouni. The MOIS agent Nasimeh Naami, met Saadouni on the Internet from inside Iran in 2004. The two got married in 2005 remotely and two years later, in February 2007, Naami went to the Netherlands with her original Iranian passport and applied for asylum in Belgium. The couple began their collaboration with the MOIS after Naami went to Belgium.

The honey trap has been increasingly used by the MOIS to lure individuals into either collaborating with the regime. It has also been used to attract Iranians in exile to neighboring countries, where they have been abducted and forcefully taken to Iran.

Acting as a sleeper cell, the couple were in active communication with an MOIS liaison officer in Tehran.

The appeals court judgment refers to a wiretapped conversations between Naami and Saadouni in which the former instructs the latter as to what to say during his interrogation. The judgement reads:

> *The results of the wiretapping the conversation between the accused Amir Saadouni and Nasimeh Naami in the detention center of FGP Antwerp on July 18, 2018 (see the following official report No. 101479/2019 dated September 11 of the wiretapped conversations) are undeniable. The defendant Nasimeh Naami repeatedly tells the defendant Amir Saadouni what he needs to explain the issues. The two also discussed what they should say about the explosives, their role in the plot and the consequences. The following is part of their recorded conversation:*

Naami: You should also say it was you who drew all the plans and that Nasimeh had nothing to do with it. Tell them even though I was not with her, Nasimeh went straight to bed at around 8:00 PM when she came home from work. She always told me that he was tired. Also tell them that you admit that you had collected information for several years. But you don't accept that you were planning to kill people. When you talk to them, try to use my name as little as possible. Tell them he (Assadi) told you in Vienna that he wanted to give you a devise that makes a noise when you throw it. That's it. Say that you were deceived by the diplomat. We have to prove this. We have to prove this. They need to understand that we didn't know it was a dangerous thing, nor did we intend to kill anyone.

When discussing the explosive, the couple were recorded as saying:

Saadouni: Say we were with our Jewish landlord from 2006 to 2010. I have never even stolen anything. How can I kill people? Isn't this a joke? We must tell the truth Nasimeh, why should we lie?

Naami: Yes, I know, but unfortunately that thing was in our car! And you and I took it from him like two idiots.

Saadouni: I know

Naami: How I are we! How could you not even check inside that bag?

Saadouni: That night I did not sleep until morning because I was terrified.

Naami: I had a bad feeling, but on the other hand, I thought he was not going to lie to you. Do you remember when he told you to do this from a distance of 50 to 100 meters?

Saadouni: When I am inside the hall].

Naami: Maybe he wanted you to die too. How big was the device?

Saadouni: 300 to 400 grams of explosives.

Naami: How many people does it kill? First, he told you to throw it between the seats and you said no.

Saadouni: Nasimeh don't say that.

Naami: He told you that it makes such a loud noise that it can be heard in the hall.

Training Recruited Agents in Iran

According to the case documents, the MOIS recruits and trains agents by inviting them to go to Iran to meet them personally in hotel controlled by the Ministry. The judgment by the court of appeals includes a summary of how Saadouni and Naami began to communicate with the MOIS.

It appears from the various interrogations of the accused Amir Saadouni and Nasimeh Naami that they were first contacted by the MOIS at the end of 2007... In 2010, the first meeting between a person named "Javad" who worked for the MOIS, and the defendant Amir Saadouni took place in Brussels. Based on the above, he received 500 euros, a postal address and a phone number in order to make further calls. According to the defendant Nasimeh Naami, they agreed to cooperate with the MOIS as a couple so that they could return to Iran and their families. It is not disputed that the couple Amir Saadouni and Nasimeh Naami traveled to Iran in September 2010 to meet the MOIS. Two agents of the Ministry of Intelligence named "Javad" and "Ahmedzadeh" were waiting for them at the airport and then accompanied them to their residence. During a meeting in a hotel, in the presence of several MOIS operatives, including Javad, the couple Amir Saadouni and Nasimeh Naami were asked to gather information more actively about the People's Mojahedin. From the stamps found in the passport of the accused Nasimeh Naami, it appears that she traveled to Tehran again on December 23, 2010. Accused Amir Saadouni also stated that "Ahmedzadeh" called him and introduced himself as an intelligence officer. In 2012, he ordered the couple to go to Iran, which they did. Accused Amir Saadouni met with "Ahmedzadeh" who asked him to put more effort in the matters entrusted to him. According to the defendant Amir Saadouni, he had another trip to Iran in early 2013, where he stayed in a safe apartment for four days, with two intelligence officers, one named "Mohammed" and the other named "Haji". ... He was again asked to have a more active role to enter the People's Mojahedin Organization. From the statements by the defendant Amir Saadouni, it appears that by the end of 2013, the couple was informed that they would be rewarded for the services they had performed for MOIS. When "Mohammed" was their MOIS handler, they received a total of 6,000 euros. But according to the defendant Amir Saadouni, "Mohammed" informed him in the summer of 2015 that moving forward, a person living in Europe, specifically named Daniel [pseudonym for Assadi], would be replacing him. He was then informed by email that the next meeting with "Daniel" would take place in Munich. Defendant Amir Saadouni also stated that during that period he was again pressured by Muhammad to continue his collaboration [with the MOIS].

Communication Methods

The Appeals Court judgment wrote the following about how the MOIS communicated with Assadi when his mission began:

The first meeting between the couple Amir Saadouni and Nasimeh Naami and Assadollah Assadi (known as Daniel) took place in Munich in August 2015, when he informed them that he was employed at the Iranian Embassy in Vienna. He also gave them an email address to keep in touch with and an envelope with €4,000 to cover their expenses.

After another meeting was arranged in Iran in November 2015, and several other meetings took place in different European locations between the couple Amir Saadouni and Nasimeh Naami and Assadollah Assadi.

Moreover, the remarks by the defendants Amir Saadouni and Nasimeh Naami and the results of the work done on the confiscated mobile phones and computers make it clear their communications with Assadi in coded language to the extent possible (see the following official report with number 512662/19 dated June 3, 2019) and the use of mobile phones to exchange of short messages would be protected. Three different phone numbers used by the couple were identified: one was linked to the defendant Amir Saadouni and two numbers were linked to the defendant Nasimeh Naami. On June 28, 2018, the couple obtained a mobile phone containing an Austrian SIM card during a meeting with Assadi in Luxembourg. Defendant Amir Saadouni also said that mobile phone numbers changed almost every eight months. As for Asadullah Assadi, it was found that he used an Austrian mobile phone number to communicate. In total, seven different numbers were identified. According to the defendant Amir Saadouni, Assadollah Assadi was only allowed to use very simple mobile phones whose batteries are easily removed so that they could be traced when used. The analysis of the Samsung Galaxy J3 mobile phone and the statements of the accused Amir Saadouni (see statements dated May 14, 2019) also show that messages were exchanged with Assadollah Assadi via Telegram.

Amir Saadouni and Nasimeh Naami met Assadi, every three to four months, and were carefully planned in advance. The agreements made in this regard were recorded in coded language by e-mail or text message before holding the meetings. The meeting location was always determined by Asadullah Assadi and had to meet various criteria such as the absence of surveillance cameras, avoidance of crowded areas and preferably not in public places. On the other hand, restaurants, bars, and train wagons met these criteria.

As for the relationship between Arefani and Assadi, the Belgian prosecutor office report states: " Arefani was recruited by the MOIS between 1988 and 2000 and came out of Iran and in Brussels Paris took part in activities such as video recording or home repair. He also went to Paris and Denmark, the United Kingdom and Ashraf in Albania. Arefani was an important source of information and had regular contact with Assadi. The details are recorded in his notebooks. Arefani had several mobile phone devices and cameras to send videos. Thousands of video clips were found, in which he had recorded MEK gatherings as well as MEK offices. He had also recorded the names of 55 important anti-regime dissidents in his notebook. He has had coded messages with and Austrian telephone number and sent and received messages via SMS since 2015. He also had meetings (with Assadi) in different countries…. Saadouni admitted that Arefani gave a lot of information to Assadi. Arefani was tasked with ensuring that the couple (Saadouni/Naami) performed their job well. Arefani was the principal agent on the ground until the end of the event. Assadi has been waiting for Arefani to send him information and control (the operation). This group wanted to carry out the plot as a big operation and actually achieve the result as a major operation.

Intelligence Agent Posing as Secular Atheist

One of the tactics used by the MOIS agents to hide their real identity is the claim to being a critic of the regime, a human rights activist opposed to the regime, or a secular atheist, thereby naturally distancing themselves from the regime and enabling them to infiltrate political opposition groups.

To easily infiltrate dissident political groups, Mehrdad Arefani posed as a poet who was opposed to the fundamentalist rulers of Iran. Meanwhile, based on the documents in the case, he worked with Assadi in forming the terrorist cell.

Agents of the regime have two different functions. Some, like Arefani, are tasked with infiltrating the ranks of opposition groups or their supporters, while others are tasked to be part of the Diaspora opposing the regime, and at the same time engaged in an attempt to discredit the opposition.

Arefani's skillset reportedly included being a poet, writing books and moderating events, various technical and intelligence activities, the practice of martial arts and the ability to adapt himself to different political groups. All of this shows that he was a very well trained and dangerous MOIS infiltrator.

Moreover, along with another person, Arefani had set up an entity linked to Vienna-based foreign reporters and journalists, named SOS Iran. SOS introduced itself as an Iranian association working to expose human rights violations and defending victims of human rights abuses. This entity was a cover for him to easily travel to Austria to have regular contact with the Iranian regime's embassy in Vienna, where Assadi was stationed. Arefani's lawyer said in court:

> *He is a poet, he is not religious, he is not a regime spy, he is not a Muslim, he is not a terrorist, he is a leftist. The MEK exploited him... He went to Austria several times. He didn't go for skiing, but he didn't go to see Assadi either. He went to see his friends in SOS Iran and help refugees, that's all. There is nothing else. Everything he says can be proven...* [109]

Arefani himself said: "I am a writer and poet and I have five books and one in French which L'Harmattan (a publishing house in France) published." The book, "TRAVAIL AU NOIR" (Illegal Work) feigns staunch opposition to terrorism and fundamentalism. To introduce the book's translation, Arefani held a conference in Paris with his translator, Myriam Benoit.[110]

In further testimony, Arefani says, "I am a member of the Austrian Journalists Association and I have published many reports on human rights violations in Iran. I have done NGO work for 15 years and I have worked with Amnesty International and helped refugees for many years." [111]

Another tactic Arefani used to pose as an anti-regime writer and earn trust within opposition groups, was to criticize the stance taken by the Writers' Club in support of the Iranian regime's lobby. Below is a post on a social platform in December 2007: [112]

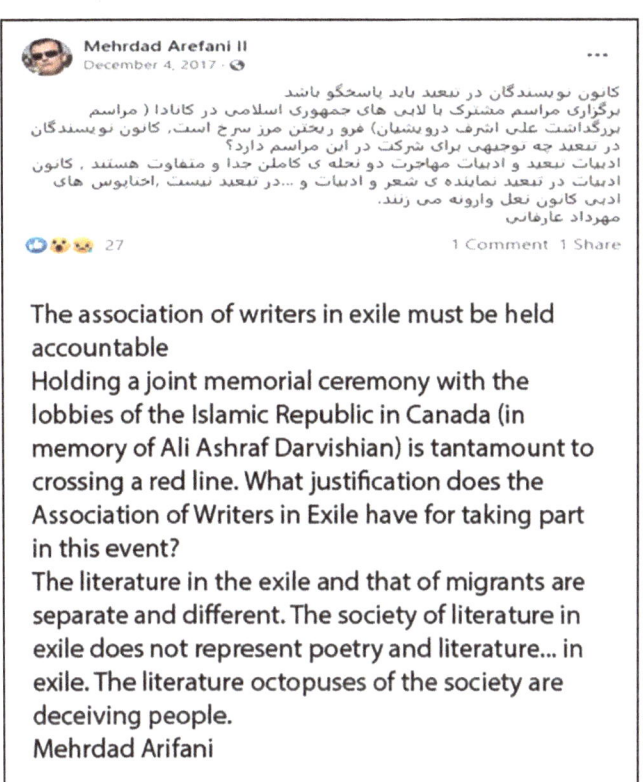

Figure 28- Arefani's post

Naami had also pretended not to be religious. To absolve Naami of responsibility in the terrorist plot, her lawyer said that Naami's family did not believe in God and had a western lifestyle. He added that Naami did not wear a scarf, was pro-western, was not a spy, did not work for the Iranian regime and was not a terrorist.

For many years, the MOIS has used the cover of human rights activists, secular intellectuals, writers, and poets who are critical of the regime, to dispel any doubt that its agents might be working with the Iranian regime, enabling them to try to infiltrate Iranian circles, and the ranks of the opposition. In many cases, the mullahs' regime has been the source of anti-Islamic slogans, and Islamophobia on social media to cover its tracks.

Intelligence Agents Abusing Refugee Status

The three terrorists who collaborated with Assadi had political asylum and later obtained Belgian citizenship. The MOIS, had provided them with Iranian passports, through the embassy in Belgium, to facilitate their travel to Iran.

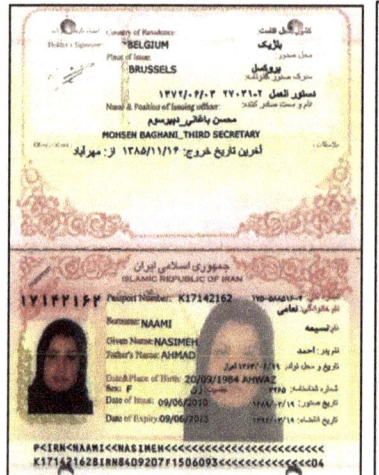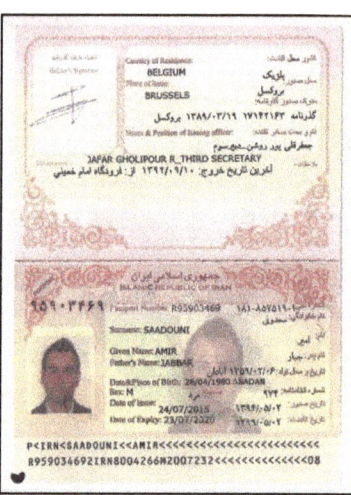

Figure 29 - Iranian passports issued in Brussels to Naami and Saadouni.

CHAPTER 6

The Response

After receiving the first reliable report about the involvement of Naami and Saadouni in a violent act in France, [113] the Belgian judiciary began taking a number of steps,[114] including:

- Wiretap and surveillance order for Naami-Saadouni issued on June 26, 2018.
- Initial indictment issued by Belgian federal prosecutor against two main defendants on June 28.
- The Belgium State Security Service received new reliable information on June 29. regarding the possibility that Arefani was involved in the same terrorist conspiracy.
- Arrest warrant issued for Naami-Saadouni couple at noon on June 30.
- Investigating judge issued European arrest warrant for Assadi in the evening of June 30, after arrest of Naami-Saadouni couple and their initial interrogations.

Initial Indictment

Only Saadouni and Naami were named in the indictment on June 28. The third "defendant" was identified as person X, as no detailed information about Arefani was yet available. Assadi was later identified in Luxembourg that same afternoon and was ordered to be arrested anywhere in Europe on June 30, at the request of the Antwerp investigative judge.

The charges in the indictment are:

To prepare for the commission of a terrorist offense referred to in Article 137, ...whereby for the purposes of this Article, "preparation" means, inter alia:

- *collecting information about locations, events, events or persons that makes it possible to take an action at those locations or during these events or events or inflicting damage on those persons, and observing those locations, events, events or persons;*

- *the possession, search, purchase, transport or manufacture of objects or substances of a nature that they could pose a danger to another person or cause significant economic damage;*

- *possessing, seeking, purchasing, transporting, or manufacturing financial or material resources, false or illegally obtained documents, computer media fluorescent immunization agents. means of transport;*

- *to have available, to look for, to purchase spaces that can provide a shelter, meeting place, meeting place or shelter;*

- *... in whatever form and by which means this claim is made. Requests that the investigating judge to proceed to a judicial inquiry...*

In the initial indictment, eight phone numbers belonging to Naami and Saadouni were identified and ordered to be wiretapped and controlled.

According to the Belgian federal prosecutor, the defendants are:

In violation of Articles 51, 52, 137, §1 and §2, °1, 138, 393 and 394 of the Belgian Criminal Code, having attempted to kill unidentified persons with intent to kill and with premeditation, as well as with terrorist intent within the meaning of Article 137, §1 of the Criminal Code, whereby the intention to commit the crime has manifested itself through external acts that constitute the beginning of the execution of that crime and only as a result of circumstances, of the want to have ceased independently of the perpetrators or have missed their effect.
[115]

The final phrase of this indictment, which will be repeated in all pursuant judicial documents, is the material basis for the terrorist offense, with the legal theme of "initiating a crime." This means that as far as the perpetrators of this crime were concerned, they had taken all necessary practical steps to commit the crime, which proved their criminal will beyond any doubt. The prevention of the crime was the direct consequence of outside intervention (police involvement and arrest).

Complementary Indictment

On June 3, 2019, after the investigation had taken its course through major stages for a year, the federal prosecutors issued a further indictment entitled "Complementary Indictment to Continue the Court's Investigation" and, in addition to the charges mentioned in the initial indictment, added the charge of "formation of a terrorist group" to the charges brought against the four defendants. The indictment reads in its fifth paragraph:

> In violation of Articles 139 and 140, §1 of the Criminal Code, having participated in any activity of a terrorist group, being a structured association of more than two persons existing for some time and acting in concert to commit terrorist offenses, as intended in Article 137 of the Criminal Code, including by providing data or material resources to a terrorist group or by financing any activity of a terrorist group in any form, for the period from 01.01.2007 to 31.12.2016: as long as he knows that his participation contributes to the commission of a crime or misdemeanor by the terrorist group for the period from 01.01.2017 to the present: while he knew or should have known that his participation could contribute to the commission of a crime or misdemeanor by the terrorist group.[116]

Two Years of Judicial Investigations

The investigation into the crime was launched on June 25, 2018, five days before the terrorist plan was implemented, and Ms. Isabel van Hoy Landt, the investigating judge in charge of the case formally announced the end of the investigation on April 28, 2020.

Extensive investigations were conducted for 23 months by the investigating judge and her assistants, judicial police investigators, experts from various fields, including explosives experts, financial experts, polygraph examiners, and others. Two other investigations, in Germany for 100 days in relation to Assadi, and in France for 20 days in relation to Arefani, were also conducted. Relevant information was also received from other countries (Germany, England, the Netherlands, Luxembourg, etc.) through judicial representation. The meticulous judicial process resulted in a case file consisting of about 15,000 pages, as all aspects of the case were thoroughly investigated.

Dozens of interrogations of Assadi and his three accomplices, Arefani, Naami and Saadouni were conducted, and dozens of interviews were conducted with officials of the NCRI, including Mrs. Rajavi,[117] Mr. Mehdi Abrishamchi, Chairman of the NCRI Peace Committee, Mr. Mohammad Mohaddessin, Chairman of the NCRI's Foreign Affairs Committee, and Abolghassem Rezaei. Several MEK supporters and Iranians residing in Belgium, who had knowledge of the three perpetrators, were also interviewed.

Private Plaintiffs

On June 30, 2018, a huge attendance of Iranians and hundreds of political figures from around the world participated in the NCRI summit. In all 25 Iranian and foreign political figures were parties to the case: [118]

1. The National Council of Resistance of Iran (NCRI)

2. Maryam Rajavi, NCRI President-elect

3. Elisabetta Zamparutti, former Italian MP and human rights personality

4. Robert Torricelli, former United States Senator

5. Roger Godsiff, British MP

6. Wesley Martin, US Army Colonel (Ret.), senior Antiterrorism/Force Protection Officer for coalition forces in Iraq

7. Ingrid Betancourt, Colombian presidential candidate

8. Sid Ahmed Ghozali, former Prime Minister of Algeria

9. Linda Chavez, former White House Director of Public Liaison

10. Tunne Kelam, former member of European Parliament from Estonia

11. Robert Blackman, British MP

12. Yves Bonnet, Director of France DST under François Mitterrand

13. Tahar Boumedra, former Chief of the UN Human Rights Office in Iraq

14. Giulio Terzi di Sant'Agata, former Italian Foreign Minister

15. Robert G. Joseph, Former US Undersecretary of State for Arms Control and International Security

16. Riad Yassin Abdallah, Former Foreign Minister of Yemen

17. Martin Patzelt, MP German Bundestag

18. Antonio Tasso, Italian MP

19. Struan Stevenson, former Member of European Parliament (MEP), President of the European Iraqi Freedom Association (EIFA)

20. Jean-François Legaret, Former Mayor of Paris 1st Arrondissement

21. Pierre Bercy, President of French New Human Rights Association

22. Farzin Hashemi, NCRI Representative in International Court Affairs

23. Sanabaragh Zahedi, Chairman of the NCRI Judiciary Committee

24. Hossein Abedini, Deputy Director of the NCRI Representative Office in the United Kingdom

25. Javad Dabirian, Deputy Director of the NCRI Representative Office in Germany

On Assadollah Assadi's Interrogations

Assadollah Assadi was arrested on the afternoon of July 1 enroute from Germany to Austria, about 400 kilometers from the Austrian border. He was accompanied by his wife and two sons.

During the first interrogation, in response to the police officers, who asked him what he was doing on German soil, he replied that he had come to Germany for a holiday. His wife, however, did not know she was in Germany.

In Germany, the police tried to interrogate him twice, but he refused to cooperate and answer any questions. During Belgian interrogations, he said that because the German police mistreated him, he refuses to cooperate.

He was briefly interrogated by Belgian judicial authorities several times, but a detailed interrogation was not conducted to deal with all the issues. During these interrogations, he acted as a sophisticated intelligence officer of the MOIS and maintained his position as a sitting diplomat and claimed he should be released. Interestingly, his defense lawyer never challenged his role as the mastermind of the terrorist plot.

He answered questions in only five interrogation sessions. On one occasion, he demanded a meeting with Belgian police officials and threatened the Belgian government that if he is not released there will serious consequences for Belgian interests.

Three interrogations are noteworthy:

- On February 25, 2019, he was questioned about the three other accomplices and Assadi said he did not know them.

- On May 28, 2019, he was questioned about his journey, and said nothing of significance.

- On March 4, 2020, excerpts of the Belgian State Security Agency report about Assadi were read back to him and he gave evasive answers when questioned about it.

Assadi did not cooperate in any stage of the interrogations, stated his unwillingness to respond, and cited his diplomatic status.

He anticipated the Belgian judicial authorities would accept that he was an official diplomat and would deal with him accordingly. Judicial authorities, however, treated him like a suspected terrorist, both in Germany and Belgium, a fact confirmed by the completed investigation. His treatment as a suspected terrorist led him to become very irritated and aggressive.

He said he did not know the other three defendants and went further by saying that they were from the MEK themselves.

Excerpts of his interrogations are listed below.

Excerpts of Assadi's Interrogations

October 10, 2018

In this interview, he said, "I want to exercise my right to remain silent, especially as long as I have not been able to consult with my lawyer. I have two lawyers in Belgium. My consulate in Munich told me that they have spoken to two lawyers in Belgium for me… You are notifying me that I am a suspect for two reasons: A. being a criminally involved in acting for terrorist assassination. B. Preparing for an attack.

February 25, 2019

Question: Can you please introduce yourself?

Answer: I am Assadollah Assadi. I am a government official of the Islamic Republic of Iran in Vienna. I am a diplomat of the Islamic Republic of Iran in Europe. I have been in Vienna since 2014. I am still active and I still receive a salary… I worked in the political section of the embassy. We had two embassies in Vienna. One embassy is for relations with the United Nations. I am at the other embassy, whose job is to maintain relations with Austria. I was an embassy worker who pursued political issues with Austria.

Question: Are you familiar with the name Amir Saadouni?

Answer: No.

Question: You have never been in contact with Amir Saadouni?

Answer: I said that I did not know the person.

Question: Do you insist that you do not know Amir Saadouni?

Answer: I'm saying I do not know this person.

Question: Do you know Nasimeh Naami?

Answer: I think you have a number of people and that's why you want to know if I know these people. I said from the beginning that I deny the charges. In doing so, I want to say that I don't know these people. If you allow me, I will tell you something. The people involved in this case are MEK spies... I have a lot of respect for you in relation to the investigation, but I have no confidence in the investigative process...

I have always trusted the Belgian police and judiciary and was ready to cooperate with its investigation, but since I was informed that my diplomatic immunity was no longer accepted, I have lost my trust. Something else happened that caused me to lose trust. That's where I realized that I had been placed on the international list of terrorists before this was proven by facts. It feels to me like a boxing match where my hands are tied from behind and the opponent can fight with his hands free. Because my feeling is that my hands are tied behind my back, I can't defend myself.

Question: Many signs in the investigation point to the fact that you know Amir Saadouni, Nasimeh Naami and Mehrdad Arefani well or were in contact with them. Are you standing by your statements that you don't know these people?

Answer: Yes, I insist that I don't know these people.

May 17, 2019

I don't want to make any statements. I want to exercise my right to remain silent.

May 28, 2019

Question: What was your itinerary?

Answer: For a long time, I intended to travel with my family to the Netherlands. I wanted to take my children to Holland. In the Netherlands I had booked two hotels, one for each night.

Question: How long was it that you were planning to travel?

Answer: I don't remember that well. I can't even remember the date of the trip properly.

Question: How did you book hotels in the Netherlands and through which email address did you book the hotels?

Answer: I did this from booking.com with my family's email account. I don't remember the accurate email address; it wasn't my official email.

Question: You were traveling in a rental car where and when did you rent it?

Answer: The court was told that I requested to have a car with a German number, which is absolutely not real.

Question: Can you describe in detail your itinerary and the places you've visited with your family?

Answer: I almost don't remember anything. I've seen places along the way, but I can't remember where I've been. I know I spent a night in Belgium.

Question: Do you remember the countries you visited or crossed on the route to the Netherlands?

Answer: No, I can't remember that.

Question: How long were you on the way?

Answer I don't remember. It was a few days, but I can't say exactly how many days I was traveling. I'm under psychological pressure.

Question: Have you been in contact with other people during the trip?

Answer: No, I was just in touch with my family.

Question: Do you remember which city you have resided in Belgium?

Answer: It was a small town. I can't remember the name.

Question: Have you been in Luxembourg?

Answer: No, you tell me that the investigation has shown that I was in Luxembourg with my family. As for the investigation, I noted that I don't agree with how your investigation is conducted. You mostly follow politics. No real investigation is done. Even before the investigation is completed, I have been seen as a criminal. That's why I don't believe in the investigation you're doing.

June 2, 2019

After several calls and follow ups, the interrogation was finally scheduled for this date and time and was supposed to be held via videoconference. But just before the meeting, Assadi announced that he wanted to exercise his right to remain silent.

August 2, 2019 - Short interview to advise of new charges

In this interrogation, the spread of the expansion and addition of new charges was notified to Assadi, in particular membership in a terrorist group has been added to the previous charges.

Question: Do you agree with the extended investigation?

Answer: No, I don't agree with extending the investigation.

Question: Do you want to add something to your statements?

Answer: I just want to add again that I am a diplomat and wish to bring up my diplomatic immunity. I wish the Vienna Conventions would be respected. In connection with the new facts, I will defend myself in criminal court.

March 4, 2020

Question: Information provided to us by our country's security agency shows that you are, an MOIS officer, the Ministry of Intelligence and Security in Iran, who operates under diplomatic cover at the Iranian Embassy in Vienna, Austria. What would you like to explain?

Answer: We do not have the post of Iranian Ministry of Intelligence at the Embassy in Vienna. I worked at the embassy. There are several posts at the Iranian embassy, but there is no intelligence service at all. I'm not an intelligence service officer. I was just a diplomat affiliated with the embassy, I am a political expert.

Question: You are affiliated with Section 312 of the Ministry of Intelligence, a section deemed by the European Union to be a terrorist organization. In this position, you are responsible for directing informants (sources/agents). Would you like to explain this?

Answer: What do you mean by section 312? You tell me that this agency is considered a terrorist organization by the European Union. The name of section 312 is not known to me. You ask me if I was responsible for dispatching the officers. My answer is no.

Question: You were the operational commander of the plan to attack the annual MEK conference in Villepinte, France. Do you want to explain this?

Answer: No, I wasn't the operational commander of the plan.

Question: Two days before the attack in Villepinte, you handed over lethal explosives containing TATP to Amir Saadouni and Nasimeh Naami, two of your own agents. Would you like to explain this?

Answer: No, I deny that I have delivered explosives, and I deny that Nasimeh Naami and Amir Saadouni are my agents. I don't have that position, let alone these two people working for me.

Question: The plan to carry out the attack was not your own initiative, but was influenced and directed by the Iranian regime. Would you like to explain this?

Answer: No, I'm not aware of that.

Question: Do you want to explain something yourself?

Answer: The only country that can take my immunity is Iran. No other country has the right to take my diplomatic rights away. I want to reaffirm my diplomatic immunity. Every diplomat has made a commitment to his country to honor the secrets of his job. A diplomat is not allowed to say anything about his missions. If a diplomat does not comply with the rules, he or she will be punished by his own country.

Assadi Threatens Belgian Government

The following is an excerpt of an official minute of an interrogation of Assadi, which was done at the request of Assadi.

On Monday, March 9, 2020, about 16h15, our services are contacted by the warden of the prison of Beveren. We are informed that ASSADI Assadolah wishes to have a conversation with (police officer, case officer)...

Before starting the conversation, we inform him that we will make a transcript of the conversation which will be processed in the case file. ASSADI agrees and declares that it is his intent that what he says is noted and added to the case...

- *ASSADI starts by saying he wants to speak partially about the case, but that this is not related to his own self...*

- *He prefers to have this conversation and not an interrogation. His goal is to point something out to the Belgian authorities and to provide information with which the Belgian State can make use of or can take into account...*

- *[Assadi discusses regime talking points on the MEK]*

The result of the enquiry in which he has taken part, is very important because the citizens of Iran and the neighboring countries are interested in the outcome of this.

It is not only about the ordinary people who have died by the hands of MEK and NCRI but also about the ones left behind.

These survivors are armed and fight against America.

They are situated in Iran but also in Iraq, Lebanon, Yemen and Syria. They have their day jobs but besides this they are armed and fight against America.

The decision in this investigation will have an influence on how they will react.

How the Belgian system will determine how this group will react.

How the Belgian System will act, will decide how the group will react.

According to Assadi Assadolah we (Belgium) do not realize what is going to happen, in the event of an unfavorable verdict.

He repeats that they are all armed and that they are watching from the sidelines to see if Belgium will support them or not. If they get the feeling that Belgium does not support them, Assadi does not know what can happen – however, a bad outcome will certainly have an influence on what can happen…

He says it is simple for us to figure out the pieces of the puzzle.

He states that we (the Belgian authorities) do not understand that it is very difficult to get out of trouble that we created.

When we ask what problems we created, he replies that those who work on this enquiry will be condemned if they are not against the MEK.

It is now decided what will happen in the future.

He says that we do not have a strategy to contain what will happen next.

Assadi's Legal Objections

Assadi and his lawyers raised various legal objections during the limited number of interrogations he had with judicial authorities, and during the defense that his lawyers presented in court. The objections all hinge on a claim of some form of diplomatic immunity and alleged violations of the law during his arrest, detention, and treatment in prison. However, Assadi and his defense lawyers refused to appeal the court verdict to a higher court, even though they could have appealed all the way up to the Belgian Court of Cassation (the highest court of the land). This showed that they do not seriously believe in the legal viability of those claims and do not see any chance of achieving success in the appeal.

The objections raised by Assadi's lawyers are a variety of issues that the Antwerp lower court addressed and rejected. Most notably, he claims diplomatic immunity, which we consider later in this chapter, because of the importance of this point.[119] However, Assadi also claimed that:

- The Iranian regime granted him diplomatic immunity and no other jurisdiction or authority may take it away

- His right to a fair trial and the right to defend himself were violated

- He was interrogated without his lawyer being present

- His wife and children were interrogated in the first session without the assistance of a lawyer

- He was prevented from consulting privately with Iranian regime embassy officials at the time of his arrest

- Conditions of his detention in Germany were unduly harsh

- Conditions of his detention in Belgiumwere also harsh

- He was unfairly subjected to terrorist designation and assets seizures

- No accurate explanation was given for the surveillance conducted on him

- Information provided by Belgian State Security Service was unsatisfactory

All of the objections arise from the underlying claim that his own claim of diplomatic immunity insulates him from prosecution by both Belgian and German authorities. However, this claim is baseless for multiple reasons. His charge of involvement in a major act of terrorism is in direct contravention of the Vienna Convention of Diplomatic Relations. Furthermore, Assadi was arrested outside of his country of service, and besides Austria withdrew his diplomatic immunity on July 1.

Nevertheless, Germany and Belgium, provided Assadi with special privileges due to diplomatic relations with the ruling regime in Iran, and allowed Iranian embassies and consulates to actively intervene, as well as giving Assadi the opportunity to meet high-ranking Iranian Foreign Ministry officials in prison. Such priviliges are normally denied to a prisoner charged with terrorism.

Diplomatic Immunity

It can be said that Assadollah Assadi, once charged with attempted terrorist murder, was essentially unable to competently claim diplomatic immunity. Technically, his diplomatic immunity in Austria where he nominally served as the third highest ranking embassy official, was limited to Austrian territory. His presence in Germany, was in his own words, a personal trip for a holiday. A diplomat spending his holiday in another country is not subject to the Vienna

Convention on Diplomatic Relations. If carrying a bomb from Tehran to Vienna to Luxembourg and delivering it to two other terrorists was a "diplomatic" mission that the Iranian authorities had assigned him, he should have confessed to this, and it was plainly in violation of the Vienna Convention. The spirit of the Vienna Convention is to facilitate diplomatic relations between sovereign states, and anyone who commits a terrorist crime by misusing this Convention has in fact renounced its founding principles.

As the Antwerp Lower Court ruled on February 4, 2021: *"His unofficial activities, of which he is suspected, do not fit at all within the limits permitted by international law, and it cannot be the intention of the contracting parties to allow diplomatic immunity to cover the acts of which the fourth defendant is suspected."*

Diplomatic immunity is a status claimed by Assadi and the Iranian regime. The alleged status was an excuse for him to evade answering questions from judicial authorities and to avoid attending trial. After the lower court issued a verdict against him, he appealed the sentence of 20 years in prison, but then withdrew the appeal under the same pretext. He and his lawyer as well as the Iranian regime claimed that they did not recognize the court's competency to try Assadi on the charges. In so doing, they declared their refusal to submit themselves to the justice system of a democratic state with separation of powers, an insult to the Belgian judiciary.

Assadi's claim of immunity in both the German and Belgian judicial systems came under close scrutiny. In Germany, the regional court and the Federal Court rejected the objections of Assadi and his lawyers, and the Bamberg High Court ordered his extradition to Belgium. (Refer to Appendix L).

In Belgium, the first objection his lawyers raised was the alleged incompetence of the Belgian court to investigate Assadi's charge. In January 2019, the Second Branch of the Supreme Court of

Belgium rejected the appeal and restored the case to the investigating authority in Antwerp for a normal review:

Court of Cassation, second chamber:[120]

"...The judgment which, along with the grounds for the claim of the Federal Prosecutor, finds that the plaintiff did not enjoy diplomatic immunity, that he was regularly arrested and that the warrant of arrest is regular, justifies that decision."

As the Lower Court of Antwerp has adequately addressed the developments in the case in its February 4, 2021, ruling, and has reasonably rejected this claim, it is fitting to acknowledge parts of the court's ruling:[121]

The fourth defendant argues that he is a diplomatic official and enjoys immunity under the Vienna Convention on Diplomatic Relations of 18 April 1961. Moreover, he argues that he could not have been arrested in Germany and then extradited to Belgium in view of his personal immunity, to which he is entitled under the aforementioned Convention.

Given his immunity, he cannot be prosecuted in the Belgian courts.

There is no dispute that at the time of his arrest, the fourth defendant was a member of the diplomatic staff (third counsellor since 23 June 2014-diplomatic passport D9016657 of 26 April 2014) and that he was accredited to the Iranian state in Austria. He held a diplomatic passport. He can be considered a diplomatic official (Article 1.e Vienna Convention) until 2 July 2018 (date of withdrawal of immunity by the Austrian authorities).

Under Belgian criminal law, anyone who commits a crime on Belgian territory is punishable, regardless of the nationality of the offender(s). The Belgian courts have jurisdiction to hear all elements and circumstances of the crime that form an indivisible whole of that crime on Belgian territory. This means that actual conduct of a crime that is partly committed in Belgium and partly committed abroad can be prosecuted in Belgium. Perpetrators who participate abroad in a crime committed in Belgium can be prosecuted in Belgium.

International law is based on the sovereignty of independent states, which are all treated equally. The Vienna Convention is a special regulation regarding this sovereignty and determines the way in which states deal with diplomatic personnel.

From the way the treaty came into being and the subsequent interpretation of the treaty, it is clear that the Vienna Convention codified customary law on diplomatic personnel and that all (important) rules are contained in it.

The provisions on diplomatic exchange are bilateral arrangements between the sending and receiving state and are based on the principle of reciprocity. In this sense, the Vienna Convention must also be interpreted restrictively and does not create obligations towards other states that are alien to the bilateral arrangements between the sending state and the receiving state, with the exception of Article 40 of the Vienna Convention.

The Vienna Convention stipulates in its Article 31 :

"The diplomatic official shall enjoy immunity from the criminal jurisdiction of the receiving State."

The immunity which a diplomatic official acquires is only an immunity from prosecution in the host state, being an executive immunity.

A diplomat can indeed commit offences in another country and be prosecuted for them in a country other than the host state (in this case, Austria). Also, the offences he committed as a co-perpetrator from Austria can perfectly be prosecuted in Belgium.

Austria, precisely because of the sovereignty of independent states, cannot offer immunity from prosecution in another country.

Austria withdrew the immunity of the fourth defendant on 2 July 2018 (application of Article 9 of the Vienna Convention), but this relates only to possible criminal proceedings in Austria for offences for which the Austrian judiciary has jurisdiction.

The diplomat concerned is then declared "persona non grata" and is given the opportunity to leave the country within a well-defined limited period.

However, this is completely irrelevant, as the crimes in question were committed partly in Belgium and partly in other EU countries, such as Luxembourg and Italy, and this is completely unrelated to the immunity enjoyed by the fourth defendant in Austria.

In any case, fourth defendant does not enjoy any immunity in respect of criminal proceedings for offences (of participation) in Belgium.

The fourth defendant argues that he was wrongfully arrested in Germany and invokes Article 40 of the Vienna Convention. Because of his wrongful arrest in Germany, he was wrongly extradited to Belgium and is wrongly on trial before this court.

The court refers to the judgment of the Indictment Division of Antwerp and the subsequent judgment of the Court of Cassation in the context of pre-trial detention.

By judgment of 18 December 2018, the K.I. ruled: "From the factual information in the criminal file, it appears that the accused was on holiday in Belgium and Germany. On 1 July 2018, he was arrested in Germany when he was on his way to his diplomatic duty station in Austria..., the accused did not enjoy his diplomatic immunity. He was arrested and detained according to the regulations. The warrant of arrest is conforming the regulations.

In its judgment of 2 January 2019, the Court of Cassation ruled:

It follows from these provisions that immunity and privileges shall be accorded by the receiving State of the diplomat and by a third State when the diplomat is in transit in the territory of a third State in order to take up his duties at his post or when he returns to his own country.

Transit, as referred to in the first sentence of Article 40(1) of the Vienna Convention, which should be interpreted strictly, means only transit which is related to the diplomatic mission, i.e. the journey from the country of origin to join the diplomatic mission or to return to the country of origin, or the journey from the diplomatic mission to the country where the diplomat is on a diplomatic mission or, after fulfilling this mission, to return from this country to the diplomatic mission. A return from a third country where the diplomat is on holiday to the place of employment is alien to the exercise of the diplomatic mission and therefore does not constitute transit within the meaning of Article 40, first sentence, of the Vienna Convention."

The German judiciary also came to the conclusion, both at the time of the deprivation of liberty/arrest and in the further procedure leading to his extradition, that the defendant was on holiday, moreover, did not hold a diplomatic post in Germany and therefore could not claim his diplomatic status either.

As it is raised again by fourth defendant, the court fully concurs with the judgment of the Court of Cassation in the context of pre-trial detention.

Diplomatic exchanges and all the rights (for the diplomat) and obligations (for the receiving state) arising from them are bilateral arrangements between the sending and receiving states, as provided for in the Vienna Convention.

The Convention does not require direct transit between the sending and receiving states. One can pass through a third country to go to its diplomatic post in the receiving state or to return to the sending state. There is therefore an exception to the rule of bilateral agreement between the sending and receiving states. The Convention of Vienna stipulates that third countries, which are foreign to the diplomatic relationship between the sending state and the receiving state, must grant passage to diplomatic officials and thus, in a sense, respect the immunity/personal inviolability of the diplomatic official. This exception must therefore be interpreted restrictively. Thus, the transit is strictly limited to this specific movement or a movement to a country other than the host state for the purpose of a specific diplomatic mission.

There is no immunity if you are in a third country for purely personal reasons.

From the observations made during the observation, the road check, the renting of the vehicle (from 25 June 2018 to 2 July 2018) and their route of travel (Germany, Luxembourg, Netherlands, Liege,...), it is undeniable that the fourth defendant was on holiday with his family and was therefore not on a diplomatic mission or diplomatic journey.

The argument that fourth defendant is trying to make that his immunity as a diplomat is comparable to the total immunity of foreign heads of state and ministers in all countries does not hold water and cannot be derived from any rule of international law, case law or custom. Nowhere does it say that diplomatic immunity has such a wide scope.

Finally, reference can be made to Article 38 of the Vienna Convention: "Except in so far as a receiving State grants additional rights and immunities, a diplomatic official who is a national of, or permanently resident in, that State shall enjoy immunity from jurisdiction and immunity only in respect of official acts performed in the exercise of his functions".

The claim shows that fourth defendant is suspected of not being a diplomat in reality. He is said to be an Iranian intelligence officer who acted as a runner for his European informants. His status as a diplomat was possibly abused in order to commit crimes elsewhere in Europe and even to smuggle an explosive device from Iran to Europe under diplomatic cover. He is suspected of being the (co-) organizer of a possible foiled fatal attack in France. These actions cannot possibly be considered as (normal) diplomatic activities, performed within the framework of his function.

The actual activities of which the accused is suspected, if proven, even violate Article 3 of the Convention.

This article states that the functions of a diplomatic mission include: ".... to promote the Interests of the sending state and its nationals, within the limits permitted by international law in the receiving state". His unofficial activities, of which he is suspected, do not fit at all within the limits permitted by international law, and it cannot be the intention of the contracting parties to allow diplomatic immunity to cover the acts of which the fourth defendant is suspected.[122]

Significance of the Lower Court's Ruling

The lower court's handed down its verdict on February 4, 2021, and sentenced Assadollah Assadi to 20 years, Mehrdad Arefani to 17, Nasimeh Naami to 18 and Amir Saadouni to 15 years in prison.

The strong conviction and heavy sentences handed down to Assadi and his three accomplices are significant.[123] The sentence for Assadi is the maximum possible and as are the sentences for the other three accomplices. The sentence shows that the gravity and severity of the crime that Assadi and his accomplices sought to carry out is very high in the eyes of the Belgian judges and judiciary. It shows that the court was convinced that law enforcement intervention prevented the crime, otherwise, as far as these four individuals are concerned, all the foundations for committing the crime were laid: all material preparations and plans were fully formed and existed. The court fully recognized the defendants' criminal will to commit the crime. The legal element of the ruling is not ambiguous.

The stripping of Belgian citizenship from Assadi's three agents and accomplices, Saadouni, Naami, and Arefani in the sentence also sent an important message to other regime agents in Europe that they cannot feel safe and secure to abuse European citizenship to commit crimes.

Confiscation of all available assets belonging to the three agents is another very important aspect of this sentence as their motivation for committing the crime was nothing but financial gain. The confiscation of funds appropriately denies them of the illicit gain that they sought. However, it is quite likely that the Naami-Saadouni couple could have removed significant portions of their assets from the reach of the law.

Arefani, an experienced and skilled agent of the Iranian regime's intelligence apparatus, was able to essentially erase his past, unlike Saadouni and Naami. However, the Belgian judiciary's skilled investigation established his guilt with certainty. Two facts established in the case about Arefani offer very strong indication of his complicity: one that he had told people in Paris on the same day (June 30, 2018), that he would not return to Belgium with them via bus. Another is that every time he returned from his trips to Austria he deposited cash into his bank account.

Antwerp Appeals Court Decision

Assadi 's lawyer initially filed the appeal, but later withdrew his appeal at a preliminary hearing. The three other defendants appealed.

Although Assadi's refusal to appeal was portrayed by the Iranian regime as a refusal to accept the court's decision and its competency, in reality, Assadi and his bosses surrendered to the lower court's decision knowing that he has no chance to change the verdict rendered by the lower court . In other words, Assadi and the Iranian regime confessed to their perpetration of state terrorism.

As part of the other defendants' appeal, Naami's lawyer, continued to claim that, despite the court's careful analysis, the seized explosive substance was not a bomb but some sort of fireworks. In response to the lawyer's demand, the court convened a special session, and the testimony of explosives experts[124] further strengthened the prosecutor's indictment, and it became clear that the extent of the bomb's lethality, given the closed space of the assembly hall and the presence of tens of thousands of people, could have been much worse than previously thought. In relation to the outcome of the Appellate Court, it is better to include the press release issued by the Court itself, which summarizes the outcome of the court's detailed reviews. The press release follows.

Press Release by Antwerp Appeals Court

Case SAADOUNI - NAAMI - AREFANI

(Assadollah ASSADI is no longer in the case to the extent of the appeal)

1.

The defendants are charged under indictment A as perpetrator or co-perpetrator with attempted murder with a terrorist intent under Article 137§1 of the Penal Code. This indictment targets the annual conference of MEK on 30 June 2018 in Villepinte, France.

The court is of the opinion that there cannot be the slightest doubt that from the very beginning it was the intention of the defendants to detonate the professionally assembled explosive device (IED), by means of a remote control, at the large annual MEK congress in Villepinte, where thousands of participants were to be present, and this with the intent to kill. The defendants acted in a premeditated and coordinated manner.

The assertion of defendants Amir SAADOUNI and Nasimeh NAAMI that they were under the impression that the explosive device would only cause noise and fireworks and that it was never the intention to kill people, is considered implausible by the Court in light of the criminal information at hand. Beforehand, everything was prepared in detail and the modus operandi to be used was discussed at length, whereby it was finally decided that the intention was to detonate the EID inside.

Furthermore, the court considered that the defendant Mehrdad AREFANI, who had been present for some time near the exit of the congress hall, was well aware of the imminent bombing. Through his operational mobile phone, he was able to communicate directly with the principal (Assadollah ASSADI), who had devised the entire plan and who also directed the defendants Amir SAADOUNI and Nasimeh NAAMI.

Moreover, the dossier data sufficiently indicated that the planned attack, in the given specific factual context, aimed at

- to strike at the MEK, and to instill serious fear in Iranian political refugees, who reside in various European countries and feel protected by our democratic constitutional state.

- to instill serious fear in France and possibly other (European) states that were involved in this internationally public, heavily attended conference or that supported the organizers of this conference.

2.

In addition, the defendants were prosecuted under indictment D for participation in a terrorist group in the period from 1 January 2015 to 30 June 2018.

The Court is of the opinion that the elements of the criminal file before it leave no doubt that Assadollah ASSADI and the aforementioned accused were already actively involved in MOIS and, more specifically, in Department 312, for a long time. In this regard, it is undisputed that Assadollah ASSADI came into the picture from 2015 as the intelligence officer linked to MOIS and Department 312 and since March 2018 was also the operational commander of the planned attack on the annual MEK conference in Villepinte.

The couple Amir SAADOUNI - Nasimeh NAAMI, on the instructions of Assadollah ASSADI, gathered information on MEK during the incrimination period provided for under Indictment D, after which the information gathered was transmitted to Department 312 of MOIS. As to their involvement in the planned attack in Villepinte, it should be emphasized that they 1° saw no reason to receive the IED, 2° subsequently manipulated this IED in accordance with the directives of Assadollah ASSADI and 3° set off with this IED to Villepinte.

During this period, the accused, Mehrdad AREFANI, also collected information on MEK and has been transmitting it to Assadollah ASSADI since 2015. Regarding his involvement in the planned attack in Villepinte, the Court emphasizes that he 1° had important information concerning the organization and security of this congress, 2° was present at the congress and 3° was in possession of an operational mobile phone that was exclusively used for his contacts with Assadollah ASSADI.

The court also points to the incriminating results of the financial investigations from which it appears that the defendants have generated a lot of financial benefits, arising from the facts included in charge D.

3.

In terms of sentencing, the court was of the opinion that the proven facts are very serious and testify to a criminal mindset, in which financial motives prevailed over human lives. The actions alleged by the defendants constitute a real and very serious threat to social order and public safety, as well as to the safety of individual citizens.

According to the court, for these reasons a strong punishment is required.

SAADOUNI - 18 years (aggravated)
NAAMI - 18 years (confirmation)
AREFANI - 17 years (confirmation)

4.

Finally, the court upheld the public prosecutor's claim for revocation of the Belgian nationality of each of the accused and ruled that the accused lose Belgian nationality as a result of this revocation.

It was pointed out in this regard that the proven offences show intolerance and anti-social behavior and are not compatible with the values inherent in Belgian citizenship. According to the court, the defendants seriously breached their obligations as Belgian citizens and abused their Belgian nationality by knowingly participating in a terrorist group for a considerable time and their active involvement in the preparation and execution of the foiled bomb attack on the MEK conference in Villepinte on 30 June 2018. The court further considers that the actions alleged by the defendants show that they 1° do not recognize the fundamental rules and values of our Western society and 2° constitute a real danger for the Belgian and international public order and for the security of the State, its institutions and citizens.

CHAPTER 7

The Judgment

Antwerp District Court's Judgement

The district court of Antwerp issued its ruling on February 4, 2021. All four defendants initially appealed the ruling. However, Assadi, the mastermind of the terror plot, withdrew his appeal, confirming his sentence of 20 years in prison. The Court of Appeals heard the case of the three other defendants and issued its ruling on May 10, 2022, confirming the decision of the District Court, with one major change, increasing the sentence for Saadouni from 15 to 18 years.

The following are excerpts of the ruling on February 4, 2021:

Grounds

> The defendants are on trial for attempted terrorist murder (charge A) and membership of a terrorist group (charge D).

> Defendants are being prosecuted for allegedly being involved in an attempt to carry out an attack on 30 June 2018 at a well-attended conference organized by the People's Mojahedin Organization of Iran/Mujahedin-e Khalq/National Council of Resistance of Iran in Villepinte (near Paris) ….

> The (senior) members of MEK and NCRI have regularly been victims of various assassination attempts in the past. On 22 March 2018, an attempted attack on the MEK camp in Albania could be foiled. This attack and other (attempted) attacks were each time attributed by MEK and NCRI or by the countries where the attacks took place to the Iranian State or one of its security services, such as MOIS.

As regards the Iranian Ministry of Intelligence and Security and Department 312

Information provided by State Security in the criminal file shows that the "Iranian Ministry of Intelligence and Security", hereinafter MOIS, was established in 1983 and has been under the authority of the Minister of Intelligence since 2013. MOIS is said to have its roots in the Shah's old secret political police (the infamous SAVAK). MOIS is said to have a central position in the Iranian security services and to receive substantial revenues. Department 312 would be a directorate dealing with the Iranian opposition abroad. It is possible that there are other government departments within Iran that were involved in this.

As for the start of the investigation

The criminal case started with an urgent report from State Security to the Federal Prosecutor's Office on 25 June 2018. State Security had received information through a partner service that a Belgo-Iranian couple might be involved in an act of violence or attempted violence in France. The information also gave the specific identity of the couple, namely first and second defendant.

On 27 June 2018, additional information came in from State Security, based on its own investigation....

State Security also found it remarkable that the first and second defendants still returned to Iran despite having problems with Iranian security forces.

Based on further investigation, State Security suspected that the violent action might be related to the well-attended MEK/NCRI conference in Villepinte (near Paris) on 30 June 2018. This conference was to be attended by international leading (political) VIPs, who were sympathetic to the Iranian opposition.

The investigation

On 28 June 28, 2018, the Federal Prosecutor's Office ordered an investigating judge to order, among other things, immediate observation of the first and second accused, as well as a tap measure on the known telephone numbers.

On 28 June 2018, during the international observation, it was found that the first and second accused moved to the Grand Duchy of Luxembourg, where they had contact with an unknown person. Following the contact, this person was identified at a traffic check as the fourth defendant, who was in possession of an Austrian identity card. He was accompanied at the time by his wife and two sons.

On 29 June 2018, additional information came from State Security that the first defendant would have contacts with an unknown person speaking in coded language.

From these contacts, it would appear that the first defendant was focused on his mission and convinced that they would succeed. There was talk of an appointment in Luxembourg and of a Playstation4, which might be a code word for a device that could be used to commit an act of violence. Second defendant was said to have a large sum of money of 15,000 euros in cash and an advance of 2,500 euros was said to have been paid for the purchase of a new Mercedes coupé vehicle.

In this information, for the first time, the third defendant was also mentioned as possibly being involved in the events that were about to take place.

On 30 June 2018, the first and second defendants were still under observation. The telephone records show that the first defendant received a call at 11h07. Some seven minutes later, the first and second accused left in their vehicle for Brussels.

Whilst travelling in their vehicle, the first and second accused received several suspicious text messages from an Austrian number, speaking in coded language. They spoke of a "device" that had to be installed. There was talk of "moving forward from 20h00 to 17h30".

The first defendant also spoke of "14h00 to 17h30" and "regular cleaning". The latter could be a code word for possible counter-observation techniques. When following the vehicle, it was indeed found that the first defendant was carrying out counter-observation techniques, by regularly switching his speed from 130 km/h to 180 km/h, which made it difficult to follow the vehicle.

At around 12h24, the vehicle of the first and second defendant ran into a traffic jam on the Brussels ring road, after which they took an exit in Woluwe-Saint-Pierre. The vehicle was stopped a few minutes later and the first and second accused were intercepted and arrested.

A perimeter of 200 meters was immediately set up and the DOVO mine clearance service arrived on the scene.

At 14h49, DOVO found a suspicious toilet bag in the trunk of the vehicle from which wires were protruding. DOVO made an RX of the toilet bag.

At about 15h15, the mine clearance service reported that it might be a detonator and that they were going to open and search the package.

At 16h25, DOVO reported a suspicious white powder, the weight of which was estimated at approximately 500 grams. During the manipulation and dismantling of the device, the white powder exploded. The DOVO robot was heavily damaged. Despite the large perimeter, a member of the special units became unwell (headache, red face and hearing damage) after being hit by the blast wave.

A yellow/gold notebook was found in the vehicle, as well as a mobile phone with only one contact, an Austrian number stored under "Daniel."

In the meantime, various searches were carried out, including at the address in Wilrijk in the home of the first and second accused, where three envelopes were found with a total of 35,690 euros in cash in a suitcase.

The Judgment

During a search of the defendant's home in Uccle, numerous CDs, video equipment, cameras and video cassettes and spyware were found.

The third defendant was arrested by the French police on 30 June 2018 in the car park of the congress in Villepinte and was immediately extradited to Belgium.

The fourth defendant was intercepted on 1 July 2018 on the German motorway at Weibersbrunn, when he was returning to Austria with his family. They were diverted to a lane rest stop, where they were further checked. Because the police dog reacted to the vehicle for the possible presence of explosives, the entire family was arrested.

No explosives were found in the vehicle and after a first interrogation, the family members of fourth defendant were released.

The fourth defendant was eventually extradited to Belgium by the German justice system.

The first and second defendants indicated at their first hearing that they were afraid of the fourth defendant, whom they knew as "Daniel." The fourth defendant was said to be waiting for a text message after the mission had been carried out. They would have to go to Cologne after their assignment, where they would meet the fourth defendant again....

Further investigation

....According to the statements of the first and second defendant, it all started in 2007, when they were asked for information by an Iranian agent "Javad". From their statements and the information concerning their flight records, it appears that the first and second defendant left together for Iran in February 2010, where they are said to have met with several MOIS agents and where pressure was again put on them.

The stamps in their passports show that they also flew to Tehran in December 2010.

Back in Belgium, they were contacted by phone by a new Iranian "runner". This one always operated from Iran. They were summoned to return to Iran in 2012. There the pressure was increased on them to give more information about the organizations, MEK/NCRI. Also, in 2013, according to his own statement, the first defendant flew to Tehran. During this meeting he noticed that the Iranian agents were also aware of when first defendant was present at the MEK/NCRI, from which he deduced that there were other informants at the MEK/NCRI. Since 2013, they were more systematically compensated for the information they provided. For example, in 2013, first defendant received monetary payments amounting to 6,000 euros.

According to first and second defendants, they were contacted in 2015 by an Iranian agent in Europe who called himself "Daniel". This concerned the fourth defendant. The couple met him for the first time in Munich in the summer of 2015. Fourth defendant had indicated that they were working for the Iranian Embassy in Vienna. They were then given a sum of money of €4,000 for expenses. They would contact each other by e-mail. Another meeting took place at the end of November 2015 at MOIS in Iran, where fourth defendant was also present. There they were asked to gather more information about the MEK/NCRI headquarters in Auvers-sur-Oise (France). Since then, meetings have taken place all over Europe, including Munich, Milan, Luxembourg and Vienna....

The analysis of the e-mails shows that first and second defendant negotiated their fees with fourth defendant, especially when they were given this particular assignment. It was clear that first and second defendant were looking for a large financial compensation. From the analysis of the bank accounts of both defendants, it was found that huge cash deposits were made by both defendants. A large sum of money was also found in their homes....

The first defendant states that he gave complete and 100% reliable information to the arresting officers during his interrogations, but it is clear from the direct listening of the conversations between the first and second defendant that they coordinated their statements and that the second defendant also gave instructions on how the first defendant should make his statements, keeping her out of harm's way as much as possible.

In all his hearings, the third defendant denied having anything to do with the attempted attack or with spying for the Iranian security services. He is an Iranian political refugee who has lived in Belgium for years. He is said to be a writer/poet, living on a limited allowance and doing some odd jobs here and there in the black (cash-in-hand)....

When he was arrested in the car park, he was in possession of a mobile phone with an Austrian number and with only one contact. This contact turned out to be the fourth defendant, and the SIM card holder of the SIM card of the third defendant's "operational mobile phone" was also found in the fourth defendant's vehicle.

Fourth defendant did not really cooperate with the investigation and denied any involvement. He complained that he was not treated as his diplomatic status required. He had nothing to do with the facts.

In his last interrogation, at his own request, he warned that armed groups would be ready to do something in Belgium if he was convicted. His defense minimizes this statement as an emotional outburst, due to the special and severe prison regime he is undergoing.

On the charge of attempted terrorist murder

In order to speak of attempted murder, it must be proved that there was an intention to kill and that there was premeditation.

As regards the intent to kill

....What is objectively certain is that, although the bomb was dismantled in a controlled state, it damaged the DOVO robot to such an extent that it was unusable...

It is therefore certain that detonating this device at a conference attended by thousands of people would have resulted in fatalities. Not only because of the explosion itself, but also because of the chaos that would have ensued.

The analysis of the messages and the statements of the first and second defendant show that the "bomb" was made in Iran. It was fine-tuned there and tested several times. According to information from State Security, it was transported in a diplomatic suitcase on a regular scheduled flight between Teheran and Vienna.

It is undisputed that the fourth defendant intended to carry out a lethal attack on a well-attended congress by giving the order to detonate this device in view of its specific content and functioning. He gave clear instructions to the first and second defendant on how to charge the device, how to wrap the device in a plastic film and how to aim the antenna during transport so that the device would not receive a Wi-Fi signal. Moreover, from the notebook that was found in the car of the fourth defendant during his interception, not only notes were found about the operation of this device, but also about a possible attack with acid or other toxic pathogenic substances. This undeniably shows the intention to kill.

The first and second accused are co-perpetrators of this attempted homicide, considering the factual actions they took: taking the device into custody, transferring it to Belgium, charging the device in accordance with the instructions and then leaving for Villepinte with the explosive material as ordered.

The first and second accused's argument cannot be followed that it was not intended to cause fatalities and that they only thought it was a kind of firework that would give a loud bang…

The investigation, including the interviews, shows that the device was to be detonated around a time when many visitors entered the hall…

Remarkable are the chat messages that were found between the first defendant and a certain "Negar". The first defendant thinks that "Negar" is an Iranian woman in Iran, with whom he chats in a loving way and has an amorous (platonic) relationship. The relationship between the first and second defendant originally started through chat (according to the first and second defendant). The first defendant is very open towards "Negar" and she is clearly aware of the plans...

These conversations are important in determining where the attack was to take place, but they will also be important in assessing the personalities of the first and second accused:

Chat conversations on 28 June 2018:

First defendant: "If it happens inside, he will personally go to his man. He said of his interview I will request for you."

First defendant: "I just wanted to ask, tell me your final decision what we should do. Do we go in or out?"

Chat conversations on 29 June 2018:

Negar (second accused): "Amir, tomorrow first check the situation and surroundings over there."

Negar (second defendant): "Should you see that it is difficult, with stress from below, inside, ok". "Should you see that it is difficult, outside, ok my dear?"

First defendant: "Ok darling."

Chat conversations on 29 June 2018 (moments later):

Negar (second defendant): "Be very relaxed with Nasim". "Tomorrow when you see that can be achieved, do it inside.

If not. Outside. Ok? Be very relaxed."

o First accused: "Ok."

o Negar (second accused): "Be very relaxed."

First accused: "Ok."

Negar (second accused): "And don't worry. Be very good mentally as well. Don't make each other nervous."

These reports show that they had orders to detonate it inside and that second defendant also urged first defendant to try it inside first.

This clearly shows that the defendants had to detonate the device in the vicinity of human presence, whether inside the hall or at the buses in the parking lot or in the baggage tent.

In addition, they knew that they had to keep their distance before detonating the device, so they had no way of knowing whether there were people around when the remote control was pressed.

It does not at all appear that first and second defendant were misled and really assumed that it was just "fireworks". The court refers to the results of the direct listening, which show that they matched their statements in this regard:...

The first and second defendant knowingly carried out orders, did not even check the device they were transporting. From the way they had to manipulate the device, it is undeniable that they had to know it was more than just "fireworks"...

As regards premeditation

There can be no dispute that there was premeditation on the part of the first, second and fourth defendants.

From the statements of the first and second defendant, it appears that around March 2018, there was talk by the fourth defendant of a device that was to be detonated. There were allegedly two meetings in Austria, one in Vienna and one on the train between Vienna and Salzburg.

The analysis of the e-mail traffic of the first and second defendant with the fourth defendant shows that the first and second defendant negotiated about the merits. For example, the e-mail traffic of March 25, 2018 shows that conditions were even set such as an increased monthly remuneration of €2,000 and an additional remuneration for their part in placing the bomb and finally the mention that the remuneration had to be looked after because they wanted to buy a house. They cited as additional arguments that they were under great stress with regard to their families and that the first defendant feared for his information position at MEK. They also praised their own specific information position with MEK.

On April 26, 2018, fourth defendant replied that there had been internal feedback with a certain "Mohsen," but that those conditions were not feasible. They had to: "continue cooking as before."

Further analysis of the e-mail traffic shows that the first and second defendant meanwhile continued to provide information about MEK, including the annual conference on June 30, 2018....

International observation and questioning of the first and second defendants show that they met the fourth defendant in Luxembourg City, where in a Pizza Hut they were handed a USB stick with the latest information, an envelope containing €18 000, a new operational mobile phone and the "bomb". The explosive was in a blue lady's toiletry bag and the second defendant put it in her handbag together with the remote control.

The fourth defendant gave clear instructions on how the bomb was to be charged and made operational. It had to be wrapped in black plastic foil and a safety perimeter had to be respected. For activation, the remote control had to be pressed for three minutes. The antenna had to be pushed down during the movement, so that it would not connect to Wi-Fi signals.

On June 29, 2018, various messages were exchanged between the two operational mobile phones of the first and fourth defendant. These show, among other things, that the explosive was charged in accordance with instructions and wrapped in plastic film.

Just before their departure on June 30, 2018, fourth defendant sent a text message with final instructions. They should leave the operational mobile phone in their vehicle in the car park in Villepinte. They agreed to get back in touch at 17h30 and would see each other again in Cologne after the attack. The investigation showed that the fourth defendant was staying with his family near Cologne....

As regards the terrorist offence

Article 137 Sw. stipulates: "A terrorist offence is an offence defined in §§ 2 and 3 which, by its nature or context, can seriously damage a country or an international organization and which is intentionally committed with the aim of seriously frightening a population or unlawfully compelling the government or an international organization to perform or refrain from performing an act, or seriously destabilizing or destroying the fundamental political, constitutional, economic or social structures of a country or an international organization"...

As regards the role of the third defendant in this charge

....On 30 June 2018, third defendant was at least the eyes and ears of fourth defendant on the premises during the attack that was to take place. He also had to do other things for the fourth defendant at the time when the attack took place. He was at least a lookout, but his task must have been more extensive. His role in the preparations was also crucial, given that, given his role in previous editions, he had concrete information regarding the organization and security of the congress.

The court unequivocally concludes from all these facts that the third defendant was aware of and actively involved in the attack that was to take place on June 30, 2018, and is therefore a co-perpetrator in the attempted terrorist murder.

It cannot even be ruled out that there were other people involved or ready for this attack.

On the charge of participating in a terrorist group (charge D)

The third defendant also provided his services purely for financial gain, without any ideological conviction....

It is absolutely certain that the first, second, third and fourth defendants formed a terrorist group. They gathered information about the organizations and the members of these organizations. On the basis of this obtained information, they organized themselves to carry out an attack on one of the most important annual meetings of these Iranian opposition parties.

However, it can be unequivocally inferred from the criminal record that there is a greater involvement than these four defendants.

The court refers, inter alia, to the observations set out below.

It is clear from the statements of the first and second defendant that they were first recruited and run by agents operating out of Iran. They both stated that they worked for the intelligence service MOIS. They regularly returned to Iran, where they had meetings with various people from MOIS.

Their statements also show that the fourth defendant also worked for the intelligence service MOIS and that they had to go to Iran for consultations under him as well. In Iran, they met not only fourth defendant but also other agents of MOIS.

Fourth defendant operated from an Iranian diplomatic cover. He did not carry out diplomatic activities but ran informers in Europe. Working under diplomatic cover without actually carrying out these activities can only be done with the consent of those responsible within the Iranian state.

From the statements of the first and second accused and from the analysis of the e-mail messages and audio recordings made by the first, second and third accused, it appears that first the original runners and later the fourth accused gathered information about MEK.

Neither Iran nor MOIS distanced themselves from the activities of the fourth defendant.

From the analysis of the e-mail messages between the first/second and fourth defendants and from the statements of the first and second defendants, it is sufficiently clear that the explosive device was manufactured and certainly tested in Iran. On the basis of the declassified State Security Note of September 7, 2020, it may be deduced with an objective certainty that the explosive was taken by the fourth defendant in diplomatic baggage on a commercial flight from Iran to Austria.

The fourth defendant had considerable sums of money at his disposal to pay the first, second and third defendants and, in view of their size, these funds were not the personal funds of the fourth defendant.

The analysis of the e-mail messages shows that with regard to the financial demands made by the first and second defendant to take action, the fourth defendant himself had to obtain permission from his principals.

According to information from State Security, which is reliable for the court, the fourth defendant is an intelligence officer of MOIS and runs sources for Department 312 as an intelligence officer in Europe.

Based on these elements, the court concludes that there exists a group within the department 312 of the intelligence service MOIS, which was engaged in gathering information on the MEK/NCRI and used this information to select targets and ultimately to organize an attack on a convention of these Iranian opposition parties.

This group of which the first, second, third and fourth accused are members, together with an unspecified number of Iranian agents of MOIS, is a terrorist group according to art. 139, paragraph 1 Sw. In any case, the first, second, third and fourth accused have actively contributed to this terrorist group…

As regards the provenance of charges A and D

The attempted terrorist murder (charge A) and membership of a terrorist group (charge D) have therefore been sufficiently proven by the findings of the reporting officers on behalf of the first, second and fourth accused:

The initial info of the State Security,

Being caught in the act,

The results of the observation in Luxembourg on June 28, 2018,

The analysis of the e-mail messages sent between the first and second defendant on the one hand and the fourth defendant on the other,

The results of the search of the premises of the first and second defendant,

The results of the search of the fourth defendant's vehicle,

Speaking in coded language and erasing messages,

The observation regarding the mobile phone contacts between the first and the fourth defendant around the time of the facts,

The large sums of cash which the first and second defendant had at their disposal,

The analysis of the chat messages between "Negar" (second defendant) and first defendant,

The results of the direct listening between the first and second defendant,

The technical and expert report on IED,

The manner in which the defendants were to manipulate the IED and make it operational,

The statements made by the first and second defendant about their own roles, about each other's roles and about the role of the fourth defendant.

As regards the fourth defendant, reference can also be made to:

His contacts with the third defendant as a unique contact,

The text messages exchanged on June 17, 2018, and speaking in coded language.

Participation in attempted terrorist murder (charge A) and membership of a terrorist group (charge D) is therefore sufficiently proven on behalf of the third defendant based on the findings of the reporting officers:

The initial info from State Security and the specific info on the involvement of third-party defendant,

His presence on the ground and his conduct there,

The discovery of an operational mobile phone, the only contact being with the fourth defendant,

The analysis of text messages sent between third and fourth defendant on June 17, 2018,

The use of coded language,

The results of the search of the premises of the third defendant, where spyware was found,

The large sums of cash which the third defendant had at his disposal,

His regular trips to Austria and his depositing of money immediately after his return from abroad,

The recordings and footage that the third defendant took of the activities of the members of MEK/NCRI,

And finally, his implausible statements.

As regards sentencing

The facts of indictments A and D are mixed together in the case of the first, second, third and fourth defendant as being committed with the same intent, so that only one sentence should be imposed.

The facts of the charges are particularly serious. Attempted terrorist murder is one of the most serious crimes in the Belgian criminal code.

Defendants not only violate the sovereignty of the Belgian and French states. By attacking a well-attended conference of Iranian opposition parties, they not only undermine freedom of speech, but also the sense of security of Iranian refugees seeking safe haven in various European countries.

Both the first, second and third defendant must realize that, on the basis of the information they gave, certain people were and are still in physical danger.

Moreover, the first, second and third defendants considered human life to be secondary to their financial motives....

The sentencing of the first defendant

The first defendant immediately made statements and cooperated with the criminal investigation.

The first defendant appears naive and impressionable to the court. He indicates a sincere sense of guilt.

However, in view of the nature and seriousness of the facts, a severe effective prison sentence is appropriate.

The sentencing of the second defendant

Second defendant also made statements.

Second defendant strikes the court as very manipulative. The court refers in this sense to the direct eavesdropping between first and second defendant and to the following chat conversations of "Negar" (second defendant) :

that the second defendant influenced her husband to take part in the facts, and to set off the explosive device inside.

that the financial earnings are important for the second defendant and even a greater motive for her to cooperate with the secret service than for the first defendant.

So, her role is certainly not limited. She also forwarded information to the fourth defendant.

In addition, direct wiretaps show that the second defendant went to Iran herself, without the first defendant, and met with MOIS agents there. The criminal file shows that the fourth defendant sometimes wanted to speak only to the second defendant.

According to the court, the second defendant has more ties to MOIS than she claims to. This is clear from the chat conversations, in which she pretended to be "Negar", from her trip to Iran without the first defendant and from the subtle pressure on and influence exerted on the first defendant by the second defendant. Her role and share in the facts is therefore greater than that of the first defendant.

In view of the nature and seriousness of the facts and her concrete role in them, a severe effective prison sentence is appropriate.

The sentencing of the third defendant

The third defendant worked for years for the Iranian intelligence services purely for financial gain. He was on site and, given the findings of his operational mobile phone, it appears that he was the ears and eyes of the fourth defendant on the ground. It cannot be otherwise, given his key position, that he was fully aware of the plans that had to be carried out and that he was at least on the look-out to keep the operational leader of the attack meticulously informed and, if necessary, to make adjustments in the field. His important role is also shown by the sums of money he received from his clients.

In view of the nature and seriousness of the offences, a severe effective prison sentence is appropriate.

The sentencing of the fourth defendant

The fourth defendant is the operational brain behind the attack. He had absolutely no conscience problems with the fact that there would be fatalities.

He abused the diplomatic status to commit terrorist crimes, thus undermining the trust that can be placed in the exchange of official government officials.

A severe effective prison sentence is the only appropriate punishment.

...

As regards forfeiture

....

Regarding the third defendant

...

Third defendant was gathering information for fourth defendant at MEK almost daily. It is also likely that he was paid handsomely for this, as were the first and second defendants. It is also noteworthy that the deposits of money often took place when he returned from a trip to Austria (meeting with the fourth defendant).

CHAPTER 8

The Silence

As flawless and exemplary as was the cooperation of the security services and police of four European countries to thwart the plot against the Free Iran World Summit in Villepinte on June 30, 2018, the diplomatic reaction was disproportionate and disappointing, with the European countries choosing political expediency over principle, and even over the security interests of Europeans, which meant inaction and silence, instead a forceful and firm reaction to this blatant assault on their countries' sovereignty.

Wrong Footed from Start

In the first hours after reports about the incident became public, in a preemptive move, the clerical regime categorically denied not only its role in this terror plot, but the plot itself, preposterously describing it as a "false flag" operation. While accompanying Hassan Rouhani on a visit to Switzerland, then-Foreign Minister Javad Zarif hastily tweeted that this was a "false flag" operation.

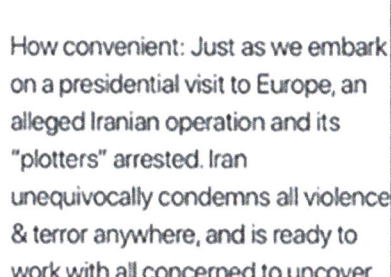

Figure 30 - Javad Zarif's tweet on the Villepinte bombing attempt

Zarif wrote, *"How convenient: Just as we embark on a presidential visit to Europe, an alleged Iranian operation and its "plotters arrested. Iran unequivocally condemns all violence & terror anywhere and is ready to work with all concerned to uncover what is a sinister false flag ploy."*

This tweet revealed the roadmap that the regime and its operatives abroad intended to follow to cover up their roles after the terror plot had been thwarted. A police official said, *"The regime had hoped that this bombing would be viewed as an internal MEK issue, which would have been seen as plausible, had we not caught their agents in the act."*

But apart from statements by regime officials on twitter to cover their tracks, Rouhani and his entourage received a red-carpet welcome in Austria, where Assadi had been a sitting diplomat.

Instead of raising even a simple objection to Zarif, whose diplomat had transported a deadly explosive to Austria onboard an Austrian Airlines flight from Tehran, then took advantage of his diplomatic status to pass through several European countries to deliver the bomb to agents with instructions on how to detonate it, the Austrian government merely, and perhaps reluctantly, agreed to revoking Assadi's diplomatic immunity.

A Feeble Reaction

Before Assadi's trial began in Belgium, in a rare statement on October 2, 2018, the French ministers of Interior, Foreign Affairs, and Finance condemned the regime's action and froze the assets of Assadi and his superior, Saeid Hashemi Moghadam, Deputy Minister of Intelligence for Internal Security, and the MOIS's Internal Security Directorate "as a preventive measure" for six months. On January 9, 2019, the European Union also included Assadi, Saeid Hashemi-Moghadam and the Internal Security Directorate of the MOIS on its list of terrorist organizations.

European Union's terrorist designations were the last and only political reaction to this matter, even after Assadi was sentenced to 20 years in prison, which he did not appeal.

Meanwhile, all concerned were fully aware of the dimensions of the terror plot, thwarted despite the expectations and wishes of the masterminds and the perpetrators, and in large measure due to the actions of the European security services.

The seriousness of the terrorist plot and the tremendous casualties it could have caused if not thwarted was not lost on the Antwerp Court of Appeal in rejecting Naami's appeal:

There is no doubt that the attack by Assadollah Assadi and his accomplices was designed with the following goals:

- *Creating serious fear in the People's Mojahedin Organization, and among Iranian political refugees living in several European countries who feel protected by the constitution of our countries.*
- *Creating serious panic in France and possibly other (European) countries involved in this international gathering, who have welcomed or supported the organizers of this conference.*

As a result, an attack of this nature and context should be seen as seriously harmful to France and possibly other European countries involved in organizing the conference of the People's Mojahedin Organization and would have caused great tension and uncertainty.[125]

Thus, there was no doubt even from the court's point of view that this terrorist plot, endangered the lives of tens of thousands of participants and political and social figures and put at risk the credibility and policies of European countries in general and France regarding refugees and their security.

But the official reaction by the European Union and its member states lacked substance and relevance and was not commensurate with the actions taken by Assadi and his superiors:

- Neither Assadi nor Saeid Hashemi Moghadam have any property in France to be seized.

- Besides conducting operations in the framework of state terrorism, the direct involvement of a regime's diplomat in this operation requires, apart from any judicial action, the adoption of appropriate diplomatic measures,

For example, the April 1997 verdict of the Berlin court regarding the assassination of Iranian dissidents in Mykonos restaurant in Berlin in 1992, where those involved were neither diplomatic staff nor even official agents of the regime, but ordinary citizens and even Lebanese nationals, confirmed that the killers were ordered and directed by the Iranian regime's hierarchy and specifically the Minister of Intelligence and the SNSC. Subsequently, all European countries summoned their ambassadors from Iran adversely affecting diplomatic ties with Tehran until November of that year.

"Let it pass" Attitude

In the case of Assadi, the passive, ambivalent, and feeble reaction of the European governments was not specific to one country. Even after the court in Antwerp confirmed the 20-year prison sentence for Assadi, the maximum possible sentence according to the Belgian law, no European official uttered a single word of condemnation.

Does the mere fact that Europe was involved in nuclear negotiations with the regime justify such a pathetic stance?

So much inaction and conciliation only embolden the other party to become more aggressive and raise the stakes as much as possible. But when you are trying to lure the other party, the price is not that important especially when the mission is to seal the deal between the two parties.

In 2005, amid negotiations between the European troika, the United Kingdom, France and Germany, and the Iranian regime, with Hassan Rouhani, as lead negotiator, news agencies revealed that the Europeans had proposed that the MEK, at the time on the EU's assets freeze list, despite absence of any proof to justify that designation, would be kept on this list, provided that the regime stop enriching uranium.

Later, in his book, entitled, "National Security and Nuclear Diplomacy," Hassan Rouhani revealed how the "centrifuges" were spinning at full speed while he was busy with negotiations with European counterparts. But 18 years later, the situation is completely different.

This time, the clerical regime and its various entities are on different terrorist lists and their fingerprints are observed on all kinds of terrorist acts in different parts of the world. As underlined in the Antwerp Court of Appeals verdict, the issue is no longer about the MEK nor the Iranian refugees living across Europe, but the credibility and security of the territory of the countries which have fallen victim to the feckless policy of appeasement.

It is not without reason that when long-term prison sentences were handed down against the perpetrators of the foiled assassination attempt in Villepinte, the clerical regime authorities reacted angrily.

When the Antwerp Court of Appeals rejected the appeal by Assadi's accomplices and finalized their verdict on May 10, 2022, the regime's Foreign Ministry spokesman said, *"In addition to his immediate release, we will follow up on the issue of compensation, restoration of dignity, and the commitment to not repeat [such acts]."*

In other words, not only did the regime fail to show any remorse for engaging in terrorism, denying the right to life, and violating other countries' sovereignty, but was also demanding carte blanche to repeat such actions and guarantees for immunity and impunity to continue to engage in similar acts in the future.

Criticism of EU Silence

The Iranian regime's use of its embassies and diplomatic services for terrorism should outrage politicians, dignitaries, journalists, media, and policymakers. This egregious abuse of international norms and laws, should dissuade all Western governments from continuing the policy of appeasing the Iranian regime.

Assadi's arrest and conviction leads any reasonable person to conclude that a lack of a decisive policy to effectively sanction the Iranian regime has emboldened the ruling theocracy to expand its terrorist activities abroad, now endangering European citizens as well as Iranian dissidents. The EU's willful disregard about human rights abuses in Iran and the regime's terrorist activities abroad, under the pretext of nuclear talks, is misguided.

Figure 31 - NCRI activists outside EU Foreign Ministers meeting in Brussels, Friday, Jan. 10, 2020. (AP).

The "Combating Terrorism Center (at West Point)," an academic institution in New York, in its report entitled, "Iran's Deadly Diplomats,"[126] dated August 2018, offers a chronology and analysis of the regime's state terrorism carried out abroad, and particularly on European soil. The report highlights the role of the Iranian regime's embassies in facilitating state terrorism and writes:

> *U.S. officials are pointing to this latest case [Assadi] as they seek to mobilize allies to counter Iran's support for terrorism around the world. Speaking on background with members of the press en route to Belgium from Saudi Arabia, on July 10, 2018, one senior State Department official made Washington's concerns very clear:*

> *'The most recent example is the plot that the Belgians foiled, and we had an Iranian diplomat out of the Austrian embassy as part of the plot to bomb a meeting of Iranian opposition leaders in Paris. And the United States is urging all nations to carefully examine diplomats in Iranian embassies to ensure their countries' own security. If Iran can plot bomb attacks in Paris, they can plot attacks anywhere in the world, and we urge all nations to be vigilant about Iran using embassies as diplomatic cover to plot terrorist attacks.'*

After listing dozens of Iranian state sponsored terrorist attacks, the report criticizes the European governments' inaction and naivety in reaction to these terror cases across Europe:

> *The international response to Iran's international terrorist activity should not be limited to law enforcement action alone. Regulatory action would also be helpful, and it is worth noting there have been calls for the European Union to designate not just Hezbollah's military wing as a terrorist group but to include the organization in its entirety, as well as expanded financial and diplomatic sanctions. European states should consider designating more Iranian institutions and personnel involved in Tehran's illicit conduct, but they should also consider working to isolate Iran diplomatically so long as Tehran continues to abuse diplomatic privilege and use its representatives abroad to murder people on foreign soil.*

> *To that end, in the wake of the Assadi affair, the State Department released timelines and maps depicting select incidents of Iranian-sponsored operational activities in Europe from 1979 to 2018, including both incidents involving Iran's proxy, Hezbollah, as well as those carried out by Iranian agents themselves. Developing an appreciation for the extent of Iranian operations in Europe over the years is important, and not just as some kind of academic exercise. As authorities in Austria, Belgium, France, and Germany dig deeper into the Assadi affair, they are likely to determine fairly quickly, as investigators invariably did in previous Iranian plots, that these are not rogue actions, but the actions of a rogue regime.*

MEP Gianna Gancia of Italy, in a written question in the European Parliament, critically asked Josep Borrell on November 17, 2020, about the Assadi case:

> *On 27 November 2020, Assadollah Assadi, an Iranian diplomat based in Vienna, will face court in Antwerp on charges of personally organizing a delivery of TATP explosives to a couple who intended to attack a gathering in Paris in the summer of 2018. Hundreds of prominent politicians from both sides of the Atlantic attended the gathering, including many European dignitaries. Assadi lost his diplomatic immunity within 48 hours and was handed over to the Belgian authorities. He has been awaiting trial ever since. While being interrogated, Assadi highlighted acts of terrorism carried out by the Iranian regime in the broader Middle East and speculated that there were a number of terrorist groups watching his case and standing ready to launch new attacks on Western soil if Belgium does not 'support them' by letting the defendant off.* [127]

1. Does the Vice-President of the Commission / High Representative of the Union for Foreign Affairs and Security Policy agree that such conduct is powerful evidence of the need for a firmer policy against the Iranian regime's threatening activities in Europe?

2. What recommendations has he made to the Government of Iran regarding the threats that its arrested diplomat Assadollah Assadi

spoke about in an attempt to influence the outcome of his trial on terrorism charges?

Given the inaction of the European Union, former Italian Foreign Minister Giulio Terzi, a civil plaintiff in the case and one of the potential targets in the Free Iran World Summit at Villepinte, criticized EU officials for their inaction. In an article appearing in "Conservative Global," on December 23, 2020, Mr. Terzi wrote:

> *Overall, however, European policy has long been based on conciliation and appeasement of the Islamic Republic. The desire to foster relations with non-existent "moderates" inside the Islamist regime has often resulted in Western policymakers turning a blind eye to abhorrent actions of the regime including actions that directly threatened the lives of Western personnel. Even more pressing and closer to home, is the trial in Belgium involving a senior Iranian diplomat – someone who answers directly to the Iranian Foreign Ministry.*
>
> *It is prudent for Borrell and other senior EU official to use the trial, its verdict scheduled for January 22, as a source of additional leverage in broader discussions over Iran's malign activities and the prospective response from EU member states.*
>
> *Within those member states, there is already substantial pressure in favor of an assertive response. In the run-up to Assadi's trial, a group of 240 European lawmakers prepared a statement addressed to Borrell, in which they urged the EU to support collective European policies that made the future of Iranian relations contingent upon the regime taking concrete steps to dismantle terrorist infrastructure and halt its malign activity on Western soil. The lawmakers stressed, 'Considering the Iranian regime's use of diplomatic cover to carry out terrorist acts, the necessary practical warnings should be given to Tehran, such as the closure of its embassies and the expulsion of its ambassadors and diplomats'.*

Referring to Mr. Borrell's tweet about his talks with Iran's Foreign Minister days after the first hearing of the Assadi case, in which

Mr. Borrell merely "*stressed the importance of preserving the JCPOA,*" Mr. Terzi criticized the current EU policy:

> *The 2018 terror plot ought to shed light on Western perception regarding political trends within the Islamic Republic. It will be a huge mistake downplaying the worst of Iran's malign activities, at the heart of Europe, as well as its brutal treatment of the Iranian people. The main and first task of every democratic government is to secure the safety and security of its citizens, and for the EU, as a union, the title 'High Representative of the Union for Foreign Affairs and Security Policy' has made the priorities very clear.*

Considering the trial of the regime's diplomat-terrorist and his accomplices in Belgium, an online panel entitled "Iran's State Terrorism and EU Policy,"[128] dated January 28, 2021, reviewed EU's policy towards Iran. Dr. Alejo Vidal Quadras, former Vice President of the European Parliament, said:

> *The Iranian regime is repressive in nature. This should make Iran a top priority in European policy. I would advise policymakers that if you want peace and stability in the region, if you want human rights to be respected in Iran, do not engage with this regime. This has been our key message to western policymakers. Do not engage with this regime, because it encourages them with their human rights violations, their terrorism, and proxy wars."* He warned, *"The Belgian judiciary will declare the ruling of the court soon. Regardless of the final outcome, we must fix our attention to the importance of this case. Because this is a ring on the bell of the European Union and European states. If they do not treat this seriously, it will be repeated. If there's another attack, it might succeed. It might be of a bigger dimension. All these governments, and the people of the External Action Service, the High Representative, the Council, they must be very attentive to the result of this trial. If they ignore it and go on with business as usual, there will be another worse attack.*

Struan Stevenson, former MEP, and a speaker at the event, reiterated:

The EU has yet to take serious measures. It has just designated two people in this enormous case. The EU is continuing business as usual and only sanctioned two people. That is unacceptable because Europe's lack of proper action has emboldened Iranian authorities in pursuing their malign activities. The Iranian government has been convinced that it has impunity no matter what it does in Europe. There are clear reasons for the EU to review our approach. European-Iranian relations must be made contingent on Iran taking concrete measures to stop its malign activities in Europe. We must also adopt practical measures to give Tehran the message that we are serious. This means closing Iranian embassies and expelling Iranian diplomats when there's serious evidence of terrorist activities.

Mr. Stevenson noted that Assadi had travelled to many countries around Europe, and that as a diplomat, these activities could not have been without the consent of his superior. He criticized the EU and Mr. Borrell for their silence:

There's no doubt that this plot was ordered by Khamenei, Rouhani, Zarif, and Intelligence Minister Mahmoud Alavi. The EU must hold all of them to account. But there has been a deafening silence from Europe. Borrell has typically said nothing.

Borrell even pledged to preserve the flawed nuclear deal and promised Iran would benefit economically from the lifting of sanctions by Europe. In his visit to Iran, Borrell didn't mention human rights violations, didn't mention the killing of unarmed protesters. A promise of an end to sanctions was the message conveyed by Borrell. The signal to the mullahs was that for the EU, trade matters, human rights does not. Borrell may be a new singer, but this is an old song. The EU has sent a catastrophic signal to Tehran by offering concession after concession. The trial of Assadollah Assadi is the tip of a massive terrorist iceberg. The regime uses its embassies as terror cells for bomb attacks and kidnappings. Borrell has a duty to protect EU citizens. His policy endangers our citizens. Borrell's silence is not acceptable. The EU must designate the IRGC as a terrorist organization and close the regime's embassies.

Former Socialist MEP, Paulo Casaca, was also critical of the EU's silence on the regime's transgressions:

> *The European External Action Service remains silent on the heinous attack of the Iranian regime against Europe. The European Union has rewarded the regime's aggressive behavior by rewarding them with a revived nuclear agreement. European institutions should reinforce European unity, uphold the rule of law, and ensure the protection of values that keep our countries together, including freedom and protection from terrorism. They must not bow to foreign terrorist powers that want us to bow before them. The regime must not enjoy impunity in causing terrorism.*

Sadly, the European Union and its member states have turned a blind eye on the implications of Iran's state terrorism on European soil and the Assadi case. The inaction, as discussed in previous chapters, has further emboldened the mullahs to continue their terrorist activities in Europe.

CHAPTER 9

The Treaty

On February 3, 2021, a day before Belgium's judiciary sentenced Assadollah Assadi to 20 years in prison, Belgian Justice Minister Vincent Van Quickenborne said[129] that "the Iranian regime likes to push for a deal or prisoner exchange."

On February 19, 2022, on the sidelines of the Munich Security Conference, the Iranian regime's Foreign Minister, Hossein Amir-Abdollahian, met with then-Belgian Foreign Minister Sophie Wilmès, and raised the Assadi matter. In late February, Iranian authorities detained a Belgian aid worker, Olivier Vandecasteele, 41, on charges of espionage.

Less than a month later, on March 11, the Belgian government signed a transfer of "sentenced persons" deal with the regime. It did not publicize the deal until June. The treaty stipulates that convicted persons can spend the remainder of their prison terms in their country of origin.

On May 11, 2022, Iranian regime President Ebrahim Raisi held a phone conversation with the Belgian Prime Minister Alexander De Croo. According to state-run media, a month later, Assadi's wife broke her silence after four years, and thanked Raisi for issuing a special order to resolve the Assadi issue.

The existence of the treaty was kept a secret until June 29, 2022, when the Belgian government submitted it to Parliament for approval. On that day, the government tabled a draft law to ratify five international agreements, including the bilateral treaty with Tehran, formally known as the "Transfer of Sentenced Persons."

According to Politico[130] on July 4, 2022, *"The Belgian government has refused to explain the immediate need for the treaty, although*

Belgian media reported Monday night that Iran has been holding a Belgian national in jail since February, potentially as leverage."

According to the proposed treaty, *"A person sentenced in the territory of a party may be transferred to the territory of the other Party, in accordance with the provisions of this Treaty, in order to serve the remaining period of the sentence imposed on him."* The treaty would allow the release of individuals like Assadi if the *"sentencing and administrating states agree to the transfer."*

According to Article 13 of the bilateral treaty, *"Either party may grant pardons, amnesties or reductions in sentences in accordance with its constitution or other laws."* So, based on this article, if repatriated to Iran, Assadi would also be able to enjoy clemency and state pardon.

While the government had hoped to ram through the legislation and limit the debate on the Treaty, fierce opposition by members of the Chamber of Representatives led to protracted debate, which delayed the adoption of the bill for a week. Ultimately, on July 20, Belgian members of parliament voted to ratify the treaty allowing prisoner exchanges with the Iranian regime. The Bill was finally adopted right before the parliament's summer break, by a vote of 79 to 41, with 11 abstentions. Significantly, many deputies in the government coalition abstained and others, while voting affirmatively, expressed their frustration and concern over the provisions of the deal.

International Reaction

On July 1, 2022, Mrs. Rajavi warned that this treaty would facilitate the release and transfer of the Iranian regime's terrorist diplomat Assadi to Iran. She called on the Belgian Parliament to refrain from passing this legislation.

International reaction to the Belgium-Iran prisoner swap treaty was intense and immediate. According to Politico on July 4, the move *"is proving far more controversial — drawing outrage from European critics of Iran, as well as members of the Iranian opposition living in exile."*

Politico added, *"Critics of the new treaty say that it will undermine the Belgian law enforcement and justice systems, literally creating a get-out-of-jail-free card for terrorists."*

"This is an erosion of the legal system," **said Michael Freilich, a Belgian MP for the Flemish nationalists N-VA, who are in opposition in the Belgian parliament.** *"Iran has made clear publicly that they don't see Assadi as a terrorist, but as a diplomat. He will be freed as soon as he steps foot on Iranian soil."*

According to The New York Times: [131]

Critics of the treaty, which was ratified late Wednesday by a vote of 79 to 41, with 11 abstentions, argue that Belgium is giving in to a form of hostage-taking by Iran." …*Iran, critics said, was pushing to secure the return of an Iranian diplomat convicted last year in Belgium to 20 years in prison for orchestrating a plot to bomb a 2018 meeting of Iranian opposition leaders in France. If the diplomat is allowed to return to Iran, he is likely to be immediately released rather than serving out his sentence there, the critics said.*

For its part, the NCRI condemned its ratification as shameful, adding that *"Belgium's vote would provide 'the highest incentive for the religious fascism ruling Iran to step up terrorism and to use hostage-taking as much as possible for the release of its arrested terrorists and agents.'"*[132]

Hundreds of international personalities, parliamentarians, and rights advocates condemned the treaty and joined calls to stop the repatriation of Assadi. Former US Attorney General Michael Mukasey wrote to the Belgian Parliament Speaker, *"As you can no doubt surmise by now, I believe this bill would disgrace your Chamber and Belgium and should not be passed. No sentient person can doubt that releasing to Iran a former diplomat of that country who was convicted of using his diplomatic status to try to commit mass murder would reward a heinous act."*[133]

In early July, 13 members of the US Congress wrote a letter to the Belgian PM, saying, *"... we implore you to uphold these precious principles and reject any cynical ploy by Iran's current "diplomats" to trade terrorists for dubiously detained Belgians."*[134] Among them were Tom McClintock, a senior member of the House Judiciary Committee.

In a letter dated July 19, 2022, the Brussels Bar Association addressed the Prime Minister, the Minister of Justice, the Minister of Foreign Affairs, the Speaker of the Parliament, and the heads of various parliamentary commissions, expressing their deep concern over the approval of such a treaty. The letter signed by the president of the Brussels Bar Association and the president of the Human Rights Institute of the Bar Association, said in part:

The French Bar Association of Brussels and its Human Rights Institute have taken note of the content of the bill of June 29, 2022, assenting to the treaty between the Kingdom of Belgium and the Islamic Republic of Iran on the transfer of sentenced persons, done in Brussels on March 11, 2022, and the Protocol of November 22, 2017 amending the Additional Protocol to the Convention on the Transfer of Sentenced Persons, signed on April 7, 2022 in Strasbourg.

It is important to note that this convention would henceforth organize the transfer to Iran of persons convicted of acts of terrorism. It is worrying to note that Article 13 of this Convention explicitly states that the parties may grant amnesty to convicted persons, pardon them or reduce the sentences pronounced against them. This is a worrying discrimination, especially in favor of named terrorists with regard to the legal principles prevailing in Belgium in terms of the execution of sentences.

Thereby the ratification of the law in Belgium, on the basis of the draft law of June 29, 2022, defined above, of a political treaty with the Islamic Republic of Iran, is considered a disturbing violation of the rule of law.

Our deep commitment to values to the rule of law, to the rights of the defense, the independence of the judiciary and respect for its decisions, can only make us wise to what we believe about the arrest in Iran, one of our compatriots. Despite these same principles, we cannot accommodate the prospect of seeing a prisoner sentenced in Belgium for acts of extreme gravity, escape from application of the punishment which was brought to him by an independent tribunal.

The International Committee 'In Search of Justice' (ISJ), led by former Vice President of the European Parliament Alejo Vidal-Quadras, former Italian Foreign Minister Giulio Terzi, former President of the European Parliament's Delegation for Relations with Iraq Struan Stevenson, and former Socialist MEP Paulo Casaca, addressed the Belgian PM: [135]

There is no doubt Assadi's terrorist plot was ordered from the highest echelons of the regime, including the Supreme Leader Ayatollah Ali Khamenei, the president at that time Hassan Rouhani and the then Foreign Minister Javad Zarif. ... There is also no doubt that if these prisoners are allowed to return to Iran, they will never be asked to serve prison sentences in that country. Indeed, they will be treated as heroes and possibly promoted. Their release from prison in Belgium would make a complete mockery of justice and send the clearest signal to the Iranian regime that they can conduct terrorist attacks in Europe with impunity. Indeed, they may even be encouraged to take further European hostages to hold as bargaining chips for future prisoner exchanges.

The British Committee for Iran Freedom (BCFIF) issued a statement regarding the deal in July. The statement, signed by Professor Lord David Alton, underscored:[136]

> *This is tantamount to releasing these convicted terrorists and allowing them to escape justice given the well-documented reputation of Iran's Judiciary to grant and uphold impunity for regime officials for serious crimes, recently expressed by the UN Special Rapporteur on Iran.*

On July 3, several US security experts and former officials, including former FBI Director Louis Freeh and Former Commandant of US Marine Corps Gen. James Conway, wrote the Belgian Parliament Speaker:[137]

> *As members of the American law enforcement and national security community, we have dedicated our lives to protecting the free world and fighting terrorism on multiple continents. That continuing commitment compels us to address what we recognize as a stunning mistake in progress: the pending 'Treaty Between the Kingdom of Belgium and the Islamic Republic of Iran on the Transfer of Sentenced Persons.'*

On July 6, at least 20 members of the European Parliament wrote a letter to Belgian parliamentarians saying, *"Such an agreement will result in more crimes and assassinations in Europe and unless we all take a firm stand, this will not be the last of these deadly terrorist plots."*[138]

Several former European leaders, including prime ministers and foreign ministers, said in a letter:[139]

> *We find this extremely problematic and dangerous. It would be a disruption of international justice and of all our anti-terrorist activities in Europe simply because it would go in the wrong direction of favoring impunity and would act as precedence to all other rogue regimes such as Russia and China to take advantage of it. With such precedence, how could we possibly stop any state-sponsored act of terrorism?*

Six hundred Iranian Americans denounced the treaty in a letter to Belgian officials, saying:[140]

In 2021, over 252 bi-partisan House members co-sponsored H.Res.118, which ... condemned Tehran's state-sponsored terrorist attacks against United States citizens and officials, specifically "the Iranian regime's terror plot against the 'Free Iran 2018–the Alternative' gathering in Paris. The resolution also called on "relevant United States Government agencies to work with European allies...to hold Iran accountable for breaching diplomatic privileges, and to call on nations to prevent the malign activities of the Iranian regime's diplomatic missions, with the goal of closing them down.

At the same time, Iranian exiles held demonstrations and protests in Belgium, Austria, France, Sweden, United States, Germany, Norway, Italy, Canada, the Netherlands, Denmark, U.K., Australia, Romania, and Luxembourg.

In a statement, Amnesty International reiterated its warnings:[141]

... there is a significant risk that Iranian dissidents abroad will face increased threats and attacks from agents of the Islamic Republic of Iran if the international community, including Belgium and other European governments, fail to ensure accountability for human rights violations and unlawful acts committed by the Iranian authorities extraterritorially to crush freedom of expression and peaceful dissent.

Several Nobel Laureates, including Professor Joachim Frank and Professor Arieh Warshel, told Belgian authorities:[142]

We have found out that Belgium quietly signed a treaty with Iran that allows persons sentenced in the territory of either party to be transferred to the territory of the other party. Allowing Assadi to serve the remainder of his 20-year sentence in Iran, the state, which was responsible for the attempted terrorist bombing, would make a mockery of the rule of law and foster further impunity for the Iranian government and its officials involved in terrorism and crimes against humanity.

The Canadian Friends of a Democratic Iran (CFDI), a non-partisan NGO, said it "*is in shock and disbelief in learning of the deal between the Belgian government and the clerical regime in Iran to release convicted terrorists back to Iran."*[143]

On July 5, Mrs. Rajavi extended her gratitude to all Iranians, parliamentarians, lawyers, and political figures participating in the global campaign against the deal. *"In particular, she thanked the parliamentarians, lawyers, and demonstrators in Belgium and their persistence against sacrificing justice, democracy, and human rights,"* according to an NCRI statement. *"She noted: So far, they have brought to light many realities and discredited and condemned auctioneering values and the rule of law."*

Mrs. Rajavi added that the NCRI has *"examined various political and legal avenues and options, and will do everything in their power, to prevent the regime's terrorist diplomat from evading justice."*[144]

Abuse of Human Rights for Appeasement

The EU adopted a decision in 2008, to transfer convicted prisoners back to their EU country of nationality, aiming to facilitate the social rehabilitation of convicted persons by allowing them to serve their sentence in their home country. These transfers are governed by Council framework decision 2008/909/JHA.

In addition, compulsory transfer may take place under the Additional Protocol to the Council of Europe Convention on the Transfer of Sentenced Persons, and any bilateral prisoner transfer agreements. Iran, however, is not a signatory to the latter convention.

Belgium, therefore, laid the groundwork for the transfer of Assadi under the guise of a humanitarian measure such as the above EU decisions and conventions, by drawing up the transfer of "sentenced persons" treaty with Iran. This was a cynical ploy to use a humanitarian smoke screen to hide the scandalous deal with the devil to return a terrorist to Iran in return for a hostage who was taken precisely to free Assadi.

The treaty stands as an egregious violation of the spirit of such prisoner transfer treaties for several reasons:

The Iranian regime, as made clear earlier in this book, does not accept Assadi's conviction on terrorist conspiracy to commit mass murder in Villepinte, France. It has declared Assadi innocent, will certainly immediately release him and assign him back to his job of plotting terrorist attacks on European soil against Iranian dissidents. Therefore, there can be no pretense of transferring a convicted terrorist offender to his home country to serve out his term.

The crime of terrorism perpetrated by a serving diplomat of a country that is a state sponsor of terrorism, cannot in any way be included in a prisoner transfer treaty, because the transfer of the convicted terrorist to the country that has sent him to commit the crime of terrorism, is analogous to freeing a convicted terrorist.

Sending Assadi back to his paymasters in Iran will further encourage violence, assassinations, and terrorism against EU nationals and Iranian dissidents as the Iranian regime will perceive this as a success of its impervious violation of all international norms.

It will further embolden the regime to perpetuate its policy of taking hostage Western nationals and dual-nationals as a tool for political and security blackmailing of Western countries.

The treaty between Belgium and the Iranian regime, therefore, is a fig leaf for a very shameful Belgian capitulation to political and security blackmail by the leading state sponsor of terrorism, the religious dictatorship ruling Iran.

Legal Action after Treaty Adoption

Subsequent to the Parliament's adoption of the bill introduced by the Belgian Government around midnight on Wednesday, July 20, the NCRI, its President-elect, and a number of civil parties, including former Algerian Prime Minister Sid Ahmed Ghozali, former Italian Foreign Minister Giulio Terzi, former Colombian presidential candidate Ingrid Betancourt, Senator Robert Torricelli, former White House director for public liaison Linda Chavez, and former UNAMI human rights office chief Tahar Boumedra, filed a lawsuit at the Court of First Instance in Brussels, arguing that any treaty that would ultimately result in the release of Assadi would violate the rights of the victims to redress.

The Court rejected the filing, arguing that it should have been made prior to the bill was approved by the parliament. The lawyers of the NCRI and civil parties appealed the decision, and the Brussels Court of Appeals issued a temporary injunction, prohibiting Assadi's transfer to Tehran pending a substantive hearing by the Court of the First Instance, in which the parties, including the Government would brief the court and present oral arguments so that a final decision could be made.

The Brussels Court of First Instance convened on Thursday, July 28, and set the date for each party's submissions and the date of the oral hearing. The lawyers representing the Belgian Prime Minister and the Ministers of Justice and Foreign Affairs, attended the hearing.

It set the date for the oral hearing for September 19, 2022. This marked a significant development in the case, in that the court extended the ban on returning Assadi to Iran, pending the final decision of the Court of the First Instance and the possible decision of the Court of Appeals, should any party decide to appeal.

The Consequences

On July 20, 2022, the Belgian Chamber of Representatives finally approved the treaty with Iran's ruling theocracy to swap prisoners. The treaty, initially and secretly signed in March 2022 with the Iranian regime, was adopted with 79 votes in favor, 41 against, and 11 abstentions.

By surrendering to the Iranian regime's blackmail, Belgium is making a mockery of the rule of law and undermining its independent judiciary. While Tehran continues to flout each and every international law and norm with its ongoing egregious human rights abuses, Belgium has undermined human rights and other democratic values that Europe has long cherished.

It is naïve, to put it mildly, to believe that the Iranian regime would keep Assadi incarcerated to serve the remainder of his sentence in an Iranian jail. His return to Tehran provides the Iranian regime the opportunity to regroup, plan more attacks and feel assured that if its operatives are arrested, they will return home safe and sound.

Furthermore, the treaty legally commits Brussels to returning future terrorists to Tehran. This will undoubtedly transform Belgium into a bridgehead for the Iranian regime's terrorists and sets a dangerous precedent because other European countries whose nationals are held hostage in Iran could use the Belgian example and exchange Iranian agents, serving time for terrorist or human rights offenses in their respective countries, with their nationals incarcerated in Iran.

Apparently, Belgium has not learned any lessons from other European countries in the past. Winston Churchill once said, "An appeaser is one feeding a crocodile, hoping it will eat him last." Belgium should rest assured that thanks to this treaty, an emboldened Iranian regime will not wait long before inflicting more pain across the continent while enjoying its impunity.

APPENDICES

Appendix A
Chronology

June 2017

Assadollah Assadi and an Iranian regime cleric, Mohammad Reza Zaeri, affiliated to the MOIS, go to Paris from Vienna in a rental car, to surveil the Exposition Hall at Villepinte and the hotels in the vicinity that would house the guests.

January 1, 2017

Ali Shamkhani, Secretary of the SNSC: The hypocrites (MEK) will receive an appropriate response from Iran from where they do not know.

January 16, 2018

Mahmoud Alavi, Minister of Intelligence is quoted as saying, "The unsung soldiers of Imam Zaman will soon respond to terrorist and counter-revolutionary groups in the region."

February 11, 2018

Hassan Taeb, at the time head of the IRGC's Intelligence Organization: "In recent events, notorious groups, led by the main enemies of the nation, exploited the people's rightful economic demands to divert the demands of the nation by causing insecurity. Of course, their actions will not go unanswered, and we will slap them at the right time."

January 4, 2018

Le Figaro: "Hassan Rouhani is once again advancing the story of the MEK. Rouhani has called on Emmanuel Macron to take action against his opponents in exile"

January 9, 2018

Underscoring that the 2017 uprising had been organized by the MEK, Ali Khamenei threatened that "this will not go unanswered."

March 17, 2018

On the train between Vienna and Salzburg, Assadi communicates the issue of Operation Villepinte to Naami and Saadouni.

March 20, 2018

The Iranian regime's terrorist operations against Ms. Maryam Rajavi, the MEK, and political figures in Tirana were uncovered and foiled by the Albanian government. Albania's Prime Minister Edi Rama announced the news on April 19, 2018.

June 18, 2018

Tweet from Hesamuddin Ashna, Rouhani adviser and head of the Center for Strategic Reviews:

«Who knows, may be amid all this chaos, the wife will find her deceased husband in the hereinafter. Those looking for hot summers, should not forget the adventures of Nimroz." (Reference to the February 8, 1981 massacre of MEK leaders, including Ashraf Rajavi.)

June 22, 2018

Assadi transports bomb from Tehran on board an Austrian Airlines flight from Tehran to Vienna.

June 25, 2018

Belgian and French security officials are informed by a trusted partner source of the existence of the bombing plot against the NCRI Summit at the Villepinte.

June 28, 2018

Nasimeh Naami and ddddAmir Saadouni meet at a pizza shop in Luxembourg, delivers the bomb and returns to Belgium. In this meeting, Assadi will pay them between 18,000 and 22,000 euros.

June 28, 2018

Luxembourg police stopped Assadi and his family members and authenticated them: Asadollah Assadi, his wife Robabeh Assadi and his two sons, Hussein and Ali, were identified. All four also had diplomatic passports.

June 28, 2018

Amir Saadouni quoted Assadi in a chat that said, "If it were done inside, he would go to the Agha (Khamenei) himself personally... He said, "I'm asking for the same speech for you."

June 29, 2018

The Belgian Security Agency said in a statement that Mehrdad Arefani is likely to be involved in this violent plot along with Saadouni and Naami.

June 29, 2018

In a chat with Assadi, Saadouni says they installed the bomb's components. And they're supposed to call at 17:00 pm on the day of the ceremony and after the operation.

June 30, 2018

Naami's SMS with Saadouni on the way to Paris: "We set up the machine and "we're going to win the cup", he continued,

"Everything's all sorts." At 12: 30pm Saadouni and Naami are stopped by the police and the occupants are arrested. A bomb is found inside their vehicle, which explodes during defussion.

June 30, 2018

French police arrest Mehrdad Arefani in Villepinte parking lot.

July 1, 2018

Assadollah Assadi arrested near the city of Ashafenburg in Bavaria, Germany.

July 2, 2018

Joint press release of the Federal Prosecutor's Office and the Belgian Security Agency, outlining the bombing plot and the arrests of the terrorists.

July 2, 2018

Javad Zarif's tweet: "Just as the president's visit to Europe begins, an Iranian operation is exposed and its 'agents' are arrested. A filthy operation to give the wrong address.»

July 4, 2018

Summoning French and Belgian ambassadors and German embassy officials in Tehran to protest against the arrest of an Iranian diplomat!

July 10, 2018

A senior US State Department official: "We are working closely with the Belgians, the French, and the Germans, and to get to the bottom of this conspiracy..."

July 11, 2018

A Paris court orders the extradition of Mehrdad Arefani to Belgium. He is handed over to the Belgian authorities on July 20.

September 25, 2018

Expulsion of an Iranian diplomat from France. A month later, Reuters announces the news as to confirm.

October 2, 2018

The French government sanctions Assadollah Assadi, Seid Hashemi Moqaddam, and the Ministry of Intelligence's Internal Security Directorate and puts them on its terrorist watch list.

October 2, 2018

Reuters: Iran's Intelligence Ministry, controlled by Ali Khamenei, ordered a foiled attack against an Iranian exiled opposition group meeting near Paris in June.

October 2, 2018

The French ministers of state, foreign affairs and economy issue a joint communiqué, referring to the "plan to attack" the MEK conference on French soil, writing that "this action is extremely serious and cannot go unanswered."

October 9, 2018

Assadollah Assadi is extradited from Germany to Belgium. The Bamberg State Supreme Court agrees to the attorney general's request.

November 19, 2018

EU foreign ministers back France's move to sanction the Ministry of Intelligence and two Iranian citizens accused of attempting to bomb the NCRI gathering in Villepinte, call for the designation to be implemented EU-wide.

19 December 2018

The Kindom of Belgium places Assadollah Assadi, Amir Saadouni and Nasimeh Naami on the list of individuals involved in the money laundering of terrorism.

19 December 2018

Iranian Ambassador to Albania, Gholam Hossein Mohammadnia, and his deputy, Mustafa Rudaki, are expelled from Albania for their involvement in a March 2018 terrorist plot against the MEK's Nowruz (New Year) celebration in Tirana.

January 8, 2019

The Council of Ministers of the European Union places the Internal Security Division of the Ministry of Intelligence, Saeed Hashemi Moghaddam and Assadollah Assadi on the terrorist list. Mike Pompeo says Washington "strongly supports" Europe's new actions against Iran.

January 22, 2019

Ali Majedi, the regime's ambassador to Germany, says the Europeans have documents that we cannot deny.

May 1, 2019

The NCRI's US Reprentative Office publishes book "Iran's Emissaries of Terror" and introduced at a press conference. A section of the books deals with the Villepinte case.

June 3, 2019

The third indictment of the Belgian federal prosecutor against the defendants charges them with membership in a terrorist group.

October 23, 2019

Albanian police chief reveals the terrorist network of the Quds Force in that country. An individual in Tehran, named Payman and an operative named Ali Reza Naghashzadeh from Austria were members of the network. The network was behind the foiled terror plot against MEK's March 2018 event.

November 4, 2019

Mrs. Maryam Rajavi testifies for seven hours. The schematic for the hierarchy in the decision-making process for the terrorist plot is handed over to the Judicial officials.

July 15, 2020

The first session of the preliminary trial is held. The court upholds the prosecutor's indictment against the defendants. With this trial, the proceedings begins.

July 15, 2020

Eric Van Der Sypt, spokesman for the Belgian Prosecutor General's Office, announces the charges against the four suspects as "initiating murder of a terrorist nature" and "participation in the actions of the terrorist organization."

July 30, 2020

A second preliminary trial is held in Antwerp to set the deadlines for the exchange of briefs. Assadi was not present at the meeting.

November 27, 2020

The first session of the Antwerp trial. Assadi did not attend. Other defendants showed up.

December 3, 2020

The second session of the Antwerp trial.

February 4, 2021

Antwerp cout announces ruling: Assadi is sentenced to 20 years, Naami, 18 years, Arefani, 17 years, and Saadouni, 15 years.

March 8, 2021

Assadi's lawyer initially appeals, but then withdraws it

May 5, 2021

The first session of the Appeals Court.

December 9 and 10, 2021

Explosives experts testify on the strength of the bomb.

February 19 , 2022

The Iranian regime's Foreign Minister meets his counterpart on the sidelines of Munich SecurityConference and discusses Assadi's case.

March 4, 2022

Final Session of the Appeals Court

March 11, 2022

Belgium and the Iranian regime sign a treaty on the exchange those convicted to spend the remainder of their sentences in their respective countries.

May 10, 2022

Court of Appeals announces ruling. Nasimeh Naami's 18-year sentence and Arefani's 17-year sentences are upheld. Saadouni's sentence is increased from 15 to 18 years.   Other convictions, including stripping Belgian citizenship of all three individuals and seizing their money and financial assets were confirmed.

May 10, 2022

Iran's Foreign Ministry spokesman Email Khatibzadeh: All phases of detention, trial and judicial order for Aasadollah Assadi have been carried out in gross violation of the provisions of the Vienna Convention on Diplomatic Rights. In addition to his immediate release, we pursue the issue of compensation, restitution, and commitment not to repeat such measures.

May 11, 2022

Ibrahim Raisi's calls the Belgian Prime Minister.

Stating that the two countries have advanced diplomatic relations over the years based on principles of respect and mutual interest, Raisi says, "Iran welcomes efforts to strengthen and expand the relations between Tehran and Brussels."

June 13, 2022

Iran regime's Foreign Ministry spokesman: It was proven what role the MKO (MEK) played in the Assadi affair. Of course, the Belgian Government set a dangerous precedent. We declare that our diplomat Mr. Assadi, should be released unconditionally, vindicated, and compensated for the damages.

June 13, 2022

Kazem Gharibabadi, Deputy Head of International Affairs for the Judiciary: "We are witnessing widespread human rights abuses against Mr. Assadi in Germany and Belgium. We call for Mr. Assadi's release and compensation as quickly as possible."

June 19, 2022

Assadollah Assadi's wife: "After about four years (exactly 1,450 days), I have still not lost hope and am waiting to hear about my husband's release. Mr. Raisi, thank you for your seriousness in pursuing my wife's release from Belgian prison."

June 24, 2022

Kazem Gharibabadi: "We are not in any meeting with the ambassadors of European countries or delegations of European countries not to deal with the MKO case"

June 29, 2022

The Belgian government presents the bill signed on March 11, 2022, to the Parliament with urgency, the first time that such a treaty had been made public.

July 4 and 5, 2022

The Belgian Foreign Affairs Commission discusses the treaty. Although the text of the treaty did not mention Assadi by name, but almost all the discussion was about returning Assadi to the regime and its consequences. The bill was passed by a vote of 10 for and 5 against.

July 13, 2022

The Iranian regime's Foreign Ministry spokesman Nasser Kanani: "Political discussions and consultations with Belgian authorities are established and close consultations are established in the jurisdiction with the Belgian government."

July 19 and 20, 2022

The bill is debated on the Belgian parliament's open stage for 12 hours and the bill was approved at midnight Wednesday, with 79 votes in favor, 41 against and 11 abstentions.

July 20, 2022

Iranian Foreign Ministry Spokesman Nasser Kanaani: Belgian lawmakers finally ratified the treaty on transferring convicts with Iran. Despite that ratification, the Belgian Court of Appeal barred Assadi's transfer, and our dialogue and contact with the Belgian government is continuing, and our position has not changed.

July 22, 2022

Following a complaint filed by the lawyer of the National Council of Resistance and party civils to the Brussels Court of Appeals, the court temporarily banned the Belgian government from transferring Assadi to Iran. The lower court had rejected the request the previous day.

July 27, 2022

The Belgian Lower Court approved the agreed deadlines between the lawyers for both parties to exchange briefs and set September 19 for the court date to discuss and review the documents of the two sides.

Appendix B

Amicus Briefs to the Court

Dignitaries at the Free Iran World Summit 2018 provide statements to the court

Several luminaries, who attended the Free Iran Summit 2018, provided statements to the Court in Antwerp during the trial of Assadollah Assadi.

While each address a particular aspect of the foiled terror plot, they all share the view that had the bombing attempt been successful, hundreds if not thousands would have been killed or wounded, including many of the distinguished attendees.

Excerpts from some of the statements follow:

Giulio Terzi, Foreign Minister of Italy (2011-2013)

"I attended the Free Iran gathering on 30 June 2018.

"On June 30, 2018, I was sitting close to my colleagues from other countries, in the seats devoted to guests of honor, close enough to NCRI's president-elect, Mrs. Maryam Rajavi, who was the main target of the foiled terrorist scheme. Like Mrs. Rajavi and all the guests, I would have run important risk against my life had the plot proceeded as planned.

"However, the fact that the criminals were not able to undertake their action thanks to the vigilance of concerned services does, in my view, not decrease the seriousness of the case.

In my understanding, damage due to not responding with ample firmness to this complex state-sponsored, state-implemented act of terror would be far greater than the eventual damage to innocent lives had the plot taken place as planned."

Robert Joseph, former Under Secretary of State for Arms Control and International Security

"Even knowing the nature of the regime beforehand, it was nevertheless shocking to learn of the attempted terrorist bombing at the 2018 gathering. I would never have thought that a peaceful event in France with tens of thousands of men, women, and children in attendance would be a target for terrorism. Any explosion in the hall, or even outside where large numbers of attendees watched the proceedings, would have resulted in huge casualties, likely hundreds killed and many, many more wounded and permanently disabled. Learning of the planned terrorist attack reinforced my view that the Iranian regime is not only the number one violator of human rights at home but also the number one state sponsor of terrorism.

"On a personal level, I have attended the annual meetings of the Iranian opposition for nearly a decade, at times with my wife. At the 2018 event, I recall vividly the enormous exhibition hall with a large VIP section where I was sitting with hundreds of parliamentarians from around the world, renowned human rights activists, and other accomplished guests from every professional field. Clearly, the main target was Mrs. Rajavi, head of the National Council of Resistance of Iran (NCRI) and sponsor of the meeting. Like the others in my section, I was sitting near Mrs. Rajavi. But there were also thousands of participants within a short distance from the VIP section. The death toll and casualties would have been in the hundreds if not more.

Based on my knowledge of the involvement of the regime in terrorism and on available information in this case, it is clear to me that the planed attack was not an isolated act by a rogue element within the Iranian government. Rather, it was a well-planned terrorist act, using diplomatic privileges for criminal purposes."

Robert Torricelli, United States Senator (1997-2003)

"I was sitting in the VIP section, not far from Mrs. Maryam Rajavi, who was the prime target of the terrorist plot. Therefore, I was certainly a potential target and as such I feel very strongly in pursuing this case until justice is done.

"While I have been aware of the terrorist nature of the Iranian regime, I never thought that they would try blowing up a huge gathering with tens of thousands of participants including high profile international dignitaries in Europe. Had they succeeded, I have no doubt that at least hundreds would have been killed and many more injured. It would have certainly been the biggest terrorist attack in Europe.

"The attempted terrorist murder in June 30, 2018 in Villepinte has affected my life. The possibility of being the target of the Iranian regime because of my involvement with the movement is no longer a theoretical issue but had it not been for the great work done by the police and other relevant institutions in Europe, many of us could have been the target of that plot."

Ingrid Betancourt, former Senator and presidential candidate in Columbia

"I would like to express first of all, how much I was shocked to feel threatened by a terrorist plot of foreign origin, on the soil of my dear country, France, while it is here that my freedom is guaranteed , that I feel protected and safe, after having been rescued from the hands of the Farc who held me hostage for more than six years, also a terrorist group from Colombia, a country which still suffers from terrorism.

"When I went to the rally on June 30, 2018, to defend the freedom of the Iranian people, I did so in solidarity with those who are experiencing human rights violations like the ones I have endured. In previous years, at the same annual gathering, my mother, my daughter and my niece have accompanied me, always in a process of commitment and solidarity. The thought that I might be in danger by going there didn't cross my mind, nor those who were with me that day.

"The place was packed. There were thousands of people from all over the world. Committed personalities but also whole families, young couples and their children, grandparents, some of Iranian origin, others not, all come to claim the freedom of the Iranian people in an atmosphere of fair, music, Colorful placards and banners for freedom I could focus on the damning facts: the use of diplomatic cover to act with impunity and across Europe; the recruitment of our nationals of Iranian origin, holders of European passports, as agents under the orders of a foreign power; the premeditation of the massacre with unlimited economic capacity, and years of elaborate upstream work to gather information, infiltrate, and plan the crime in all detail and with all calculations of space and time; the instrumentalization of the rules of the Schengen area in favor of the murderous plan; the deployment of an international strategy from the offices of Iranian ministers, etc."

Wesley Martin, Active Component Colonel (ret.), United States Army Military Police

"As a participant of "Free Iran 2018" rally outside Paris I could have been one of the casualties had the Iranian Ministry of Intelligence and Security plot succeeded. The use of the very deadly triacetone triperoxide (TATP) in the intended explosive device proves the Iranian government was intent on causing extensive damage.

"It was the diligence of police officers in Belgium, backed by German, French, and Austrian law enforcement agencies that prevented the slaughter and have now thoroughly developed the case that is before your court at this time.

"As the 2018 Paris rally was attended by scores of thousands of participants, it is obvious hundreds of people would have been killed and maimed had the Iranian attack succeeded. Attendees included current and former senior officials from governments throughout Europe, Asia, Africa, and North America. Just as important, rally participants also included citizens from these same countries, coming to show their support for Iran one day achieving President Franklin Roosevelt's four freedoms: of speech, of worship, from want, and from fear. This attack was as much against the attendees as it was against those freedoms."

Appendix C

Belgian VSSE letter to Federal Prosecutor's Office

June 25, 2018

Appendix D

Joint Press Release of the Federal Public Prosecutor

July 2, 2018

Parquet fédéral
Rue aux Laines 66/1
B-1000 Bruxelles
tél +32 2 557 77 11
fax +32 2 557 77 99

Federaal Parket
Wolstraat 66/1
B-1000 Brussel
tel +32 2 557 77 11
fax +32 2 557 77 99

Communiqué de presse du Parquet Fédéral et de la Sûreté de l'État

Persbericht van het Federaal Parket en de Veiligheid van de Staat

Ref: Gezamenlijk persbericht van het Federaal Parket en de Veiligheid van de Staat

Ref: Communiqué de presse conjoint du Parquet Fédéral et de la Sûreté de l'État

Joint press release of the Federal Public Prosecutor's Office and the Belgian Federal Intelligence and Security Agency

Bruxelles, le 2 juillet 2018
Brussel, 2 juli 2018
Brussels, the 2th July 2018

Op basis van belangrijke informatie van de Veiligheid van de Staat werd er door het federaal parket een terrorisme onderzoek geopend.

In het kader van dat onderzoek werden Amir S., geboren op 26 april 1980 en zijn echtgenote Nasimeh N, geboren op 20 september 1984, beiden met de Belgische nationaliteit maar van Iraanse origine, vandaag onder aanhoudingsmandaat geplaatst door een in terrorisme gespecialiseerde onderzoeksrechter van Antwerpen.

Zij werden inverdenkinggesteld van poging tot terroristische moord en het voorbereiden van een terroristisch misdrijf.

Beiden worden er van verdacht om op zaterdag 30 juni 2018 een bomaanslag te hebben willen plegen te Villepinte (Frankrijk) op een conferentie die daar werd gehouden door het MEK, les Moudjahidines du Peuple Iranien.

Page 1

Deze organisatie is een Iraanse oppositiepartij die reeds werd opgericht in 1965 en in 1981 buiten de wet werd gesteld door de Iraanse regering.

Op deze conferentie waren ongeveer 25.000 personen aanwezig.

Het aangehouden koppel werd, aan boord van hun voertuig Mercedes, onderschept door de speciale eenheden van de politie te Sint-Pieters-Woluwe.

Bij de doorzoeking van dat voertuig werd ongeveer 500 gram TATP en een ontstekingsmechanisme aangetroffen in een kleine toilettas.

Deze springstof werd gecontroleerd tot ontploffing gebracht door DOVO.

De federale gerechtelijke politie van Antwerpen heeft zaterdag, op vraag van de onderzoeksrechter, vijf huiszoekingen uitgevoerd, respectievelijk te Wilrijk, Boom, Ukkel, Bergen en Leuze-en-Hainaut.

Over de resultaten van deze huiszoekingen kan voorlopig niets medegedeeld worden.

Tegelijkertijd werd er te Frankrijk een vermoedelijke medeplichtige, Merhad A, geboren op 31 juli 1963, van zijn vrijheid beroofd. Twee andere personen werden in Frankrijk na verhoor vrijgelaten.

In Duitsland werd eveneens een contactpersoon van het koppel, Assadollah A., geboren op 22 december 1971, van Iraanse nationaliteit aangehouden. Het betreft een Iraans diplomaat bij de Oostenrijkse ambassade in Wenen.

Deze operatie kon enkel lukken door de informatiepositie die de Veiligheid van de Staat (VSSE) in dit dossier heeft opgebouwd. De VSSE heeft op korte termijn essentiële informatie verzameld, geëxploiteerd en verrijkt mede door een uitstekende uitwisseling met buitenlandse inlichtingendiensten. Dankzij de samenwerking tussen het Federaal Parket, de Veiligheid van de Staat, de Federale Gerechtelijke Politie van Antwerpen, DOVO en de Franse (DGSI) en Duitse gerechtelijke autoriteiten kon een terroristische aanslag vermeden worden.

Het federaal parket wenst te benadrukken dat uit de voorlopige stand van het onderzoek blijkt dat er op geen enkel moment een rechtstreekse dreiging naar België was.

Verder wordt er in het belang van het lopend onderzoek geen informatie ter zake meer verspreid.

****

Le parquet fédéral a ouvert une enquête de terrorisme sur la base d'informations importantes de la Sûreté de l'État.

Dans le cadre de cette enquête, Amir S., né le 26 avril 1980, et son épouse Nasimeh N., née le 20 septembre 1984, tous deux de nationalité belge mais d'origine iranienne, ont été placés aujourd'hui sous mandat d'arrêt par un juge d'instruction d'Anvers spécialisé en terrorisme.

Ils ont été inculpés de tentative d'assassinat terroriste et de préparation d'une infraction terroriste.

Tous deux sont suspectés d'avoir voulu commettre un attentat à la bombe le samedi 30 juin 2018 à Villepinte (France), lors d'une conférence qui y était organisée par les Moudjahidines du Peuple Iranien (MEK).

Cette organisation est un parti d'opposition iranien qui a été fondé en 1965 et qui a été interdit par le gouvernement iranien en 1981.

Quelque 25.000 personnes étaient présentes à cette conférence.

Le couple interpellé a été intercepté à bord de son véhicule Mercedes par les unités spéciales de la police de Woluwe-Saint-Pierre.

Lors de la fouille de ce véhicule, environ 500 grammes de TATP et un mécanisme de mise à feu ont été découverts dans une petite trousse de toilette.

Le SEDEE a fait sauter cet explosif de manière contrôlée.

La police judiciaire fédérale d'Anvers a exécuté samedi cinq perquisitions à la demande du juge d'instruction, respectivement à Wilrijk, Boom, Uccle, Mons et Leuze-en-Hainaut.

Rien ne peut actuellement être communiqué quant aux résultats de ces perquisitions.

Dans le même temps, un complice présumé, Merhad A., né le 31 juillet 1963, a été privé de liberté en France. Deux autres personnes en France ont été remises en liberté après audition.

Un contact du couple, Assadollah A., né le 22 décembre 1971, de nationalité iranienne, a également été interpellé en Allemagne. Il s'agit d'un diplomate iranien auprès de l'ambassade autrichienne à Vienne.

Cette opération n'a pu être menée que grâce aux informations que la Sûreté de l'État (VSSE) a collectées dans ce dossier. La VSSE a recueilli, exploité et enrichi des informations essentielles en très peu de temps, grâce notamment à un excellent échange d'informations avec des services de renseignements étrangers. Un attentat terroriste a pu être déjoué grâce à la coopération entre le parquet fédéral, la Sûreté de l'État, la police judiciaire fédérale d'Anvers, le SEDEE et les autorités judiciaires françaises (DGSI) et allemandes.

Le parquet fédéral tient à souligner qu'à ce stade de l'enquête, il n'y a eu à aucun moment une menace directe contre la Belgique.

Aucune autre information ne sera communiquée dans l'intérêt de l'enquête en cours.

****

On the basis of important information from the Belgian Federal Intelligence and Security Agency, a terrorism investigation was initiated by the Federal Public Prosecutor's Office.

Within the framework of this investigation, an arrest warrant was issued today for Amir S., born on 26 April 1980, and his wife Nasimeh N, born on 20 September 1984, both of Belgian nationality but of Iranian origin, by an Antwerp Investigating Judge specialized in terrorism.

They were charged with attempted terrorist murder and the preparation of a terrorist offence.

Both are suspected of wanting to commit a bomb attack in Villepinte (France) on Saturday 30 June 2018 at a conference held there by the MEK, *Les Moudjahidines du Peuple Iranien*.

This organisation is an Iranian opposition party that was founded in 1965 and outlawed by the Iranian Government in 1981.

Approximately 25,000 people attended the conference.

The arrested couple were intercepted, on board their Mercedes, by the special units of the police in Sint-Pieters-Woluwe.

During the search of that vehicle, approximately 500 grams of TATP and an ignition mechanism were found in a small toiletry bag.

DOVO conducted a controlled detonation of this explosive.

At the request of the Investigating Judge, the Antwerp Federal Judicial Police carried out five house searches on Saturday in Wilrijk, Boom, Ukkel, Mons and Leuze-en-Hainaut.

The results of these searches cannot be communicated for the time being.

At the same time, a suspected accomplice, Merhad A, born on 31 July 1963, was deprived of his liberty in France. Two other people were released in France after questioning.

A contact person of the couple, Assadollah A., born on 22 December 1971, of Iranian nationality, was also arrested in Germany. He is an Iranian diplomat at the Austrian Embassy in Vienna.

This operation was only possible because of the information position that the Belgian Federal Intelligence and Security Agency (VSSE) has built up in this file. In a short period of time, the VSSE has collected, exploited and enriched essential information, also thanks to an excellent exchange with foreign intelligence services. Cooperation between the Federal Public Prosecutor's Office, the VSSE, the Antwerp Federal Judicial Police, DOVO and the French (DGSI) and German judicial authorities has made it possible to prevent a terrorist attack.

The Federal Public Prosecutor wishes to emphasise that the provisional state of the investigation shows that there was at no time a direct threat to Belgium.

In the interest of the ongoing investigation, no further information will be given.

Appendix E

VSSE Letter on Assadi's Transporting Explosives from Tehran to Vienna on Passenger Plane

```
                              FEDERAAL PARKET
                              0 8 -09- 2020
   VSSE                       PARQUET FEDERAL      TRES URGENT
```

DATUM   07/09/2020
DIENST   Dienst analyse CI3A   Federaal Procureur
ONZE REF. NA/2020/1166/CI3A/284/099/1   HEEL DRINGEND
UW REF.

Federale Politie – DJSOC/Terro

FGP Antwerpen (via DJSOC/Terro)

Onderwerp: CI IRAN - Assadolah (°22/12/1971): informatie betreffende de gebruikte explosieven in de zaak Villepinte

Geachte Heren,

Onze dienst heeft de volgende informatie kunnen verzamelen in verband met de betrokkenheid van ASADI Assadolah (°22/12/1971) in de verijdelde aanval op de jaarlijkse bijeenkomst van de Iraanse Oppositiepartij - Volksmoejahedien (WIPO) in Villepinte in Frankrijk op 30/06/2018

- BEGIN –
De Iraanse inlichtingenofficier Assadolah ASADI nam het explosieve materiaal voor de aanslag mee op een commerciële vlucht van Iran naar Oostenrijk. Twee dagen voor de aanvalspoging overhandigde ASADI het explosief aan Amir SAADOUNI en Nasimeh NAAMI.
- EINDE –

Met de meeste hoogachting,

[handgeschreven handtekening]

Algemeen directeur

1/1
Staatsveiligheid – Koning Albert II laan, 6 – 1000 Brussel
Tel.: 02 205 62 11 – Fax: 02 201 57 72

.be

« Vertaling conform en ne varietur van het Frans naar het Nederlands, gedaan te Huppaye op 11/09/2020 door de beëdigde vertaalster-tolk Rosario Nunez, ingeschreven in het nationaal register der vertalers-tolken en beëdigd bij de Rechtbank van Eerste Aanleg van en te Brussel, onder het nummer ID 825595 – VTI 2031542 »
Ik zweer dat ik mijn taak naar eer en geweten nauwgezet en eerlijk heb vervuld.
FD35.97.19/18 – 18RF666   Pagina 1 / 1

Appendix F

Last exchanged SMS Messages Between the Terrorist Cell

Bijlage 3 aan 530174/2018
dd. 30/12/2018

Index	69
Text	Salam daey
	Dag, oom
Storage	Device
Status	Sent
To	
Tel	+436602227681

Index	70
Text	Khobi ? Bazi nasb shod ?
	Alles is goed? Is de spel geinstalleerd?
Storage	Device
Status	Read
Time	29-06-2018 20:08:03 UTC+02:00 (Network)
Service Center	+320301120232050
From	
Tel	+436602227681

Index	71
Text	Are bazi nasb shod bordim sobhane yeshanbe top mizanim
	Ja , de spel is geinstalleerd , we zullen zondagmorgen balspelen.
Storage	Device
Status	Sent
To	
Tel	+436602227681

Index	72
Text	Be omide khodesh. Faghat man farda 11:30 va 20:00 game bazi mikonam shoma ham blaeid hambazi beshim. Hatman
	Met hoop, ik zal morgen 11:30 en 20:00 zal spelletjes spelen en jullie moeten ook komen zodat we kunnen samen spelen.

Ik zweer dat ik mijn opdracht in eer en geweten, nauwgezet en eerlijk heb vervuld.
Voor eensluidende vertaling van het Farsi naar de Nederlandse taal,
de beëdigde vertaler – tolk, Anif Pardes, Antwerpen 29 oktober 2018

Storage	Device
Status	Read
Time	29-06-2018 20:13:25 UTC+02:00 (Network)
Service Center	+320301120232050
From	
Tel	+436602227681

Index	73
Text	Hatman miaim pansion bazi mikonim
	We zullen zeker komen om Pansion te spelen.
Storage	Device
Status	Sent
To	
Tel	+436602227681

Index	74
Text	Ok khodahafaz
	Oké, God zij met u.
Storage	Device
Status	Read
Time	29-06-2018 20:16:45 UTC+02:00 (Network)
Service Center	+320301120232050
From	
Tel	+436602227681

Index	75
Text	Age ps nasb nashod bagardim khone zaker ya berim bara sobhane?
	Indien ps = (vermoedelijk Playstation) niet geinstalleerd is dan keren we terug naar het huis van Zaker of we gaan voor het ontbijt?
Storage	Device
Status	Sent

Ik zweer dat ik mijn opdracht in eer en geweten, nauwgezet en eerlijk heb vervuld.
Voor eensluidende vertaling van het Farsi naar de Nederlandse taal,
de beëdigde vertaler – tolk, Anif Pardes, Antwerpen 29 oktober 2018

Bijlage 3 aan 530174/2018
dd. 30/12/2018

1658

To	
Tel	00436602227681

Index	76
Text	Hamon 20 ke game bazi kardim malom mishe. Bye
	Als we 20 (vermoedelijk 20:00) spelletjes spelen dan zien we wel. Dag
Storage	Device
Status	Read
Time	29-06-2018 20:19:56 UTC+02:00 (Network)
Service Center	+320301120232050
From	
Tel	+436602227681

Index	77
Text	Bashe daey
	Is goed, oom.
Storage	Device
Status	Sent
To	
Tel	+436602227681

Index	78
Text	Agar nazareton hast bazi 20 ra jelotar bekeshim
	Als u eens bent we kunnen de spel van 20 verderzetten
Storage	Device
Status	Read
Time	29-06-2018 20:21:19 UTC+02:00 (Network)
Service Center	+320301120232050
From	
Tel	+436602227681

Ik zweer dat ik mijn opdracht in eer en geweten, nauwgezet en eerlijk heb vervuld.
Voor eensluidende vertaling van het Farsi naar de Nederlandse taal,
de beëdigde vertaler – tolk, Anif Pardes, Antwerpen 29 oktober 2018

Bijlage 3 aan 530174/2018
dd. 30/12/2018

Index	79
Text	Are behtare 17:30 behtare
	Ja is beter 17:30 beter.
Storage	Device
Status	Sent
To	
Tel	+436602227681

Index	80
Text	Ok hamon 17 30 kobe , tim shoma baramde mishe ishala bye
	Ok 17:30 is goed. Jullie tijd zal uitkomen , inshallah. Bye
Storage	Device
Status	Read
Time	29-06-2018 20:24:19 UTC+02:00 (Network)
Service Center	+320301120232050
From	
Tel	+436602227681

Index	81
Text	Ok fadat bye
	Oke , dank u. Bye
Storage	Device
Status	Sent
To	
Tel	+436602227681

Index	82
Text	Salam ps rah andakhtim mirim ke jamo bebarim daey
	Dag, de "ps" hebben we gegooid en we zullen hem vrijdag meenemen ,oom.
Storage	Device

Ik zweer dat ik mijn opdracht in eer en geweten, nauwgezet en eerlijk heb vervuld.
Voor eensluidende vertaling van het Farsi naar de Nederlandse taal,
de beëdigde vertaler – tolk, Anif Pardes, Antwerpen 29 oktober 2018

Bijlage 3 aan 530174/2018
dd. 30/12/2018

Status	Sent
To	
Tel	00436602227681

Index	83
Text	Daset dorost. Fish tv ham vasl shod ya na?
	...('Daset' = vreemde word) is goed. Is de tv-fiche geïnstalleerd of niet ?
Storage	Device
Status	Read
Time	30-06-2018 11:34:41 UTC+02:00 (Network)
Service Center	+320301120232050
From	
Tel	+436602227681

Index	84
Text	Are hamash jore
	Ja , alles is in orde.
Storage	Device
Status	Sent
To	
Tel	+436602227681

Index	85
Text	Afarin be shoma . Pansion ba khodet nabar , beza too doroshke bashe , man az sat 2 moratab miram nezafat ta 17:30
	Is zeer creatief van jullie. Je moet de Pansion niet mee nemen. Laat in ...(doroshke = vreemde woord) zijn , ik zal vanaf 2 uur regelmatig gaan schoonmaken tot 17:30.
Storage	Device
Status	Read
Time	30-06-2018 11:41:11 UTC+02:00 (Network)

Ik zweer dat ik mijn opdracht in eer en geweten, nauwgezet en eerlijk heb vervuld.
Voor eensluidende vertaling van het Farsi naar de Nederlandse taal,
de beëdigde vertaler – tolk, Anif Pardes, Antwerpen 29 oktober 2018

Bijlage 3 aan 530174/2018
dd. 30/12/2018

Service Center	+320301120232050
From	
Tel	+436602227681

Index	86
Text	Ok man atrafe 6 miaim pansio mohtaje doa
	Oke, ik zal rond 6 komen naar Pansio , nood van gebeden.
Storage	Device
Status	Sent
To	
Tel	+436602227681

Index	87
Text	Dast hagh be hamraton.
	De hand eer met jullie.
Storage	Device
Status	Read
Time	30-06-2018 11:44:30 UTC+02:00 (Network)
Service Center	+320301120232050
From	
Tel	+436602227681

Index	88
Text	Toye zamin bazi narid pansion . Bad az khoroj berid berid badan berid pansion
	In de speltuin jullie moeten niet gaan in Pansion. Na de uitgang gaan ,gaan naar de Pansion.
Storage	Device
Status	Read
Time	30-06-2018 13:06:40 UTC+02:00 (Network)
Service Center	+320301120232050
From	

Ik zweer dat ik mijn opdracht in eer en geweten, nauwgezet en eerlijk heb vervuld.
Voor eensluidende vertaling van het Farsi naar de Nederlandse taal,
de beëdigde vertaler – tolk, Anif Pardes, Antwerpen 29 oktober 2018

Appendix G

Assadi's Instructions on How to Use the Bomb and his Codebook

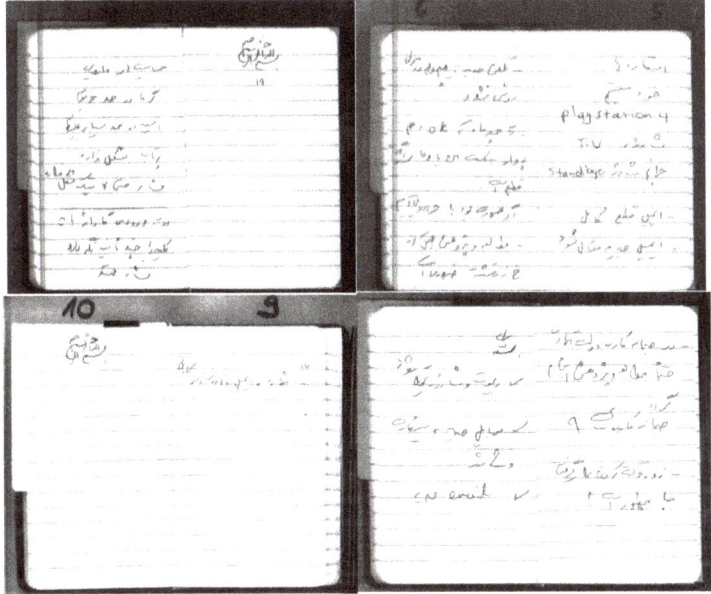

Appendix H

Assadi's Funds Transfer Receipts to his Terrorist Accomplices

```
BUNDESKRIMINALAMT
Asservat
Nr.: 0.47
Sachbearbeitende Org.-Einheit
ST 24
Aktenzeichen / Tagebuchnummer
ST 24-050006/18/GBA 3 BJs 28/18-1
Gegenstand  weiß, Papier
13 x DIN A5-Blätter mit
           arab. Schrift
Sichergestellt / Beschlagnahmt am
01.07.2018
in
Weibersbrunn/Aschaffenburg
Name des Beamten


Dienststelle des Beamten
KPI Unterfranken
Unterschrift
```

APPENDICES

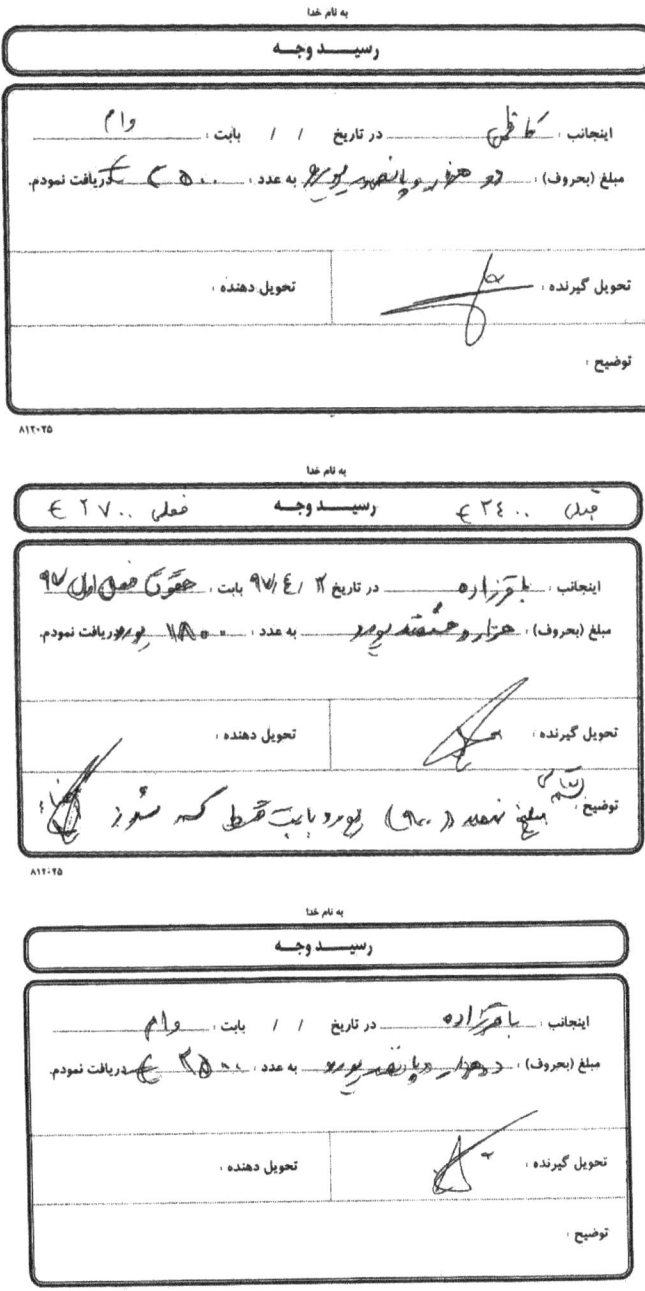

DIPLOMATIC TERRORISM

به نام خدا

رسید وجه

اینجانب: باقرزاده .... در تاریخ / / .... بابت ۹۷
مبلغ (بحروف): .... به عدد: ۵۰۰۰ .... دریافت نمودم.

تحویل گیرنده:
تحویل دهنده:

توضیح:

به نام خدا

رسید وجه

اینجانب: .... در تاریخ / / .... بابت: ....
مبلغ (بحروف): .... به عدد: .... دریافت نمودم.

تحویل گیرنده:
تحویل دهنده:

توضیح:

به نام خدا

رسید وجه

اینجانب: .... در تاریخ / / .... بابت: هزینه های مأموریت فصل ۹۷
مبلغ (بحروف): .... به عدد: .... دریافت نمودم.

تحویل گیرنده:
تحویل دهنده:

توضیح: ۸۰۰ تردد
+ ۳۰۰€ اقامت صفرف [ف اول ۹۷]
+ ۱۹۰۰€ مانده قبل [قرار دارم بردم]
۹۰۰€ مانده قبل

جمع مانده: ۲۰۰۰ €

AZ: GBA 3BJs 18/18-1 - St24 050006/18

Asservat Nr.: 0.47

Blatt1 1:
Im Namen Gottes
früherer (Betrag) 3000,00 EUR
Quittung bzw. Empfangsbestätigung
Jetziger (Betrag) 3300,00 EUR

Ich **Kazemi** (habe) am 03.04.97 (iranischer Zeitrechnung) (24.06.2018) wegen des Gehaltes des ersten Abschnitts (Quartals) des Jahres 97 (2018) den Betrag in Worten zweitausendvierhundert in Zahlen 2.400,00 EUR erhalten.
Empfänger: Unterschrift

Handschriftliche Fußnote;
Im Namen Gottes,
Erklärung: Der Betrag in Höhe von 900,00 EUR wurde wegen der Verbindlichkeitsrate abgezogen.
Unterschrift

Blatt 2:
Im Namen Gottes
Quittung bzw. Empfangsbestätigung

Ich Kazemi (habe) wegen der Schulden (Verbindlichkeiten) den Betrag in Worten zweitausendfünfhundert in Zahlen 2.500,00 EUR erhalten.
Empfänger: Unterschrift

Blatt 3:

Im Namen Gottes
Quittung bzw. Empfangsbestätigung

Ich Kazemi (habe) am 02.04.97 (iranischer Zeitrechnung) (24.06.2018) wegen der Kosten (Aufwand) des ersten Abschnitts (Quartals) des Jahres 97 (2018) den Betrag in Worten fünftausend in Zahlen 5.000,00 EUR erhalten.
Empfänger: Unterschrift

Blatt 4:
Im Namen Gottes
früherer (Betrag) 2.400,00 EUR
Quittung bzw. Empfangsbestätigung
Jetziger (Betrag) 2.700,00 EUR

AdÜ: Anmerkung des Übersetzers

AZ: GBA 3BJs 18/18-1 - St24 050006/18

Ich **Bagherzadeh** (habe) am 02.oder 12. 04.97 (iranischer Zeitrechnung) (23.06. oder 03.07.2018) wegen des Gehaltes des ersten Abschnitts (Quartals) des Jahres 97 (2018) den Betrag in Worten eintausend und achthundert in Zahlen 1.800,00 EUR erhalten.
Empfänger: Unterschrift

Handschriftliche Fußnote;
Im Namen Gottes,
Erklärung: Der Betrag in Höhe von 900,00 EUR wurde wegen der Verbindlichkeitsrate abgezogen.
Unterschrift

Blatt 5:
Im Namen Gottes
Quittung bzw. Empfangsbestätigung

Ich **Bagherzadeh** (habe) wegen der Kosten (Aufwand) des ersten Abschnitts (Quartals) des Jahres 97 den Betrag in Worten fünftausend in Zahlen 5.000,00 EUR erhalten.
Empfänger: Unterschrift

Blatt 6:
Im Namen Gottes
Quittung bzw. Empfangsbestätigung

Ich **Bagherzadeh** (habe) wegen der Schulden (Verbindlichkeiten) den Betrag in Worten zweitausend und fünfhundert in Zahlen 2.500,00 EUR erhalten.
Empfänger: Unterschrift

Blatt1 7:
Im Namen Gottes
Quittung bzw. Empfangsbestätigung

Ich Nawid (habe) wegen der administrativen Kosten (Aufwand) des ersten Abschnitts (Quartals) des Jahres 97 (2018) den Betrag in Worten eintausend und sechshundert in Zahlen 1.600,00 EUR erhalten.
Empfänger: Unterschrift fehlt (AdÜ)

Handschriftliche Fußnote;
Im Namen Gottes,
Erklärung:
+ 200,00 EUR Besuch
+ 300,00 EUR Gehaltserhöhung (erster 97)
+1.1100,00 jetzige bzw. aktuelle Unterstützung (ich hatte versprochen)
Summe: 1.600,00 EUR.
___,00 frühere Unterstützung bzw. Hilfe
___me der Hilfen: 2.000,00 EUR
AdÜ: Anmerkung des Übersetzers

118

AZ: GBA 3BJs 18/18-1 - St24 050006/18

Blatt1 8
Im Namen Gottes
Quittung bzw. Empfangsbestätigung

Ich Nawid habe einen Laptop erhalten.
Empfänger: Unterschrift fehlt (AdÜ)

Für die Richtigkeit

Meckenheim, 01.08.2018   Dr. A. Karim Wasiri

AdÜ: Anmerkung des Übersetzers

Appendix I

Judgement of Belgium Court of Cassation (Supreme Court)

First and Last Page

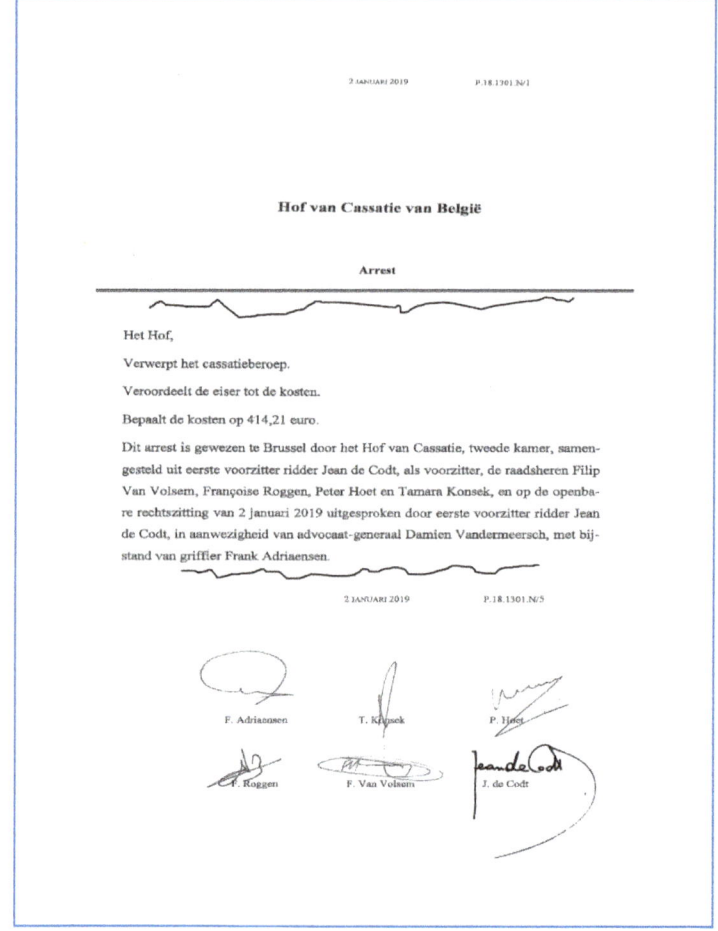

Appendix J

Judgement of Belgium Tribunal of First Instance

First and Last Page

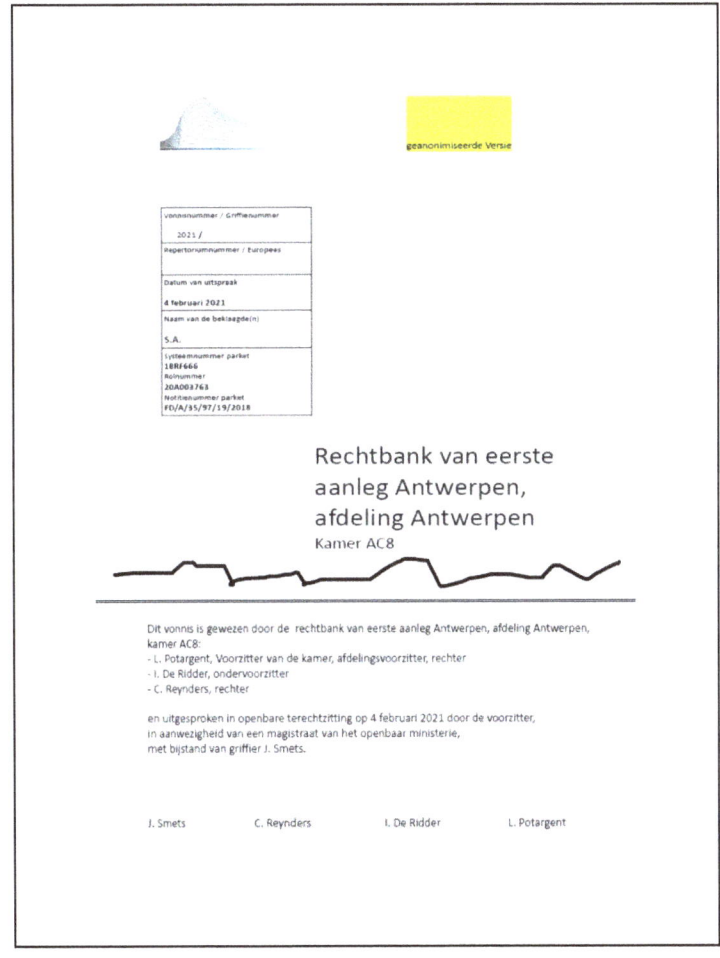

Appendix K

Judgement of Belgium Court of Appeals

First and Last Page

Kopie
Afgeleverd aan: mr. VANREUSEL Rik
Vrij van griffierecht - art. 280,2° W.Reg.

Aroodnummer
C / / 2022

Repertoriumnummer
2022 /

Datum van uitspraak
10 mei 2022

Rolnummer
2021/FP/4
BANDOUM Asto

Notitienummer parket-generaal
FD35.97.19-1B

☐ Meedegedeeld aan de ontvanger

Hof van beroep
Antwerpen

Arrest

kamer C2
correctionele zaken

Dit arrest is gewezen te Antwerpen door het hof van beroep, kamer C2, samengesteld uit:
mevrouw J. DE SLOOVERE   Raadsheer, dd. Voorzitter,
de heer Chr. NYS   Raadsheer,
mevrouw V. FONTAINE   Raadsheer,

en op de openbare terechtzitting van **woensdag 10 mei 2022**
uitgesproken door mevrouw J. DE SLOOVERE, Voorzitter,
in aanwezigheid van het lid van het Openbaar Ministerie zoals vermeld in het proces-verbaal van de terechtzitting,
met bijstand van mevrouw Yevgenia PSCHENITCHNA, griffier.

Y. PSCHENITCHNA   V. FONTAINE

Chr. NYS   J. DE SLOOVERE

Appendix L

General Public Prosecutor's Office in Bamberg, Germany
Extradition Permission for Assadollah Assadi

Ausfertigung

Generalstaatsanwaltschaft
Bamberg

230 Ausl A 118/18   01. Oktober 2018

Auslieferung des iranischen Staatsangehörigen Assadollah Assadi, geb. 22.12.1971 in Khorramabad/Iran, derzeit JVA Würzburg, zuletzt wohnhaft Kirchmergasse 5, Wien/Österreich

aus der Bundesrepublik Deutschland an das Königreich Belgien zur Strafverfolgung wegen versuchten terroristischen Mordes und Vorbereitung eines Attentats

Auslieferungsbewilligung:

Die Auslieferung des iranischen Staatsangehörigen Assadollah Assadi, geb. 22.12.1971 in Khorramabad/Iran, aus Deutschland an das Königreich Belgien zum Zwecke der Strafverfolgung wegen der im Europäischen Haftbefehl des Gerichts Erster Instanz Antwerpen vom 30.06.2018, Az. 2018/102, Notiz-Nummer AN35.97.19.18, bezeichneten Straftat des versuchten terroristischen Mordes und der Vorbereitung eines Attentats wird bewilligt.

Auf die Beachtung des Grundsatzes der Spezialität wird nicht verzichtet, weil auch der Verfolgte hierauf nicht verzichtet hat.

Der Verfolgte befand sich für das Auslieferungsverfahren vom 01.07.2018 bis 09.07.2018 in Haft. Im Übrigen bestand ein Untersuchungshaftbefehl des Bundesgerichtshof wegen des in der Bundesrepublik Deutschland gegen den Verfolgten geführten Verfahrens.

gez. Dr. Rosenbusch
Oberstaatsanwalt

Für den Gleichlaut der Ausfertigung
mit der Urschrift

Bamberg, 02. Oktober 2018
Die Urkundsbeamtin der Geschäftsstelle
der Generalstaatsanwaltschaft Bamberg

Schmitt
Justizangestellte

Appendix M

Assadollah Assadi Confirmed as Member of MOIS Unit 312

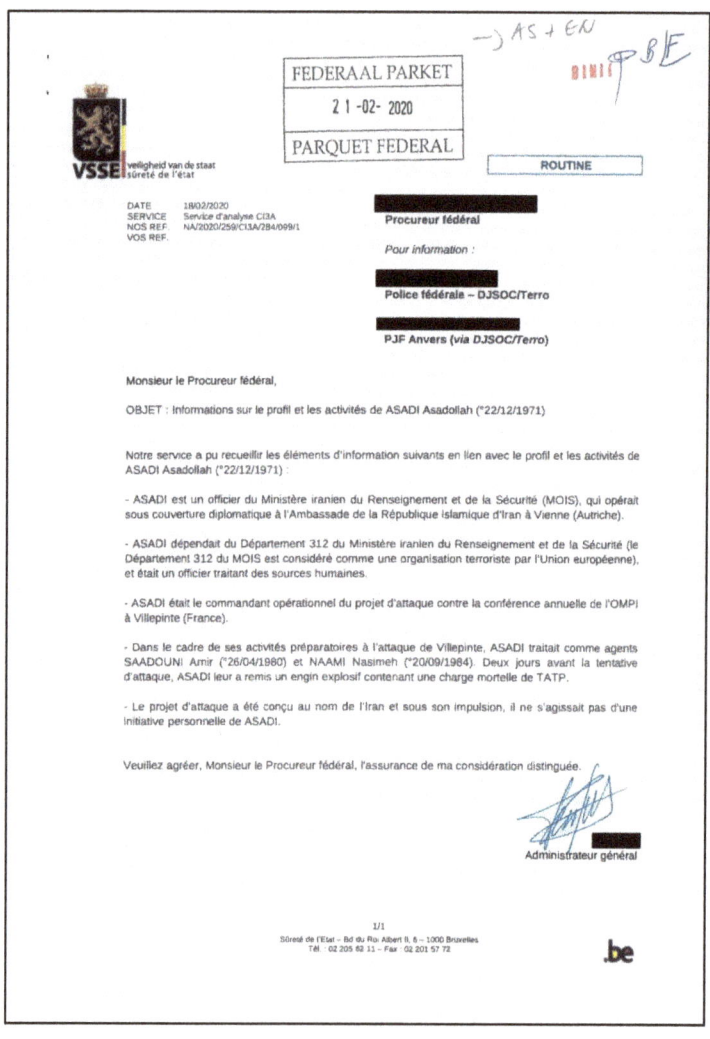

Appendix N

List of Iran Regime Officials Meeting with Assadi in Prison

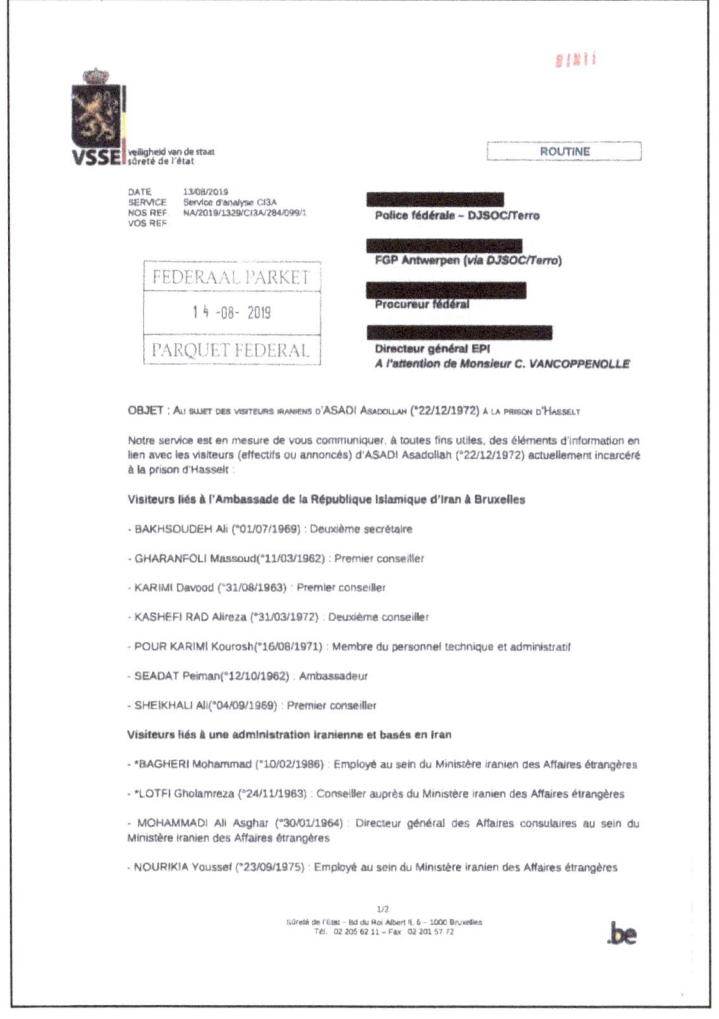

DATE : 12/09/2019
REF : NAJ2019/1329/C/SA/2394/099/3

- *SHAHROKHIAN Mojtaba (°19/04/1978) : Conseiller

Concernant les individus mentionnés ci-dessus et dont le nom est précédé d'un astérisque (*), notre service ne peut pas confirmer formellement la fonction annoncée de ces visiteurs, en l'absence d'informations propres complémentaires.

Autres visiteurs

- RAHNAMA Mohsen (°06/07/1964) : Médecin d'origine iranienne basé en Belgique

- RAZAVI FAR(D) Behzad (°10/06/1972) : Avocat d'origine iranienne basé en France

Veuillez agréer, messieurs, l'assurance de ma considération distinguée.

Administrateur général

Sûreté de l'Etat – Bd du Roi Albert II, 6 – 1000 Bruxelles
Tél. 02 205 62 11 – Fax : 02 205 57 72

Appendix O

Assadollah Assadi Promises Gift for Completed Bombing Job

Part of WhatsApp chat conversations between Amir Saadouni and Negar in Iran. This is the evening chat on June 28, 2018, and just after the Naami-Saadouni couple met Assadollah Assadi in Luxembourg, who handed them the bomb. In this chat, Saadouni quotes Assadi: "If you send everyone away, I will set a date for you on Sunday, the day after the wedding day in Ali's country. He will give us gifts... He said that if it was done inside, he would go himself to his old man... He said, "I will appeal to him to mention you in his speech." To clarify, Assadi told him that if they could detonate the explosives in a way to kill a considerable number in the hall, he would set an appointment with them in Germany the day after the incident on Sunday and give them gifts. Saadouni continues that Assadi told him that if the explosion took place inside the Villepinte rally hall, Assadi would go to his own leader (Khamenei) and ask him to talk about Naami and Saadouni in his speech.

Bijlage 1 aan 500064/2019
dd. 02/01/2019

Status: Sent
Platform: Mobile

28-06-2018 17:48:21(UTC+0)Direction:Outgoing, 32483609877@s.whatsapp.net (Amir)

اگه همه فروختن ، یکشنبه یعنی فردا روز عروسی تو کشور علی باهاتون قرار میزارم ، هدیه بهمون میده

Als jullie alles verkocht hebben, zondag, dus dag na de trouw zal ik in het land van Ali met jullie afspreken. Hij zal ons belonen

Status: Sent
Platform: Mobile

28-06-2018 17:47:12(UTC+0)Direction:Outgoing, 32483609877@s.whatsapp.net (Amir)

گفت اگه داخل انجام شد ، شخصا خودش میره پیش آقاش ... گفت از نطق همون واسه شما درخواست میکنم

Hij (of ze) zei als het binnen gebeurt, gaat hij zelf persoonlijk naar zijn meneer.

Hij (of zij) zei van zijn gesprekken zal ik voor jullie aanvragen. (*nota tolk: rare zin)

Status: Sent
Platform: Mobile

28-06-2018 17:48:05(UTC+0)Direction:Outgoing, 32483609877@s.whatsapp.net (Amir)

فقط خواستم بگم تصمیم نهایی تو بگو که ما چی کارکنیم ، بریم داخل یا بیرون

Ik wou gewoon vragen, zeg mij jouw finale beslissing wat we moeten doen. Gaan we naar binnen of buiten?

Status: Sent
Platform: Mobile

28-06-2018 17:48:51(UTC+0)Direction:Outgoing, 32483609877@s.whatsapp.net (Amir)

میدونم از کار امدی خسته ، من فردا راستی صبح زود ، ذاکر بیرخونه مادربزرگ ، عصرش باید ماشین یخچالدار بیا رم تحویل بدم

Ik weet dat je van je werk komt en moe bent. Ik moet morgenvroeg Zaker naar het huis van grootmoeder meedoen. 's Avonds moet ik de auto met geïntegreerde koelkast brengen en afgeven.

Status: Sent

Ik zweer dat ik mijn opdracht in eer en geweten, nauwgezet en eerlijk heb vervuld.
Voor eensluidende vertaling van het Farsi naar de Nederlandse taal,
de beëdigde vertaler – tolk, identiteit bij onze diensten gekend, Antwerpen 02 januari 2019

Appendix P

Statement by US Embassy in Belgium

https://be.usembassy.gov/extradition-of-iranian-official-asadollah-assadi-for-role-in-paris-terrorist-plot/

Extradition of Iranian Official Asadollah Assadi for Role in Paris Terrorist Plot

Home | News & Events | Extradition of Iranian Official Asadollah Assadi for Role in Paris Terrorist Plot

Press Statement
Michael R. Pompeo
Secretary of State
Washington, DC

October 10, 2018

Authorities in Germany announced yesterday the extradition of Asadollah Assadi, an Iranian official working under diplomatic cover, to Belgium for his role in the disrupted Iranian terrorist plot to bomb a political rally near Paris, France on June 30. The scale of this plot, which involved arrests of numerous suspects across Europe – including in Belgium, France, and Germany – reminds us that Iran remains the world's leading state sponsor of terrorism. This plot also lays bare Iran's continued support of terrorism throughout Europe. We support our European allies in exposing and countering the threat that Iranian-backed terrorism poses around the world. The United States will continue working with our partners and allies to confront the threat posed by the Iranian regime.

Appendix Q

US Congress, 115th Congress, H. RES. 1034

Introduced in House (07/26/2018)

115TH CONGRESS
2D SESSION

H. RES. 1034

Condemning Iranian state-sponsored terrorism and expressing support for the Iranian people's desire for a democratic, secular, and non-nuclear republic of Iran.

IN THE HOUSE OF REPRESENTATIVES

JULY 26, 2018

Mr. MCCLINTOCK (for himself, Mr. GOSAR, and Mr. POE of Texas) submitted the following resolution; which was referred to the Committee on Foreign Affairs

---

RESOLUTION

Condemning Iranian state-sponsored terrorism and expressing support for the Iranian people's desire for a democratic, secular, and non-nuclear republic of Iran.

> Whereas, on July 2, 2018, the Belgium Federal Prosecutor's Office announced the foiling of a terrorist plot against the "Free Iran 2018 – the Alternative" gathering held on June 30, 2018, in support of the Iranian people's quest for freedom;
>
> Whereas the Free Iran gathering had commenced to show support for the Iranian opposition leader Mrs. Maryam Rajavi's 10-point plan for future Iran, that calls for universal right to vote, free elections, and advocates gender, religious and ethnic equality, and adheres to a market economy;
>
> Whereas the plan calls for establishment of a republic in Iran based on separation of religion and state and envisions a non-nuclear Iran;
>
> Whereas the plan commits to the abolition of Sharia Law, practiced by the Iranian regime, and a foreign policy based on peaceful coexistence and international and regional peace and cooperation, as well as respect for the United Nations Charter;

Whereas senior governmental, military, and public security officials in Iran have for decades ordered or committed egregious human rights violations and acts of terror;

Whereas a senior Iranian diplomat based in the Iranian embassy in Vienna, Austria, was also arrested in connection with the planned terror plot while in Germany;

Whereas the Iranian diplomat has been charged in Belgium in connection with the terrorist plot and in Germany with "activity as a foreign agent and conspiracy to commit murder";

Whereas a senior Department of State official said on July 10, 2018, that "Iran uses embassies as cover to plot terrorist attacks.", and that "The most recent example is the plot that the Belgians foiled, and we had an Iranian diplomat out of the Austrian embassy as part of the plot to bomb a meeting of Iranian opposition leaders in Paris.";

Whereas the Department of State official has urged "all nations to be vigilant about Iran using embassies as diplomatic cover to plot terrorist attacks";

Whereas Secretary of State Mike Pompeo expressed concern about Iran's use of its embassies to plan terrorist activities in Europe, including the "plot to bomb an Iranian opposition group rally in France on June 30, 2018";

Whereas several prominent former United States Government officials, three retired United States generals, congressional staff, and thousands of United States citizens participated at this gathering, and

Whereas a large bipartisan group of Members of Congress supported H.R. 4744, and have expressed support for "efforts made by the people of Iran to promote the establishment of basic freedoms that build the foundation for the emergence of a freely elected, open, non-corrupt and democratic political system": Now, therefore, be it

Resolved, That the House of Representatives —

(1) condemns past and present Iranian state-sponsored terrorist attacks against United States citizens, United States officials, and Iranian dissidents;

(2) condemns the Iranian regime's terror plot against United States citizens and other participants of the "Free Iran 2018 – the Alternative" gathering in Paris;

(3) calls on relevant United States Government agencies to work with European allies to identify and bring to justice the Iranian officials behind this plot;

(4) stands with the people of Iran who are engaged in continuing, legitimate, and peaceful protests against an oppressive, corrupt regime; and

(5) recognizes the rights of the Iranian people and their struggle to establish a democratic, secular, and non-nuclear republic of Iran.

Appendix R

US Congress, 117th Congress (2021-2022), H. RES. 118

IV

117TH CONGRESS
1ST SESSION
H. RES. 118

Expressing support for the Iranian people's desire for a democratic, secular, and nonnuclear Republic of Iran and condemning violations of human rights and state-sponsored terrorism by the Iranian Government.

IN THE HOUSE OF REPRESENTATIVES

FEBRUARY 11, 2021

Mr. MCCLINTOCK (for himself, Mr. SHERMAN, Mr. WEBSTER of Florida, Mr. FITZPATRICK, Mr. LOUDERMILK, Mr. BABIN, Mr. CRENSHAW, Mr. BILIRAKIS, Mr. NORMAN, Mr. FLEISCHMANN, Mr. HICE of Georgia, Mr. GAETZ, Mr. GROTHMAN, Mr. MAST, Mr. MEUSER, Mr. GRIFFITH, Mr. COHEN, Mr. BACON, Mr. RUIZ, Ms. CRAIG, Mr. PETERS, Mr. LAMALFA, Ms. CHU, Mr. PERRY, Mr. LUETKEMEYER, Mrs. WAGNER, Mr. CALVERT, Mr. GREEN of Tennessee, Ms. BROWNLEY, Ms. STEFANIK, Mr. AGUILAR, Mr. BRIGGS, Mr. CARTWRIGHT, Miss RICE of New York, Mrs. WALORSKI, Mrs. LESKO, Mr. BUDD, Mr. WALTZ, Mr. BURCHETT, Mr. COURTNEY, Mr. WOMACK, Mr. STANTON, Ms. GRANGER, Mr. LAMBORN, Mr. STAUBER, Mr. ZELDIN, Mr. HARDER of California, Mr. ALLEN, Mr. BERA, Mr. PAYNE, Mr. CLOUD, Mr. WENSTRUP, Mr. JOHNSON of Louisiana, Mrs. NAPOLITANO, Ms. JACKSON LEE, Mr. BUCSHON, Mr. ROUZER, Mr. TIMMONS, Mr. STEUBE, Mr. RUTHERFORD, Mr. BURGESS, Mr. WEBER of Texas, Mr. BRADY, Mr. HUDSON, Mr. LATTA, Mr. ROGERS of Kentucky, Mrs. MCBATH, Miss GONZÁLEZ-COLÓN, Mr. VICENTE GONZALEZ of Texas, Mr. LAHOOD, Mr. FERGUSON, Mr. ESTES, Mrs. RODGERS of Washington, Mr. KATKO, Mr. CLINE, Mr. KELLER, Mr. DIAZ-BALART, Mr. GUTHRIE, Mrs. FLETCHER, Mrs. MILLER of West Virginia, Mr. ADERHOLT, Mr. CRAWFORD, Mr. WILSON of South Carolina, Mr. SMITH of Missouri, Ms. MALLIOTAKIS, Mr. GONZALEZ of Ohio, Mr. YOUNG, Mr. GUEST, Mr. BARR, Mr. GOODEN of Texas, Mr. TAYLOR, Mr. LARSON of Connecticut, Mr. COSTA, Mr. DESJARLAIS, Mr. AUSTIN SCOTT of Georgia, Mr. SCHWEIKERT, Mr. MOORE of Alabama, Ms. WILSON of Florida, Mrs. HARTZLER, Mr. EMMER, Mr. FULCHER, Mr. MOOLENAAR, Mr. NEHLS, Mr. JOHNSON of Ohio, Mr. WESTERMAN, Mr. HAGEDORN, Mr. ALLRED, Mr. HILL, Mr. HUIZENGA, Mr. PHILLIPS, Mr. NEWHOUSE, Mr. BROOKS, and Mr. AMODEI) submitted the following resolution; which was referred to the Committee on Foreign Affairs

RESOLUTION

Expressing support for the Iranian people's desire for a democratic, secular, and nonnuclear Republic of Iran and condemning violations of human rights and state-sponsored terrorism by the Iranian Government.

Whereas beginning in 2017, and continuing for several months after protests erupted in more than 100 cities, the Iranian regime suppressed such protests with repressive forces that resulted in at least 25 deaths and 4,000 arrests, including decorated wrestling champion Navid Afkari, who was later executed in September 2020 amidst international outrage;

Whereas, on November 15, 2019, popular protests against the Iranian regime began and rapidly spread to at least 100 cities throughout the country, and reports indicate that Iranian security forces used lethal force and about 1,500 people were killed during less than two weeks of unrest, and thousands more were detained during these protests;

Whereas, in the 116th Congress, the House of Representatives passed House Resolution 752, "Supporting the rights of the people of Iran to free expression, condemning the Iranian regime for its crackdown on legitimate protests, and for other purposes.";

Whereas House Resolution 752 urges the Administration to work to convene emergency sessions of the United Nations Security Council and to work with United States partners and allies to condemn the ongoing human rights violations perpetrated by the Iranian regime and establish a mechanism by which the United Nations Security Council can monitor such violations;

Whereas according to a September 2, 2020, Amnesty International report, detained protesters were subjected to "widespread torture including beatings, floggings, electric shocks, stress positions, mock executions, waterboarding, sexual violence, forced administration of chemical substances, and deprivation of medical care";

Whereas, from January 11 to 13, 2020, protesters gathered across Iran chanting against Iran's Supreme Leader Ali Khamenei and the Islamic Revolutionary Guard Corps after it shot down a Ukrainian passenger plane killing 176 civilians, and Iranian authorities deployed tear gas and live ammunition against the protesters;

Whereas the Iranian regime has routinely violated the human rights of Iranian citizens, including by implementing ongoing, systematic, and serious restrictions of freedom of peaceful assembly and association and freedom of opinion and expression, including the continuing closures of media outlets, arrests of journalists, and the censorship of expression in online forums such as blogs and websites;

Whereas the Iranian regime has killed or arrested more than 860 journalists since 1979;

Whereas the Iranian regime has lured three political activists to Iran's neighboring countries, where they were abducted and transferred to Iran, of which one, Ruhollah Zam, was executed on December 12, 2020;

Whereas the Iranian regime has arbitrarily and brutally suppressed ethnic minorities, including Iranian Kurds, Baluchis, and Arabs, as well as religious minorities such as Christians, Jews, Baha'is, Zoroastrians, and even

Sunni Muslims and deprived them of their basic human rights, and has in many cases executed them;

Whereas, in the 115th Congress, the House of Representatives passed H.R. 4744 calling on the United States to "condemn Iranian human rights abuses against dissidents, including the massacre in 1988 and the suppression of political demonstrations in 1999, 2009, and 2017, and pressure the Government of Iran to provide family members detailed information that they were denied about the final resting places of any missing victims of such abuses";

Whereas the killings were carried out on the orders of a judge, an official from the Ministry of Intelligence, and a state prosecutor, known to the prisoners as "Death Commissions", which were formed on July 19, 1988, and undertook proceedings in a manner designed to eliminate the regime's opponents;

Whereas Amnesty International described as a "momentous breakthrough" marking a "turning point" the September 3, 2020, communication by seven United Nations human rights experts, regarding information that "between July and September 1988, the Iranian authorities forcibly disappeared and extrajudicially executed thousands of imprisoned political dissidents affiliated with political opposition groups in 32 cities in secret and discarded their bodies, mostly in unmarked mass graves", as United Nations experts warned that "the situation may amount to crimes against humanity";

Whereas the United Nations calls on the international community to take action to investigate the cases through the establishment of an international investigation;

Whereas the United States should be involved in any establishment of an international investigation into the 1988 extrajudicial killings of Iranian dissidents;

Whereas senior Iranian Government, military, judicial, and security officials have for decades ordered or committed egregious human rights violations and acts of terror;

Whereas the Iranian people have been deprived of their fundamental freedoms for which reason they rejected monarchic dictatorship and are opposing religious tyranny;

Whereas, on June 30, 2018, tens of thousands of people gathered in Paris at the Free Iran gathering where they supported advocates for a democratic, secular, and nonnuclear Republic of Iran, and showed support for the opposition leader Mrs. Maryam Rajavi's 10-point plan for the future of Iran, which calls for the universal right to vote, free elections, and a market economy, and advocates gender, religious, and ethnic equality, a foreign policy based on peaceful coexistence, and a nonnuclear Iran;

Whereas, on July 2, 2018, the Belgian Federal Prosecutor's Office announced it had foiled a terrorist plot against the "Free Iran 2018–the Alternative" gathering held on June 30, 2018, in support of the Iranian people's struggle for freedom;

Whereas several prominent bipartisan former United States Government officials, several retired United States generals, congressional staff, and thousands of American citizens participated in that gathering;

Whereas Assadollah Assadi, a senior Iranian diplomat based in the Iranian Embassy in Vienna, Austria, was arrested in Germany in connection with the planned terror plot in Paris;

Whereas the Iranian diplomat has been charged in Belgium in connection with the Paris terror plot and in Germany with "activity as a foreign agent and conspiracy to commit murder";

Whereas, on February 4, 2021, a court in Belgium sentenced Iran's diplomat Assadollah Assadi to the maximum sentence of 20 years imprisonment for his role in planning to plant a bomb at the Free Iran gathering in 2018, and his 3 accomplices were given jail terms of 15 to 18 years and stripped of their Belgian citizenship;

Whereas Assadi took an Iranian-made bomb from Iran to Europe on a commercial flight, and delivered it to his accomplices with the aim of causing mass casualties at the Free Iran gathering in Paris in 2018;

Whereas the Belgium court found "that the four defendants are part of a larger terrorist group within a specific Iranian intelligence service. This appears from the sums of money paid to the defendants, the way information was gathered, the meetings in Iran, the use of diplomatic status, and the making and testing of the explosive device in Iran itself.";

Whereas, on July 10, 2018, a senior Department of State official said, "Iran uses embassies as cover to plot terrorist attacks", and that "The most recent example is the plot that the Belgians foiled, and we had an Iranian diplomat out of the Austrian Embassy as part of the plot to bomb a meeting of Iranian opposition leaders in Paris.";

Whereas, in January 2019, the European Union (EU) included the Internal Security Division of the Iranian Ministry of Intelligence and Security (MOIS), and two of its officials on the EU terror list in connection with the Paris bomb plot;

Whereas according to the Select Iran-Sponsored Operational Activity in Europe, released by the Department of State on July 5, 2018, "Two Iranian operatives were arrested on charges of terrorism by Albanian authorities", for a bomb plot against the March 2018 New Year gathering of thousands of Iranian opposition members in Tirana;

Whereas, in December 2018, the Government of Albania expelled Iran's Ambassador, Gholamhossein Mohammadnia, and MOIS station chief in Albania, Mostafa Roudaki, for planning terrorist activities against Iranian dissidents and members of the People's Mojahedin Organization of Iran (PMOI/MEK);

Whereas, in January 2020, the Government of Albania expelled two other Iranian diplomats also for planning terrorist activities against the MEK;

Whereas the expulsion of the Iranian Ambassador by the Government of Albania is a positive and important step, which sends the right message that no Iranian embassies should be used for plotting terror and conducting spying activities against dissidents;

Whereas Iran's malign activities in the Balkans, specifically its presence and activities in Albania, pose a serious threat to United States national security interests;

Whereas the Department of State has urged "all nations to be vigilant about Iran using embassies as diplomatic cover to plot terrorist attacks"; and

Whereas the United States Government arrested two Iranian nationals in August 2018 who had acted on behalf of the

8

MOIS to conduct covert surveillance in the United States against officials of the National Council of Resistance of Iran for a target package, which, according to the Department of Justice Federal complaint, may include "apprehension, recruitment, cyber exploitation, or capture/kill operations", and that they pleaded guilty and were sentenced to imprisonment: Now, therefore, be it

1 *Resolved*, That the House of Representatives—
2 (1) condemns past and present Iranian state-
3 sponsored terrorist attacks against United States
4 citizens and officials, as well as Iranian dissidents,
5 including the Iranian regime's terror plot against
6 the "Free Iran 2018–the Alternative" gathering in
7 Paris;
8 (2) calls on relevant United States Government
9 agencies to work with European allies, including
10 those in the Balkans where Iran has expanded its
11 presence, to hold Iran accountable for breaching dip-
12 lomatic privileges, and to call on nations to prevent
13 the malign activities of the Iranian regime's diplo-
14 matic missions, with the goal of closing them down,
15 including the Iranian Embassy in Albania;
16 (3) stands with the people of Iran who are con-
17 tinuing to hold legitimate and peaceful protests
18 against an oppressive and corrupt regime; and

9

1 (4) recognizes the rights of the Iranian people
2 and their struggle to establish a democratic, secular,
3 and nonnuclear Republic of Iran.

Appendix S

Press Release by Three French Ministers
French Minister of Interior, Minister of European Affairs, and Minister of Economy and Finances

Ministère de l'Intérieur
Ministère de l'Europe et des Affaires Etrangères
Ministère de l'Economie et des Finances

Le 2 octobre 2018

Communiqué de presse

Une tentative d'attentat a été déjouée à Villepinte le 30 juin dernier.

Cet acte d'une extrême gravité envisagé sur notre territoire ne pouvait rester sans réponse.

Par arrêté du 2 octobre 2018 du ministre d'Etat, ministre de l'Intérieur et du ministre de l'Economie et des Finances et sans préjudice des résultats de l'action pénale entreprise contre les initiateurs, les auteurs et les complices de ce projet d'attentat, la France a pris des mesures préventives ciblées et proportionnées sous la forme de l'adoption des mesures nationales de gels des avoirs de M. Assadollah Asadi et de M. Saeid Hashemi Moghadam, ressortissants iraniens, ainsi que de la Direction de la Sécurité intérieure du Ministère du Renseignement iranien.

En prenant cette décision, la France rappelle sa détermination à lutter contre le terrorisme, en particulier sur son propre territoire.

Pour Jean-Yves Le Drian, « l'attentat déjoué à Villepinte confirme la nécessité d'une approche exigeante dans nos relations avec l'Iran ».

Gérard Collomb réaffirme sa « détermination à tout mettre en œuvre pour prévenir toute forme de terrorisme, d'où qu'elle vienne ».

Bruno Le Maire souligne que « nous devons assécher les canaux de financement des terroristes afin de mettre fin à leurs actes intolérables. Nous agissons au niveau national avec fermeté et nous continuons à renforcer les dispositifs au niveau international ».

Service de presse de Gérard COLLOMB, ministre d'État, ministre de l'Intérieur
01 49 27 38 53 - sec1.pressecab@interieur.gouv.fr
Service de presse de Jean-Yves LE DRIAN, ministre de l'Europe et des Affaires Etrangères
01 43 17 57 93 - presse.cabinet@diplomatie.gouv.fr
Service de presse de Bruno LE MAIRE, ministre de l'Economie et des Finances
01 53 18 41 13 - presse.mineco@cabinets.finances.gouv.fr

TRANSLATION:

Press release

An attempted attack was foiled in Villepinte on June 30.

This extremely serious act envisaged on our territory could not remain unanswered.

By order of October 2, 2018 of the Minister of State, Minister of the Interior and the Minister of Economy and Finance and without prejudice to the results of the criminal action taken against the initiators, authors and accomplices of this project of the attack, France took targeted and proportionate preventive measures in the form of the adoption of national measures to freeze the assets of Mr. Assadollah Assadi and Mr. Saeid Hashemi Moghadam, Iranian nationals, as well as of the Directorate of Internal Security of the Iranian Ministry of Intelligence.

By taking this decision, France is reaffirming its determination to fight terrorism, in particular on its own territory.

For Jean-Yves Le Drian, "the foiled attack in Villepinte confirms the need for a demanding approach in our relations with Iran".

Gérard Collomb reaffirms his "determination to do everything possible to prevent all forms of terrorism, wherever it comes from".

Bruno Le Maire stresses that "we must dry up the terrorist financing channels in order to put an end to their intolerable acts. We are acting firmly at the national level and we continue to strengthen the mechanisms at the international level".

Appendix T
Belgian Official Gazette

BELGISCH STAATSBLAD — 24.12.2018 — MONITEUR BELGE 102207

Bijlage bij het koninklijk besluit van 19 december 2018 tot aanvulling van de lijst van personen en entiteiten bedoeld in artikelen 3 en 5 van het koninklijk besluit van 28 december 2006 inzake specifieke beperkende maatregelen tegen bepaalde personen en entiteiten met het oog op de strijd tegen de financiering van het terrorisme.

Lijst van de personen toe te voegen aan de lijst van personen en entiteiten bedoeld in artikelen 3 en 5 van het koninklijk besluit van 28 december 2006 inzake specifieke beperkende maatregelen tegen bepaalde personen en entiteiten met het oog op de strijd tegen de financiering van het terrorisme:

1. NAAMI NASIMEH (NRN 84.09.20-558.87)
2. SAADOUNI AMIR (NRN 80.04.26-403.40)
3. ABU HAMISA FAHED (NRN 91.08.11-455.18)
4. ASSADI ASSADOLLAH (geboren op 22/12/1971)

Gezien om gevoegd te worden bij Ons besluit van 19 december 2018 tot aanvulling van de lijst van personen en entiteiten bedoeld in artikelen 3 en 5 van het koninklijk besluit van 28 december 2006 inzake specifieke beperkende maatregelen tegen bepaalde personen en entiteiten met het oog op de strijd tegen de financiering van het terrorisme.

FILIP

Van Koningswege :
De Vice-Eerste Minister en Minister van Financiën,
A. DE CROO

Annexe à l'arrêté royal du 19 décembre 2018 complétant la liste des personnes et entités visée aux articles 3 et 5 de l'arrêté royal du 28 décembre 2006 relatif aux mesures restrictives spécifiques à l'encontre de certaines personnes et entités dans le cadre de la lutte contre le financement du terrorisme.

Liste des personnes à ajouter à la liste des personnes et entités visée aux articles 3 et 5 de l'arrêté royal du 28 décembre 2006 relatif aux mesures restrictives spécifiques à l'encontre de certaines personnes et entités dans le cadre de la lutte contre le financement du terrorisme.

1. NAAMI NASIMEH (NRN 84.09.20-558.87)
2. SAADOUNI AMIR (NRN 80.04.26-403.40)
3. ABU HAMISA FAHED (NRN 91.08.11-455.18)
4. ASSADI ASSADOLLAH (né le 22/12/1971)

Vu pour être annexé à Notre arrêté du 19 décembre 2018 complétant la liste des personnes et entités visée aux articles 3 et 5 de l'arrêté royal du 28 décembre 2006 relatif aux mesures restrictives spécifiques à l'encontre de certaines personnes et entités dans le cadre de la lutte contre le financement du terrorisme.

PHILIPPE

Par le Roi :
Le Vice-Premier Ministre et Ministre des Finances,
A. DE CROO

FEDERALE OVERHEIDSDIENST WERKGELEGENHEID, ARBEID EN SOCIAAL OVERLEG

[2018/205447]

12 DECEMBER 2018. — Koninklijk besluit waarbij algemeen verbindend wordt verklaard de collectieve arbeidsovereenkomst van 6 september 2018, gesloten in het Paritair Comité voor de bewakings- en/of toezichtsdiensten, betreffende de rechtsbijstand (1)

FILIP, Koning der Belgen,
Aan allen die nu zijn en hierna wezen zullen, Onze Groet.

Gelet op de wet van 5 december 1968 betreffende de collectieve arbeidsovereenkomsten en de paritaire comités, inzonderheid op artikel 28;

Gelet op het verzoek van het Paritair Comité voor de bewakings- en/of toezichtsdiensten;

Op de voordracht van de Minister van Werk,

Hebben Wij besloten en besluiten Wij :

Artikel 1. Algemeen verbindend wordt verklaard de als bijlage overgenomen collectieve arbeidsovereenkomst van 6 september 2018, gesloten in het Paritair Comité voor de bewakings- en/of toezichtsdiensten, betreffende de rechtsbijstand.

Art. 2. De minister bevoegd voor Werk is belast met de uitvoering van dit besluit.

Gegeven te Brussel, 12 december 2018.

FILIP

Van Koningswege :
De Minister van Werk,
K. PEETERS

Nota
(1) Verwijzing naar het *Belgisch Staatsblad* :
Wet van 5 december 1968, *Belgisch Staatsblad* van 15 januari 1969.

SERVICE PUBLIC FEDERAL EMPLOI, TRAVAIL ET CONCERTATION SOCIALE

[2018/205447]

12 DECEMBRE 2018. — Arrêté royal rendant obligatoire la convention collective de travail du 6 septembre 2018, conclue au sein de la Commission paritaire pour les services de gardiennage et/ou de surveillance, relative à la protection juridique (1)

PHILIPPE, Roi des Belges,
A tous, présents et à venir, Salut.

Vu la loi du 5 décembre 1968 sur les conventions collectives de travail et les commissions paritaires, notamment l'article 28;

Vu la demande de la Commission paritaire pour les services de gardiennage et/ou de surveillance;

Sur la proposition du Ministre de l'Emploi,

Nous avons arrêté et arrêtons :

Article 1er. Est rendue obligatoire la convention collective de travail du 6 septembre 2018, reprise en annexe, conclue au sein de la Commission paritaire pour les services de gardiennage et/ou de surveillance, relative à la protection juridique.

Art. 2. Le ministre qui a l'Emploi dans ses attributions est chargé de l'exécution du présent arrêté.

Donné à Bruxelles, le 12 décembre 2018.

PHILIPPE

Par le Roi :
Le Ministre de l'Emploi,
K. PEETERS

Note
(1) Référence au *Moniteur belge* :
Loi du 5 décembre 1968, *Moniteur belge* du 15 janvier 1969.

Appendix U

Terrorist List of the European Union

Official Journal of the European Union — 9.1.2019

ANNEX

List of persons, groups and entities referred to in Article 1

I. PERSONS

1. ABDOLLAHI Hamed (a.k.a. Mustafa Abdullahi), born 11.8.1960 in Iran. Passport number: D9004878.

2. AL-NASSER, Abdelkarim Hussein Mohamed, born in Al Ihsa (Saudi Arabia), citizen of Saudi Arabia.

3. AL YACOUB, Ibrahim Salih Mohammed, born 16.10.1966 in Tarut (Saudi Arabia), citizen of Saudi Arabia.

4. ARBABSIAR Manssor (a.k.a. Mansour Arbabsiar), born 6.3.1955 or 15.3.1955 in Iran. Iranian and US national. Passport number: C2002515 (Iran); Passport number: 477845448 (USA). National ID no.: 07442833, expiry date 15.3.2016 (USA driving licence).

5. ASADI Assadollah, born 22.12.1971 in Teheran (Iran), Iranian national. Iranian diplomatic passport number: D9016657.

6. BOUYERI, Mohammed (a.k.a. Abu ZUBAIR, a.k.a. SOBIAR, a.k.a. Abu ZOUBAIR), born 8.3.1978 in Amsterdam (The Netherlands).

7. EL HAJJ, Hassan Hassan, born 22.3.1988 in Zaghdraiya, Sidon, Lebanon, Canadian citizen. Passport number: JX446643 (Canada).

8. HASHEMI MOGHADAM Saeid, born 6.8.1962 in Teheran (Iran), Iranian national. Passport number: D9016290, valid until 4.2.2019.

9. IZZ-AL-DIN, Hasan (a.k.a. GARBAYA, Ahmed, a.k.a. SA-ID, a.k.a. SALWWAN, Samir), Lebanon, born in 1963 in Lebanon, citizen of Lebanon.

10. MELIAD, Farah, born 5.11.1980 in Sydney (Australia), Australian citizen. Passport number: M2719127 (Australia).

11. MOHAMMED, Khalid Shaikh (a.k.a. ALI, Salem, a.k.a. BIN KHALID, Fahd Bin Adballah, a.k.a. HENIN, Ashraf Refaat Nabith, a.k.a. WADJOOD, Khalid Adbul), born 14.4.1965 or 1.3.1964 in Pakistan, passport number 488555.

12. ŞANLI, Dalokay (a.k.a. Sinan), born 13.10.1976 in Pülümür (Turkey).

13. SHAHLAI Abdul Reza (a.k.a. Abdol Reza Shala'i, a.k.a. Abd-al Reza Shalai, a.k.a. Abdorreza Shahlai, a.k.a. Abdolreza Shahla'i, a.k.a. Abdul-Reza Shahlaee, a.k.a. Hajj Yusef, a.k.a. Haji Yusif, a.k.a. Hajji Yasir, a.k.a. Hajji Yusif, a.k.a. Yusuf Abu-al-Karkh), born circa 1957 in Iran. Addresses: (1) Kermanshah, Iran, (2) Mehran Military Base, Ilam Province, Iran.

14. SHAKURI Ali Gholam, born circa 1965 in Tehran, Iran.

15. SOLEIMANI Qasem (a.k.a. Ghasem Soleymani, a.k.a. Qasmi Sulayman, a.k.a. Qasem Soleymani, a.k.a. Qasem Solaimani, a.k.a. Qasem Salimani, a.k.a. Qasem Solemani, a.k.a. Qasem Sulaimani, a.k.a. Qasem Sulemani), born 11.3.1957 in Iran. Iranian national. Passport number: 008827 (Iran Diplomatic), issued 1999. Title: Major General.

II. GROUPS AND ENTITIES

1. 'Abu Nidal Organisation' — 'ANO' (a.k.a. 'Fatah Revolutionary Council', a.k.a. 'Arab Revolutionary Brigades', a.k.a. 'Black September', a.k.a. 'Revolutionary Organisation of Socialist Muslims').

2. 'Al-Aqsa Martyrs' Brigade'.

3. 'Al-Aqsa e.V.'.

4. 'Babbar Khalsa'.

5. 'Communist Party of the Philippines', including 'New People's Army' — 'NPA', Philippines.

6. 'Directorate for Internal Security of the Iranian Ministry for Intelligence and Security'.

7. 'Gama'a al-Islamiyya' (a.k.a. 'Al-Gama'a al-Islamiyya') ('Islamic Group' — 'IG').

Appendix V

Iranian Regime Assassination Attempt on Maryam Rajavi in June 1995

The New York Times

SUNDAY, JUNE 25, 1995

U.S. Asserts Iranians Plotted To Disrupt Rally in Germany

By ELAINE SCIOLINO

WASHINGTON, June 24 — Iranian diplomats working out of their embassy in Bonn plotted to disrupt a huge opposition rally in Germany last week, perhaps with the intention of assassinating a leading Iranian dissident, American intelligence officials said today.

At about the same time, Germany asked two Iranian intelligence officials to leave the country because of evidence that they were planning potentially lethal operations from German territory, the American officials said. The expulsions did not appear to be specifically linked to the plot.

German Foreign Ministry officials denied any knowledge of the plot or the expulsions, although they abruptly banned the opposition leader, Maryam Rajavi, from entering the country to address the rally.

But United States officials said they confirmed the incidents both with German officials and through independent American intelligence-gathering efforts in Germany.

The American disclosure of the incident in Bonn is likely to embarrass the German Government and may further divide the Clinton Administration and its allies in Europe and Asia about how to deal with Iran.

For the United States, evidence of an Iranian-inspired plot in Europe is just more proof that Iran is, as Washington claims, an "outlaw state" that spends hundreds of millions of dollars a year on terrorism and has embarked on a "crash" course to develop nuclear weapons. The evidence is certain to be seized on by the Administration to bolster its uncompromising though much-criticized campaign to undermine the Teheran Government through economic means.

Both American and German intelligence concluded last year that Iran is using its embassy in Bonn as an informal headquarters of the Iranian intelligence services in Europe, and as a base from which to watch its 100,000 citizens in Germany and to buy militarily useful technology and equipment.

The German determination to remain silent about the plot and expulsion underscores the vast difference in approach between the United States and Iran's major trading partners, which have refused to join the American economic embargo. They argue that the best means of changing Iran's behavior is to embrace it, rather than isolate it.

President Clinton acknowledged that difference in a news conference earlier this month when he said, "I don't know that we're on the same wave length" with the allies, adding, "the evidence is that constructive engagement with the Iranians has, at least so far, failed to produce any positive results."

Most of the allies would agree with the American case — despite official denials in Teheran — that Iran is positioning itself to become a nuclear power, building its arsenal of chemical weapons and ballistic missiles, undermining Middle East peace efforts, and supporting terrorist groups and acts worldwide.

But the Europeans and the Japanese contend that the United States, with its relentless name-calling and sweeping charges often without concrete proof, has tended to distort the Iranian threat for domestic political reasons, including a desire to neutralize an anti-Iranian Congress. There is also a strong perception abroad that the anti-Iranian stance of the United States reflects the increased influence of Israel in shaping American perceptions of Iran, at a time when Iran is strongly supporting terrorist groups determined to undermine Middle East peace talks.

Iran has done little to help the Europeans and Japanese justify their conciliatory approach, as shown most recently by Teheran's rejection on Thursday of an appeal from the 15 European Union nations to lift the death threat imposed against the novelist Salman Rushdie.

Early last week, when the German Government abruptly banned Mrs. Rajavi, the Iranian opposition leader, from entering Germany, officials explained that as the head of a movement determined to violently overthrow the Government of another country, she was not welcome.

But American intelligence officials concluded that there was another reason as well: the discovery by German intelligence that Iran's embassy in Bonn was assembling a team from the terrorist group the Party of God to violently disrupt the rally, and perhaps to assassinate Mrs. Rajavi.

Since Germany has led the Europeans in defending what it calls a "critical dialogue" with Teheran that is based on high-level exchanges and efforts to boost trade, it is not surprising that German authorities have kept quiet about the alleged plot, but have clung to the official line.

"We cannot allow cause for the violent overthrow of a government from our own territory," said Sabine Sparwasser, a Foreign Ministry spokesman in Bonn. Asked whether Germany has asked for the expulsion of two Iranian diplomats, she added, "To my knowledge there have been no recent cases where we told Iranians from the embassy to leave."

Officials in the office of Bernd Schmidbauer, the intelligence coordinator for Chancellor Helmut Kohl and the senior German official involved in contacts with Iran, declined comment on any matter involving Iran. It was Mr. Schmidbauer who infuriated the Clinton Administration after he allowed Ali Fallahian, the head of Iran's intelligence services, to visit Germany in 1993, and tour intelligence headquarters in Wiesbaden.

Of all the arguments the Administration has made against Iran, its case that Iran supports terrorism has been the most difficult to make. That is because American officials say they are reluctant to disclose information that could reveal intelligence sources and methods in gathering the information and thus compromise the operations involved.

Appendix X

Images and Figures

Figure 32 - Robabeh Assadi.

Figure 33 - Ali Assadi.

APPENDICES

Figure 34 – Assadi's eldest son, Hossein.

Figure 35- Assadollah Assadi's passport showing his position in Vienna as the "third counsellor"

Figure 36 - Saadouni Naami couple's car under police inspection following their arrest.

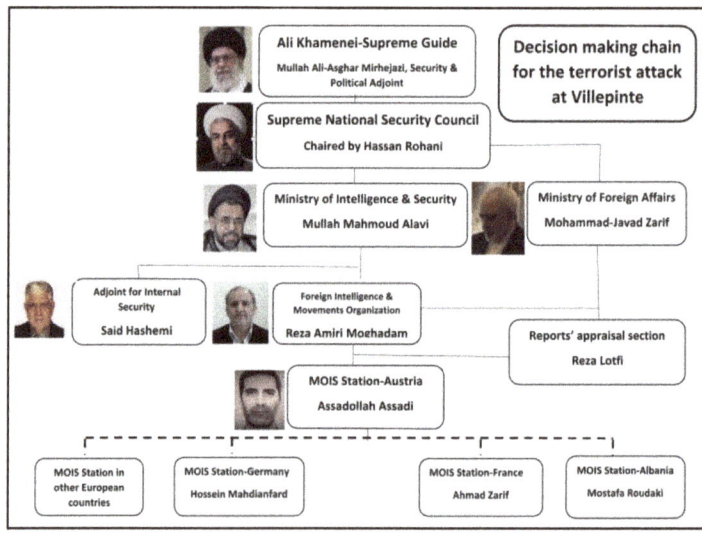

Figure 37 - Decision making chart.

ENDNOTES

[1] The NCRI, parliament of the Iranian Resistance, voted unanimously on August 28, 1993, to elect Maryam Rajavi as "president-elect for the transitional period" after the overthrow of the clerical regime. Within six months, a transitional government will hold popular elections for a constituent assembly and resign. The constituent assembly will appoint a new government and draw up the country's new constitution within a two-year period. Mrs. Rajavi's position as president of the country shall end after the new constitution is ratified and a new president is elected.

[2] Based on reliable information provided by Maryam Rajavi, a witness in the case.

[3] Goodenough, P. (2022, July 21). 'Pact With the Devil': Critics Slam Belgium-Iran Deal That Could See Terrorist Diplomat Sent Home | CNSNews. CNSNews. https://www.cnsnews.com/article/international/patrick-goodenough/pact-devil-critics-slam-belgium-iran-deal-could-see

[4] Ibid.

[5] The Iranian regime's Intelligence Ministry recruits and trains female agents in sexpionage, to lay a honey trap, luring vulnerable men via female intelligence agents. In MOIS lexicon, these trained female agents are dubbed "Swallows" (*parastoo*).

[6] On the news that the Iranian regime had made extensive efforts, particularly through diplomatic channels, to stop the Resistance gathering, French political figures supporting the

Resistance wrote a letter to President Emmanuel Macron demanding his outspoken opinion in defense of freedom of expression at the Iranian Resistance Conference in France. Just before the event, Macron's chief of staff responded formally to the letter, declaring that freedom of expression in France was guaranteed.

[7] The ruling was issued on May 10, 2022, by the Belgian Court of Appeals for three defendants, Mehrdad Arefani, Nasimeh Naami, Amir Saadouni. Assadollah Asadi refused to appeal.

[8] During initial interrogations, Amir Saadouni recounted some information about the terrorist plot, particularly the role of Asadollah Asadi. But he gradually tried to justify his own actions during subsequent interrogations. This was especially the case after he spoke privately in prison with Nasimeh Naami on July 18. That is, Naami outlined her narrative to him in this meeting. It is interesting that Saadouni tries a lot to say Naami is not an influential party in the plot!

[9] At his September 25, 2018 interrogation, Saadouni, for example, responded to the police by saying, "The game is installed," I mean, by packaging, the explosives I took from Daniel. His November 23, 2018 interrogation is specifically devoted to questioning about the codes used in the communications. Some of the questions in this case: Q: What is the exact meaning of "for 24 people, 12 euros per euro"? Q: What exactly does "number of 28 boxes of soaps " mean? A: 28 is the date and 14 euros means the hour. Q: Can you tell which meeting this is about? A: It was about the appointment in Luxembourg.Q: What is the order of "buy very luxurious potatoes"? A: Luxury means Luxembourg, potatoes meant nothing. I already knew where it was, Q: What is the exact

meaning of "for 24 people, 12 euros per euro"? Answer: 24 people means date, 12 euros means hours. By 24 people I mean in the next 24 months. Q: What exactly does "15 euros each" mean? A: In this way, we mean from 12 noon to 3 p.m. 15€ means hours and 28 is date.

[10] Mohsen is in the hierarchy of the Ministry of Intelligence above Assadollah Assadi, and generally Assadi checks sensitive and sometimes even regular matters with him. Usually, the money paid is all with Mohsen's approval. Sometimes relocation of Saadouni's workplace for several days also requires Mohsen's approval.

[11] The contents of this report are essentially taken from a Luxembourg police report that had Assadi and his accomplices under control and surveillance on the day Assadi met with his agents in Luxembourg, on June 28, 2018. The report was later written up on September 4, 2018. Document Specifications: DEEL 10 - E.O.B. - FRANKRIJK - LUXEMBURG - OOSTENRIJK - NEDERLAND - U.K. – ZWEDEN - 7EOB – LUXEMBURG - 2 - 40-84 - SCHRIJVEN LUXEMBURG + BIJLAGEN

[12] These remarks are quoted from pages 18 to 23 of the SMS reports exchanged between the Naami-Saadouni couple and Assadi. Document Specifications: File 13- document 233 - 233 - 18-530174 - 1673-1636UITLEZEN – VERTALING DEEL 13 - ALGEMEEN DEEL 3

[13] There was a long-running conversation between Naami and Saadouni inside the prison that the police recorded and filed. The police have come to varying conclusions about the couple's conversation. In parts of the police report it is said: *Nasimeh Naami asks Amir Saadouni not to say that she was aware*

of the task that Assadollah Assadi had given them. Nasimeh Naami wants Amir Saadouni to say that only he [Saadouni] sent emails from his personal computer. According to the above information, we may conclude that Nasimeh Na'ami is telling Amir Saadouni what he should be saying.

14 The photos from the Luxembourg police report (except for the photos taken during the police stop) were obtained from city cameras after Assadi was identified and arrested by the police.

15 According to Saadouni, Assadi had always avoided going to Belgium for security reasons. and had not even once met them in Belgium. The question is why did he go to Belgium himself after delivering the bomb to them in Luxembourg on the afternoon of June 28, 2018? That night he stayed at the *Hotel Ibis Budget* in Leige. In addition to the two duplex rooms that he had booked for himself, his wife, and his two sons, he had also booked two more rooms (one for two persons and one for three persons). For whom did he book these two rooms? Who did he meet that night in Liege? Why did he book all four rooms for two nights?

16 At 8:00 AM, Assadi drove the Ford to a carwash. As a trained military specialist in Iran, Assadi knew that TATP leaves traces that can be tracked by police dogs. He knew then that he must return to Vienna, as quickly as possible. He would be safe at the embassy - See article in Belgium's De Morgan newspaper 20 February 2020.

17 "I like to see castles and visit them often," Assadi says when questioned by German police five days later. "I've been to many castles." Burg Brennberg in Wiesent. The family is driving on the highway at 9:47 a.m. ... Article in Belgium's De

Morgan newspaper. February 20, 2020. DE CONINCK, DOUGLAS and 2021. "Citytrippen met een bom in de koffer: hoe een Iraanse diplomaat zelfs zijn eigen gezin voor de gek hield." Demorgen. February 20, 2021. https://www.demorgen.be/nieuws/citytrippen-met-een-bom-in-de-koffer-hoe-een-iraanse-diplomaat-zelfs-zijn-eigen-gezin-voor-de-gek-hield~bbcaa6b0/.

[18] Document 233 File 13 - SMS text between Asadi and Saadouni

[19] See endnote 3.

[20] "Maryam Rajavi's Ten Point Plan for Future Iran - NCRI." NCR-Iran. https://www.ncr-iran.org/en/maryam-rajavis-ten-point-plan-for-future-iran/.

[21] Hall, Benjamin. 2018. "'Free Iran' rally held in Paris." Video. July 2, 2018. https://video.foxnews.com/v/5804468884001#sp=show-clips.

[22] Sciolino, Elaine. 1995. "U.S. Asserts Iranians Plotted to Disrupt Rally in Germany." June 25, 1995. https://www.nytimes.com/1995/06/25/world/us-asserts-iranians-plotted-to-disrupt-rally-in-germany.html.

[23] Ibid.

[24] According to Weekly Standard, September 12, 2012, Hossein Mousavian "was the Iranian ambassador to Germany when Iranian agents machine-gunned Iranian-Kurdish dissidents at the Mykonos restaurant in Berlin in 1992. In the early 1990s, [former Iranian president Ali Akbar Hashemi] Rafsanjani and [current Iranian Supreme Leader Ali] Khamenei, then working in tandem, gave orders to Iranian intelligence to assassinate several annoying dissidents in Europe and Turkey." In April 1997 a German court ruled Iranian leaders

and ministers, including Mousavian, were directly involved in the Mykonos restaurant assassination. More from The Weekly Standard: "We know that Iranian ambassadors, though most likely not players in the planning of these assassinations, were kept apprised of the operations and were instrumental in the post-kill whitewashing of the Islamic Republic. Mousavian was quite active on the German scene—he remained ambassador until 1997—denying Iranian culpability. In 1997 Tehran's guilt was proven beyond a shadow of a doubt in a German court, and an arrest warrant was issued for the intelligence minister, Ali Fallahian. Fallahian's men would not have moved without a green light from Khamenei and Rafsanjani. We can assume that the Central Intelligence Agency thoroughly debriefed Mousavian in exchange for his refuge. That's fair game in power politics and espionage. (Why Princeton University—especially former ambassador Daniel Kurtzer, now at the Woodrow Wilson School, who strongly supported Mousavian's appointment— would want to give a fellowship to someone who has so much blood swirling around him is a different question.)"

25 "Patterns of Global Terrorism 1997 - Iran." Www. April 1, 1998. https://www.refworld.org/docid/4681071fc.html.

26 "Albania, host of Iranian dissident camp, expels two Iranian diplomats | Reuters." Reuters. January 15, 2020. https://www.reuters.com/article/us-albania-iran-expulsion-idUSKBN1ZE27X.

27 Koleka, Benet. 2019. "Albania says it foiled Iranian plot to attack exiled dissidents | Reuters." Reuters. October 23, 2019.

https://www.reuters.com/article/uk-albania-iran-idINKBN1X22CN.

[28] Mero, Armand, Lipin, Michael and 2019. "Albania Names Iranian, Turkish Members of Alleged Terrorist Cell." Voanews. October 23, 2019. https://www.voanews.com/a/europe_albania-names-iranian-turkish-members-alleged-terrorist-cell/6178051.html.

[29] Moniquet , C. & . (2019). IRAN - Terrorism in Europe., p28.

[30] Sands, David R. and 2022. "Iranian exile dissident group calls off summit after terror threat - Washington Times." Washington Times. July 23, 2022. https://www.washingtontimes.com/news/2022/jul/23/iranian-exile-dissident-group-calls-summit-after-t/.

[31] 2022. "Hillsborough: Timeline of the 1989 stadium disaster - BBC News." BBC. April 8, 2022. https://www.bbc.com/news/uk-england-merseyside-47697569.

[32] Der Spiegel, July 26, 2010

[33] 2015. "Hajj stampede: At least 717 killed in Saudi Arabia - BBC News." BBC. July 24, 2015. https://www.bbc.com/news/world-middle-east-34346449.

[34] 2005. "BBC NEWS | Middle East | Iraq stampede deaths near 1,000." News. August 31, 2005. http://news.bbc.co.uk/2/hi/middle_east/4199618.stm.

[35] Refer to the press conference organized by the National Council of Resistance of Iran in Brussels on August 8, 2018, attended by international lawyer William Bourdon (France) and several private plaintiffs of the case, including international dignitaries who participated at the Villepinte

gathering, such as former Italian Foreign Minister Giulio Terzi and former US Senator Robert Torricelli.

36 State-run Kayhan daily, July 11, 2018.

37 State-run daily Kayhan, "What happened to the return of the honor of the Iranian passport", July 11, 2018. <http://kayhan.ir/fa/mobile/news/136854/1326>

38 Document dated November 22, 2018: E-mails exchanged between Assadi, Naami and Saadouni, page 112.

39 Refer to the press conference of the NCRI in Brussels on August 8, 2018.

40 Evidence no. 1, Folder 18, File 6 - Review of the red notebook.

41 Evidence no. 1, Folder 1, File 5 - Assadi's green notebook.

42 Evidence no. 1, Folder 9, File 5 - Assadi's Nokia 105 phone.

43 Evidence no. 1, Folder 16, File 6 - Review of Assadi's Alcatel phone, which was most likely used for only contacting Amir Saadouni.

44 Pictures in this phone could be related to MOIS officials as well.

45 Evidence no. 1, Folder 16, File 6 - Review of Assadi's iPad.

46 Evidence no. 1, Folder 13, File 6 - Review of Assadi's USB drive.

47 Evidence no. 1, Folder 11, File 7 - Contents of Assadi's Asus computer.

48 Evidence no. 1, Folder 3, File 5 - Some of the documents seized from Assadi.

49 Evidence no. 1, Folder 3, File 5 - Reviewing some of the items Assadi carried with himself.

[50] Evidence no. 1, Folder 10, File 5 - Reviewing Assadi's passport and stamps in the passport.

[51] See endnote 1 above.

[52] Iran SOS. Wuk. https://www.wuk.at/en/iran-sos/

[53] "iran sos – MUK IM WUK." Iransos. undefined NaN, NaN. https://iransos.com/muk/index.php/tag/iran-sos/.

[54] https://www.tribunezamaneh.com/archives/40343

[55] *Iran's Emissaries of Terror: How mullahs' embassies run the network of espionage and murder*, published by the US Representative Office of the National Council of Resistance of Iran, 2019, page 67.

[56] According to Saadouni's confessions on May 14, 2019, and according to documents in the court case, Assadi had proudly talked about the assassinations of opponents, including the 2017 assassinations in the Netherlands, as the work of the Islamic Republic.

[57] The Associated Press, "Trump thanks Albania for expelling Iranian diplomats", December 20, 2018. <https://apnews.com/article/5f1edb0b69094a54a10e9445afe6b877>

[58] This document was submitted to the Belgian Federal Prosecutor's Office on February 21, 2020.

[59] "Official Journal of the European Union." Official Journal of the European Union 65 (4 February 2022) :L25/3 to L25/4. https://eur-lex.europa.eu/legal-content/EN/TXT/PDF/?uri=OJ:L:2022:025:FULL&from=EN

[60] Document dated October 30, 2018 of the Belgian police investigation (including the schedule of Assadi's trips to Iran since he was stationed in Vienna in 2014).

[61] Belgian police investigation documents dated September 7, 2020.

[62] Independent Arabia, "Intelligence source: Iranian explosives were transported on a civilian plane to carry out a terrorist attack in Paris 2018", June 24, 2019. <https://www.independentarabia.com/node/35311/>

[63] Belgian police investigation document dated August 28, 2019 (report on Assadi's last trip to Tehran).

[64] Ibid.

[65] Statements of the prosecutor in the afternoon session of the second day of Assadi's trial on November 27, 2020.

[66] België: DOVO | Defensie (mil.be) https://www.mil.be/nl/onze-missies/belgie-dovo/

[67] The police investigation report about the bomb, which was handed over to the investigative judge on February 12, 2019.

[68] French police investigation document at the request of the Belgian police - document number 102/2018 - registered in the file dated February 12, 2019.

[69] Ibid.

[70] A copy of Zaeri's driving license at the car rental company, which is among the registered documents of the case.

[71] Khamenei's official website <https://farsi.khamenei.ir/page?id=27523>

[72] Document dated October 30, 2018 from the Belgian police investigation (including the schedule of Assadi's trips to Iran since he was stationed in Vienna in 2014)

[73] Investigation documents of the case, including photos of Naami's passports.

[74] The aforementioned document was in the file dated October 30, 2018.

[75] See The Routledge Handbook of Terrorism Research, Alex Schmid (ed.), Routledge, 2013. <routledge.com/The-Routledge-Handbook-of-Terrorism-Research/Schmid/p/book/9780415520997>

[76] See "Types of Terrorism", Britannica, <https://www.britannica.com/topic/terrorism/Types-of-terrorism>

[77] See definition of "state terrorism" in Merriam-Webster dictionary.

[78] L'Administrateur général or VSSE.

[79] Document dated February 18, 2020 - Belgian police investigation addressed to Ms. Van Lowe, the federal prosecutor.

[80] Statements of the prosecutor in the afternoon session of the second day of Assadi trial on November 27, 2020.

[81] Judgment of Antwerp court, paragraph 4.6.30

[82] Judgment of Antwerp court, paragraph 4.6.31.

[83] Press conference of the National Council of Resistance of Iran, Brussels, August 8, 2018.

[84] Ibid. Hossein Amir Abdollahian became the Minister of Foreign Affairs in the Ebrahim Raisi administration.

[85] Reuters, "France points finger at Iran over bomb plot, seizes assets", October 2, 2018. < https://www.reuters.com/article/us-france-security/france-points-finger-at-iran-over-bomb-plot-seizes-assets-idUSKCN1MC12X>

[86] BBC News, "France blames Iran for foiled Paris bomb plot", October 2, 2018. <https://www.bbc.com/news/world-europe-45722523>

[87] Ibid.

[88] The New York Times, "E.U. Imposes Sanctions on Iran Over Assassination Plots", January 8, 2019. <https://www.nytimes.com/2019/01/08/world/europe/iran-eu-sanctions.html>

[89] Judgment of Antwerp court, paragraph 4.6.30.

[90] US State Department, "Background Briefing on Meeting with Saudi Officials", July 10, 2018. <https://2017-2021.state.gov/background-briefing-on-meeting-with-saudi-officials/index.html>

[91] Ibid.

[92] US State Department, "Supporting Iranian Voices", July 22, 2018. <https://2017-2021.state.gov/supporting-iranian-voices/index.html>

[93] United States Mission to the United Nations, "Remarks at a UN Security Council Briefing on the Middle East", November 19, 2018. <https://usun.usmission.gov/remarks-at-a-un-security-council-briefing-on-the-middle-east/>

94 Document dated May 20, 2019 - a summary of some of Naami's and Saadouni's statements during interrogations.

95 Investigation document dated August 26, 2019.

96 Combating Terrorism Center at West Point, "Iran's Deadly Diplomats", Matthew Levitt, Volume 11, Issue 7, August 2018. <https://ctc.usma.edu/irans-deadly-diplomats/>. This report was republished by the Washington Institute for Near East Policy. <https://www.washingtoninstitute.org/uploads/Documents/opeds/Levitt-20180808-CTCSentinel.pdf>

97 *Eskorte nach Teheran: Der österreichische Rechtsstaat und die Kurdenmorde,* Peter Pilz, Ibera-und-Molden-Verlag, 1997. <https://www.goodreads.com/book/show/17886768-eskorte-nach-teheran>

98 *Iran's Emissaries of Terror: How mullahs' embassies run the network of espionage and murder,* published by the US Representative Office of the National Council of Resistance of Iran, 2019.

99 State-run 24 News, "Zarif: I consider Meydan and diplomacy to be fundamental and complementary", April 28, 2021. https://www.24-news.ir/news/70116/-ظریف-میدان-دیپلماسی-مقوم-مکمل-می-دانم

100 Payam Aftab, Full text of the confidential interview of Mohammed Javad Zarif with Saeed Lilaz, April 25, 2021. https://www.payam-aftab.com/fa/mosahebe/95230/-متن-کامل-مصاحبه-محرمانه-محمدجواد-ظریف-سع

101 Ibid.

102 Javad Zarif at the Munich Security Conference, February 20, 2019. Watch on YouTube: "[MSC|2019] 26. Talk: Statement

by Mohammad Javad Zarif followed by Q&A". https://www.youtube.com/watch?v=uhvp0M6JNuQ

[103] One of the people that was exposed in the organizational chart was Reza Lotfi, a senior official of the Ministry of Intelligence, who visited Assadi in August 2019. When the org chart was presented, this trip and meeting had not yet been disclosed.

[104] State-run Asr-e Iran daily, No. 2350, January 9, 2018. <https://asre-iranian.ir/?nid=2350&pid=2&type=0>

[105] State-affiliated Blogh News, "Shamkhani's reaction", January 1, 2018. <bloghnews.com/news/338233/-واکنش-شمخانی-رفتار سعودی-ها-اغتشاشات-اخیر>

[106] "Minister of Intelligence: Imam Zaman's soldiers will soon respond to groups - Tasnim Political News | Tasnim." Tasnimnews. January 16, 2018. https://www.tasnimnews.com/fa/news/1396/10/26/1629804/ وزیر-اطلاعات-سربازان-امام-زمان-عج-به-زودی-پاسخ-کوبنده-ای-به-گروهک-ها-می-دهند.

[107] State-run Fars News, "Creation of new security threat grouplets is on the agenda of enemies of the revolution", February 11, 2018. https://www.farsnews.ir/news/13961122001051/-ایجاد گروهک%8C%80%E2های-ضدامنیتی-جدید-در-دستور-کار-دشمنان-انقلاب- است

[108] See endnote 1 above.

[109] https://iransos.com/muk/index.php/tag/iran-sos/

[110] https://www.decitre.fr/livres/travail-au-noir-9782343062945.html

111 https://www.wuk.at/en/iran-sos/

112 https://www.tribunezamaneh.com/archives/40343

113 The first document of this case is dated June 25, 2018, signed by the head of the Belgian Authority.

114 All these judicial decisions were made by the investigating judge in this case, Ms. Van Hoylandt.

115 In this way, the charge attributed to the subjects of this case is "initiation of a crime" in the legal term. Initiating a crime means that there are all material preparations and preparations as well as the criminal will to commit a crime, but a foreign agent prevents the crime from occurring.

116 Article 137 of the Penal Code was changed on the first of 2017 to reflect that for a terrorist group to exist it is not necessary for the individuals to "know" that their participation in the terrorist group would result in the crime, but rather they knew or "should have known" that the group played such a role.

117 For Mrs. Rajavi's testimony, the Belgian judicial authorities gave judicial representation to the French authorities, and the French authorities went to Auvers sur Oise, France, to receive her testimony. Other testimonies were heard by the Belgian judicial authorities in Antwerp.

118 Every person of the tens of thousands of participants could be a plaintiff in this case, but for practical reasons only 25 private Iranian and foreign plaintiffs were introduced.

119 Approximately 17 pages of the 64-page ruling by the Court of First Instance of Antwerp have been devoted to investigating the objections raised by Assadi's lawyer.

[120] Judgment No. P.18.1301,N/1 dated January 2, 2019 Second Branch of Belgium's Court of Cassation.

[121] Given that Assadi's lawyer withdrew his appeal after the lower court's decision, the immunity issue was only mentioned in the Antwerp lower court's ruling, and the appellate court ruling issued on May 10, 2022, no longer considered this matter.

[122] Inspite of the court's reliable decisions that Assadi was not allowed to use the Diplomatic Immunity, the Iranian regime again says that the Belgian judiciary has acted illegally and therefore Assadi should be released, reinstated, and the damage done by the Belgian government be compensated.

[123] The lower court's ruling, in remarkably minute detail, reviewed all elements of the case of Assadi and his three accomplices and stated the facts one by one and issued verdicts based on each.

[124] Two experts testified at the hearing, one German and another Belgian.

[125] Judgment by the Antwerp Court of Appeals, May 10, 2022

[126] LEVITT, MATTHEW and 2018. "Iran's Deadly Diplomats – Combating Terrorism Center at West Point." CTCSENTINEL 11 (7).

[127] Irish, John and 2020. "Iranian diplomat warned of retaliation over Belgian bomb plot trial, document shows | Reuters." Reuters. October 9, 2020. https://www.reuters.com/article/iran-plot-france-int-idUSKBN26U28N.

128 "Online Panel on Iran's State Terrorism and EU Policy - Iran Freedom." Iranfreedom. January 28, 2021. https://iranfreedom.org/en/articles/2021/01/online-panel-on-irans-state-terrorism-and-eu-policy/20801/.

129 "SÉANCE PLÉNIÈRE." Publications officielles éditées par la Chambre des représentants CRIV 55 COM 363 (2021). https://www.dekamer.be/doc/CCRI/pdf/55/ic363.pdf

130 Moens , Barbara, Herszenhorn, David M. "Belgium paves way to send convicted terrorist to Iran – POLITICO." Politico. July 4, 2022. https://www.politico.eu/article/belgium-send-convicted-terrorist-iran/https://www.politico.eu/article/belgium-send-convicted-terrorist-iran/.

131 Erlanger, Steven. "Belgium Ratifies Prisoner-Exchange Treaty with Iran - The New York Times." NYTimes. July 21, 2022. https://www.nytimes.com/2022/07/21/world/europe/belgium-iran-prisoner-exchange-treaty.html.

132 "Treaty with Mullahs Encourages Further Terrorism and Hostage-taking," July 21, 2022. https://www.ncr-iran.org/en/ncri-statements/terrorism-fundamentalism/treaty-with-mullahs-encourages-further-terrorism-and-hostage-taking/

133 "US National Security Experts Condemn Iran- Belgium Deal to Release Terrorists," July 6, 2022. https://www.ncr-iran.org/en/news/iran-resistance/us-national-security-experts-condemn-iran-belgium-deal-to-release-terrorists/

134 "Thirteen Members of US Congress Censure Iran- Belgium Treaty to Release State Terrorists," July 6, 2022. https://www.ncr-iran.org/en/news/iran-resistance/thirteen-

members-of-us-congress-censure-iran-belgium-treaty-to-release-state-terrorists/

[135] "ISJ Committee Denounces Iran- Belgium Deal to Release Terrorists," July 4, 2022. https://www.ncr-iran.org/en/news/iran-resistance/isj-committee-denounces-iran-belgian-deal-to-release-terrorists/

[136] "British Lawmakers Censure Iran- Belgium Deal to Release Terrorists," July 4, 2002. https://www.ncr-iran.org/en/news/iran-belgium-treaty-prisoners/british-lawmakers-censure-iran-belgian-deal-to-release-terrorists/

[137] "US National Security Experts Condemn Iran- Belgium Deal to Release Terrorists," July 3, 2022. https://www.ncr-iran.org/en/news/iran-resistance/us-national-security-experts-condemn-iran-belgium-deal-to-release-terrorists/

[138] ,"MEPs Censure Iran- Belgium Deal to Release Terrorists," July 6, 2022. https://www.ncr-iran.org/en/news/iran-resistance/meps-censure-iran-belgium-deal-to-release-terrorists/

[139] "Twenty MEPs: Reject Iran-Belgium Treaty for the Sake of Peace and Security," July 8, 2022. https://www.ncr-iran.org/en/news/iran-resistance/twenty-meps-reject-iran-belgium-treaty-for-the-sake-of-peace-and-security/

[140] "Six Hundred Iranian Americans Denounce Iran- Belgian Deal to Release Terrorists," July 3, 2022. https://www.ncr-iran.org/en/news/iran-resistance/six-hundred-iranian-americans-denounce-iran-belgian-deal-to-release-terrorists/

[141] Amnesty International statement, "Belgium must ensure new treaty with Iran does not entrench impunity," July 5, 2022.

https://www.amnesty.org/en/documents/mde13/5813/2022/en/

[142] Joint letter of the Nobel Laureates to the Belgian Prime Minister, July 11, 2020. https://www.ncr-iran.org/en/news/iran-resistance/joint-letter-of-the-nobel-laureates-to-the-belgian-prime-minister/

[143] "CFDI Calls the Brussels-Tehran Deal A Shameful Treaty to Release Iranian Convicted Terrorists," July 11, 2022. https://www.ncr-iran.org/en/news/iran-resistance/cfdi-calls-the-brussels-tehran-deal-a-shameful-treaty-to-release-iranian-convicted-terrorists/

[144] Mrs. Rajavi's Message to Iranians' Demonstration in Brussels Against the Clerical Regime's Shameful Deal with Belgium, July 14, 2022. https://www.ncr-iran.org/en/ncri-statements/president-elect/mrs-rajavis-message-to-iranians-demonstration-in-brussels-against-the-clerical-regimes-shameful-deal-with-belgium/

www.ingramcontent.com/pod-product-compliance
Lightning Source LLC
Chambersburg PA
CBHW041136110526
44590CB00027B/4033